Asmund Havsteen-Mikkelsen *Complex*, Oil on Canvas, 186 × 140 cm

Letterbox, Oil on Canvas, 103 × 80 cm

Dark Interior, Oil on Canvas, 105 × 78 cm

Gym, Oil on Canvas, 155 × 100 cm

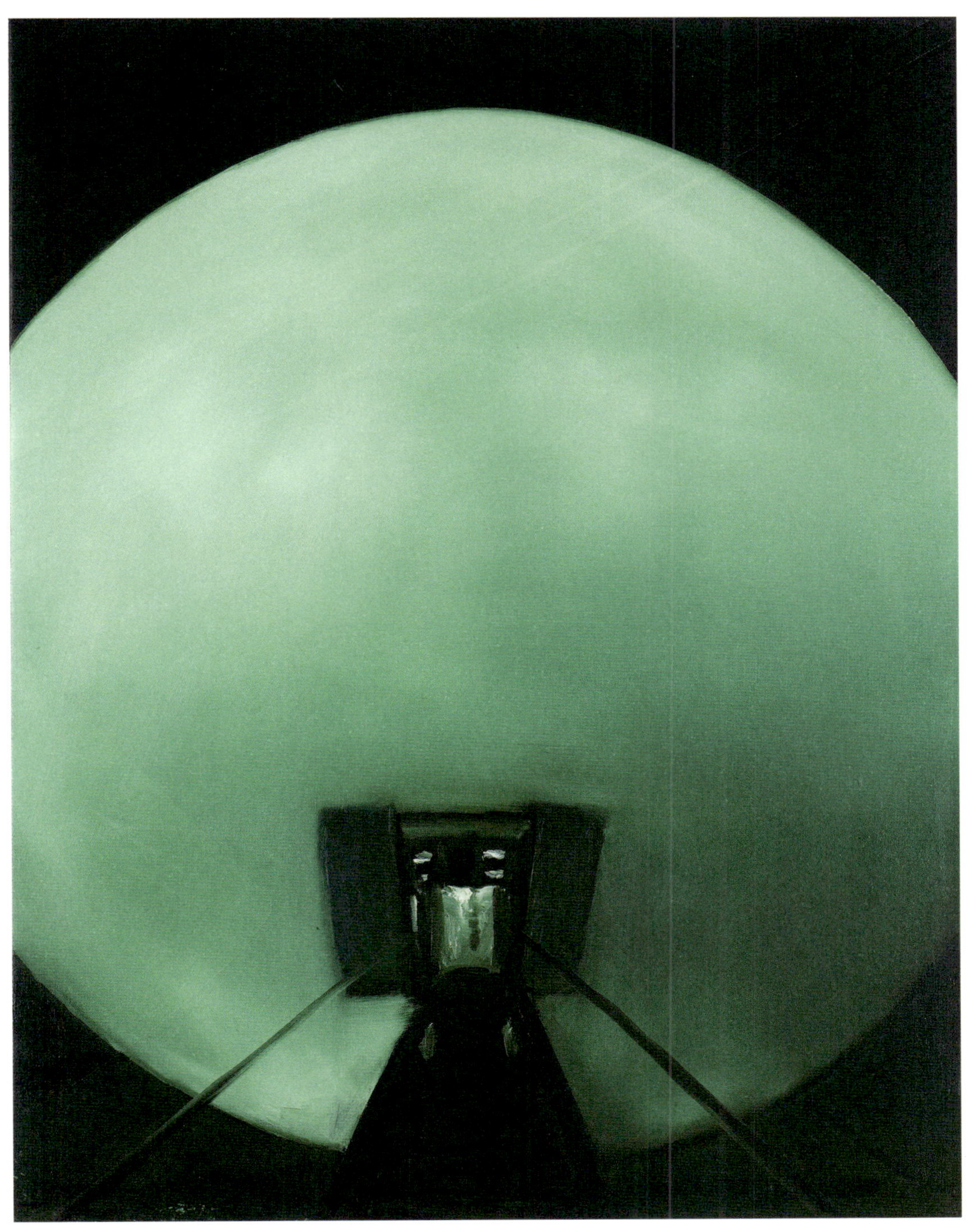

Metal Sphere, Oil on Canvas, 78 × 60 cm

Urban Pyramid, Oil on Canvas, 130 × 100 cm

Distortion, Oil on Canvas, 134 × 105 cm

Silhouettes, Oil on Canvas, 134 × 105 cm

Tilted Space, Oil on Canvas, 80 × 103 cm

Continuum, Oil on Canvas, 130 × 100 cm

Almut Grüntuch-Ernst and Armand Grüntuch in conversation with Ilka and Andreas Ruby

Andreas Ruby

You're very much perceived as a Berlin office: you've realised most of your projects here, and you repeatedly emphasise and deliberately promote this. Nevertheless, your architectural socialisation didn't take place in Berlin. Which experiences and places were influential for your development before you came to Berlin?

Almut Grüntuch-Ernst

The time in London was important to us; we came to Berlin from there more than 22 years ago. However, different paths led each of us to London and to architecture. I grew up in Schleswig-Holstein. After high school, in 1985, I went back to my birthplace to study architecture at the Stuttgart Technical University. I did my first architecture internship at a small office on the island of Sylt. After my pre-diploma, I went to London for another internship during the semester break in 1987. This developed into more – I stayed for a long internship, a so-called "Year Out", in the office of Will Alsop and then came back again on a scholarship for the AA (Architectural Association). In between, I briefly returned to Stuttgart for my diploma, but we actually moved from London directly to Berlin.

Armand Grüntuch

The time in London was important in many ways – that's where we actually met. My path there, however, was a bit different: I was born in Riga, and my family moved from there first to Israel, and then to Aachen, where I grew up and, in 1982, began my studies. The architecture school in Aachen had a good reputation. After my pre-diploma, I received funding to study abroad; consequently, I went first to Venice for a year and then, in 1987, to London, where I worked for Norman Foster.
Almut and I first met, briefly, in Stuttgart; I worked in the same studio as she for three months, preparing my design for the Schinkel competition. But we really only got to know each other in London.
At the time, many German architecture students were going to London, including, for instance, Patrik Schumacher, who came with Almut from Stuttgart, and Stefan Behling, who started with me on the same day at Foster Associates. In 1987, London was the most interesting melting pot for architects and students.

That was also the heyday of high-tech architecture in London. In which offices did you work?

I worked for Alsop & Lyall, as they were still called at the time. That was a fascinating office! Although they'd been working together for ten years, they had built relatively little. Nevertheless, they were firmly rooted in the architectural discourse. How Will Alsop could position and maintain himself between the academic and the professional world! It was a very exciting, intense time, with conceptual discussions not only among the architects, but also with engineers like Christopher McCarthy and Guy Battle.

When I first came to London, I wanted to get insight into the various offices. First, I looked at Norman Foster's office. The next morning, I wanted to drop by Zaha Hadid's. When I rang the bell at eight in the morning, she opened the door in her bathrobe – I hadn't gotten the address of her office, but her private residence! On the evening of my official interview with Zaha, I received an offer from Norman Foster – I probably could've just as easily ended up with Zaha Hadid.

In addition to the focus on high-tech architecture, there was a completely different way of thinking, which I found fascinating. It was promoted by architects like Cedric Price and leading figures of the Archigram period, like David Greene and Ron Herron, who was my teacher at the AA. I found it exciting to search for a new formal approach, in this context of unconventional thinking about architecture.

But people like Frei Otto also influenced us. The way he merges engineering and observations about nature into architectural design is impressive. His comprehensive research work is as fascinating as his ability to explain complex subjects clearly. Working with him on our competition projects for the EZB in Frankfurt and the BMW plant in Leipzig was particularly stimulating.

Were there other formative office experiences after Alsop and Foster?

Your first office experience has the greatest influence – often much more than your time at university. Foster was simply an extreme office, and probably still is today. Even back then, it was professionally run. For me, it was an important start: Foster is certainly more of an inventor's office than an architectural drawing office – above all, thanks to close collaboration with the engineers, but also thanks to special people like Jan Kaplický or Richard Horden, who emerged from there. The approach was less formalistic, but open and unbiased and actually very scientific.

Will Alsop had a different approach to architecture: Abstract painting was a starting point for his projects, for instance. Incidentally, at this time, Alsop regularly met with Otto Steidle and Massimiliano Fuksas to develop building concepts. The offices built up a network to participate in competitions together – to experience this shared authorship was hugely exciting. I also learned a certain serenity or creative openness from him, with which an architect can question the role as service provider. He often refused to take things literally. It's always important to think creatively and to question your objectives.

Other architects, more creative thinkers who haven't built very much, have also influenced us – for example, Yona Friedman. We met at a joint exhibition, the first Shanghai Biennial, and then visited him in Paris. However, it was always important for us to build. Therefore, in London, we worked on our own projects too – on the competition for the documenta exhibit hall in Kassel, for example.

Our design approach was to dynamise the central event venue. Our building could move on rails and could stand in the city or on the Friedrichsplatz. The rail system functioned pneumatically: the building was meant to rise briefly and then move onto the cantilevered platform where, today, Haus-Rucker's framework stands. They won the competition that time, too.

That sounds like Cedric Price.

It was a very English and, at the same time, very technical solution, that's right.

Architects like Patrik Schumacher and Stefan Behling remained in London and established themselves there as architects. Was that never an option for you?

I think it's extremely difficult for German architects to establish themselves in the United Kingdom. I don't know precisely what the reasons for that are, but it's virtually impossible. As a German architect, you are quite welcome in London, because you can pull your own weight there, but it's difficult to open your own office. Therefore, staying in London was never open for debate. I've simply always wanted to work independently as an architect.

Moreover, it made me increasingly frustrated that, from London, I could only experience the fall of the Berlin wall on TV – I was unbelievably curious and wanted to experience it myself.

What were your initial experiences in Berlin? How did you begin working?

When we went to Berlin together in 1991, Philipp Oswalt was just planning the workshop "Wohltemperierte Architektur" (Well Tempered Architecture) for students at Technische Universität Berlin. Armand was invited, along with Jan Kaplický from Future Systems, to lead a workshop. And I did the same with Cedric Price.

That was the first major event in Berlin in which we participated.

We were simply fascinated by the energy in this city –

– but we had the feeling that we had come too late. In 1991, we couldn't show any completed work. As a start, we both worked at the Hochschule der Künste (University of the Arts) – I worked in the Department of Building Construction as a research associate for Peter Bayerer.

And I worked, initially, with the architects at the Institute of Zamp Kelp. Later, I switched to Gerd Diel in the Department of Visual Communication.

Parallel to this, we tried to establish our own office. But we had to contend with the problem that we seemed to be too late, that many young architects had long since established themselves in Berlin.

Every beginning is difficult – we lacked a network in Berlin. But in hindsight, that probably wasn't so bad. Years later, when the construction boom collapsed, there were major upheavals in the Berlin architecture landscape; many offices closed or had to cut back drastically. In the long term, our slow and anti-cyclical path weathered that change much better.

When you came to Berlin in 1991, Hans Stimmann was appointed Senatsbaudirektor (Senate Building Director). His conservative agenda for the critical reconstruction of Berlin defined what was architecturally possible in the city for a good fifteen years. Where did you see potential for your work back then?

We returned from London relatively naive, but full of idealistic notions and extremely happy to try out new things. With our activities at the university, we had a balanced mix between the academic and professional worlds. Our first successful competition entry was for the school in Hellersdorf in 1993 – we won the competition and were also able to realise the design.

By now, we must've entered more than a hundred competitions, and we've won quite a few of them – that's where most of our projects come from. At the same time, we've worked on many smaller projects and studies. Often, these have vanished into thin air or only developed into an actual project years later.

There was a law in Berlin at the time that, in retrospect, has proven to be relatively important for architects: the Investitionsvorranggesetz (Priority Investment Law). According to this law, builders could acquire property if they could prove that they wanted to invest there, that jobs would be created, and that they would erect a building. Their investments had priority over all property claims and inheritance disputes, which were then cleared up in retrospect. In accordance with this law, many architects created corresponding preliminary notice or plans, and, depending on the situation, then sold the property to an investor or property developer. We certainly created a large number of surveys for different locations in Berlin-Mitte.

We only started building years later, and then often for completely different people. The potential property developers changed, the plots remained. So it came about that from five preliminary building permits, we realised two or three for completely different clients. Our projects at Hackescher Markt and Monbijouplatz 3 are examples of this.

Returning to Stimmann: As a glass structure, our new building at Hackescher Markt doesn't actually fit into the building period or the material world of the former Senatsbaudirektor. With his urban policy, Stimmann promoted stock building polarization among architects. For example, the division between glass and stone architects always seemed to us too unilateral. Of course, we understand that there's a need for some degree of harmonisation of the building with its plaster and stone environment, but material similarity is only one design possibility of dealing with the surrounding city. Working contextually can mean many things; it can happen through scale, form, and outline, and thereby attain far more sensitive results.

I think you have to be careful not to allow yourself to be reduced to a steel-and-glass architect. No one would get the idea of fixing fashion designers to a single material. A good cut not only needs the right material, but also the movement and contour of the body and the effect of the light in order to fully reveal its elegance. The choice of the material has to remain open, so that the right cut can be developed for each commission.

As a material, glass has no intrinsic value – it's a means to allow our buildings a greater degree of complexity and versatility.

For us, versatility and complexity are also guidelines for a basic understanding of the city. The plan for Berlin's city centre, on the other hand, tried to force urban development into a master plan that threatened to become an architectural corset. I think it's important to accept the unpredictability of a city so that it can develop further. The projection of a final ideal state inhibits energy and destroys vitality. It's much more appropriate to see and treat a city as an amalgam of many individual places.
The Senate and the planning bodies have learned something, they now take individual solutions and specific locations under closer consideration.

Many of your built projects are in Berlin-Mitte. Are there reasons for this concentration or was that also coincidence?

Both. The largest building projects naturally emerged in East Berlin after the fall of the wall; the West offered only a few sites for new buildings then. The most attractive neighbourhood in a central location at that time was the Spandauer Vorstadt.

That was no coincidence! We were engaged with this area and often pointed investors to the prime sites, so we brought the clients to the locations.

It felt like every fifth plot of land was vacant. Well, in truth, it was probably every fifteenth, but there really were quite a few vacant lots; many had been empty since the immediate post-war era. Almost all of the plots that we developed in Mitte lay fallow. The former Jewish Girl's School is an exception.

Now, at this time, the thrust of Germany's conservative architects was completely different. To them, there was no city in East Berlin; there, a city had to be built. The entire structure that the GDR had produced over forty years was considered non-functional and would have to be replaced. Thus, not a "convertible city" as you later named your German Pavilion at the Architecture Biennial in Venice in 2006, but a "replaceable city". A public discourse emerged in the competition at Alexanderplatz, where the biggest controversy at the time was between the winning project by Kollhoff and the second-place design by Libeskind. Daniel Libeskind's approach was not to demolish buildings, but to modify the existing ones. How did you position yourselves in that debate?

To be honest, at the time, I didn't know what to think of either of the approaches. The large-scale buildings of the Berlin metropolis were not our world; we concentrated on small building sites. We weren't interested in the big master plan, in which everything was assimilated, but rather in the individual building blocks of the city's ever-changing landscape and its cultural value for the city.

We were occupied with the urban development of the GDR within the framework of our first competition win, the construction of a school for mentally handicapped children in Berlin-Hellersdorf. The mono-structure of the surrounding Plattenbau housing had set a strong urban theme. That's what we picked up on: the street side of the building follows a clear, orthogonal grid, and with the modular rhythmisation of the building, we make reference to the surrounding buildings.

We won the competition because our project dealt with how disabled children in the GDR resided and lived. With horror, we realised that most of these children were permanently stuck at home in their apartments and very rarely actually went outside – school wasn't compulsory for them! Therefore, at the centre of our design for the school was that these children would receive the opportunity to build a relationship with their environment. To get them outside, we planned terraces in front of each classroom. From a distance, the school building looks more like a holiday resort.

In the nineties, a type of fragmentation occurred that marks Berlin up to the present day – namely, two completely separate scenes. The wild underground brings the city cultural capital and its international reputation. Opposed to this is a somewhat semi-official policy that gets lost in stiff representative gestures, but often doesn't have the economic capital for that type of building project. The capital city is still evolving in this area of tension. Where does Berlin stand today? Is it still the city of unimagined possibilities? Is Berlin a paradise for architects, or do you tend to be exasperated by the almost notorious inability of the city to recognise its opportunities and take advantage of them accordingly?

Both. In our work, it seems like we constantly switch between enthusiastic feelings and big disappointments. All in all, it's also true that it was very good for us to walk more difficult paths. I'm not sure it really would've been good for us back then if we'd won our first competition, for the Reichstag building.
By the way, one shouldn't equate the creative industries with the architecture scene. Everything that's creative today is usually short-lived and fleeting – from the advertising industry, to theatre sets, even to bars. These things are here today and gone tomorrow. As architects, we shape a concrete part of society: our buildings remain standing when everyone else awakens from their dream.
In the discussion about the Stadtschloss (the old royal palace) and the Palast der Republik (the seat of the parliament of the former GDR, built on the site of the Stadtschloss and then demolished after reunification), I always wished that more time had been taken. Things probably could have turned out differently.

Cedric Price would certainly have left the Palast der Republik standing. I remember that, before the demolition, someone spray-painted on the façade: "Don't worry, Palace, when I grow up, I'll rebuild you!" That came from the heart. The whole debate about the Stadtschloss, in my opinion, is mainly emotional. But if it is the case that large segments of the population have this nostalgic longing for the past and the buildings of the monarchy, then we owe them a discussion – we can't just hide it.

There is certainly a human longing for a more pictorial, more emotional architecture – these were the reasons for the emergence of postmodernism. It's undoubtedly the case that increasing complexity and functionality, as well as the virtualisation of our world and architecture, increases the need for more sensuality and emotion. Emotional compensation has always been of great importance in architecture and will probably gain even more importance. I also think that the change in our living environment creates a need for very specifically designed spaces.

Finding new ways to shape living, working, and recreational conditions has always been a challenge for architecture. It's not yet the case that people only do business in the virtual marketplace; they do it there as well as in the "physical" marketplace. They're still in the physical space twenty-four hours a day. Certain functions are shifting, but again, that creates the challenge for architecture to develop new building types and spaces.

Yes. Ultimately, people live in the physical world and the architect is the only one who assumes responsibility for this. It's important that the architect accepts this responsibility; otherwise we'll find that someone else has designed our physical world – undoubtedly the construction companies and specialists who take no account of context and quality of life. It's certainly also interesting and important to concern ourselves with problems of global perception and interpretation, but reality can only be changed in our physical world. Architecture is neither virtual nor conceptual, but quite definitely physical.

Where does Berlin stand today? Can the city continue to operate on the creative capital of its residents and its urban spaces, or does it need investors from outside who bring money into the city?

Berlin needs both impulses, because they interact in a productive way and balance each other out. For large-scale projects, the city always needs capital from outside. Nevertheless, cooperatives and other small building projects here have to be able to emerge and be supported – those are two completely different dimensions. New cooperative models are currently developing here. I find that interesting, because their members are not aiming for a division of property, but a new definition of communal and individual ownership.

Do you also experiment with such new models in your own housing projects?

Yes, we're currently conducting some exciting project discussions. The question of how the threshold between community and individual is handled spatially is always important for us. I explored that theme in my inaugural lecture at Braunschweig, "communal and individual". On the one hand, it concerns the empathy of the designer, on the other his obstinacy. But it also deals with the special relationship of personal space to community space. Architects are not only specialised in spatial limits, but also in the connection between spatial relationships – from private space to collective space and urban space.

Some of the formalities of urban development are badly outdated. In building law, there's Paragraph 34 of the German Civil Code about the "manner of the surrounding structures" – it's always a balancing process, how a building can best fit into the city. On the other hand, it's the case today that the Berlin club scene, the supposedly informal world that advocates "a city for everyone", currently wants to realise one of the largest investment projects in Berlin: the former operators of Bar 25 have been awarded, in a formal bidding process, the contract for a 90-metre high-rise directly on the Spree on the former location of the bar. This is no longer about a small cooperative, but about land worth tens of millions!

So yesterday's club owners are today's project developers?

I believe these paradigms shift constantly. In the past, we often saw that a solid institution could develop from something fun. For me, that's exactly what makes Berlin different from London, where there is hardly any transformation, because so little social fluctuation takes place among the classes.

Moreover, the coexistence of actors with different role profiles has an enormous quality in Berlin. We experienced that, for example, when we renovated the former Jewish Girls' School. There, we defined ourselves, over and above our role as designers, as moderators, working to connect the right uses with the right people in order to reprogramme the site. So not fitting the place to the programme, but, instead, finding the right programme for the place.

It's similar to a current project of ours, the former women's prison on Kantstrasse. Here, we're even the co-initiators. That's very exciting because we can design a piece of the city on a couple of completely different levels.

Many perceive the coexistence of formal and informal economies in the city as a displacement process. For the urban pioneers, the Spandauer Vorstadt has become too expensive; now they have to live somewhere else.

The question is: Do you want a vital mix in the city centre, or should the idyllic world of the rich be sequestered in the suburbs? I don't want that!

Hans Kollhoff once said on the subject of luxury living that modernity was too concerned with social housing. Mies van der Rohe also had a weakness for expensive living: his house Tugendhat cost about twenty times as much as any of the other houses in the neighbourhood. You, too, have built an array of luxury buildings. How do you feel about that? Is there actually a pent-up demand for contemporary architecture to address luxury living concepts?

The exciting thing about residential construction can be – and perhaps this is what Kollhoff meant – when you really build for an owner-occupier and develop a customised solution together with him. That's fun, no matter how large the budget is! The personal dialogue component is interesting for me.

We've actually rejected large projects for speculative residential development because the programmatic challenge was missing. We simply need the freedom to design inquiringly and to widen the horizon beyond the expectations of our clients.

But you're perceived as architects in this context. Grüntuch Ernst is associated with high-priced living – you're even considered pioneers.

We have no special interest in realising luxury apartments. For us, social housing is just as important a design challenge. Just last year, we were awarded a large social housing building project in Munich. What matters to us above all is creating attractive living spaces in the city centre, a counter-model to the single-family houses of the suburbs. To transfer the qualities of that residential typology to the dense inner city.

The clients here usually come from a privileged financial circle. About one-fifth of Berlin residents right now are owners, while the vast majority are renters. Building for yourself in Berlin, in part because of high property prices, is very expensive.

But that could also be controlled differently from the political side. If urban, public building sites were cost-effectively passed to certain users, perhaps other groups could afford their own property. There's currently something underway.

That would also deter still other groups from advancing urban sprawl. As an architect, you also have a responsibility for the scarce resource landscape.

That all strengthens urban densification, which is an important settlement policy step. It makes the inner cities more attractive and diverse places – they must not degenerate into open-air museums where you can only buy souvenirs and go for dinner in the evenings.

You can be described as situational architects – the opposite of the strategic architects, like Gehry or Coop Himmelb(l)au, who generate considerable attention through an iconographic, sustained style. Have you ever asked yourselves whether it would be better to settle on a signature style in order to guarantee an even greater recognition?

I wonder sometimes, if I were on the jury, would I recognise us? And how? Or if I created a competition design and Almut sat on the jury: would she be able to recognise my work and give me first prize? In the past, the widely used strategy was to recognise an architect by the people and trees in his plans. Now perhaps the façades are the more relevant features. If you frequently sit on juries, you quickly notice how often you can be wrong. The industry of imitators perfects every manner of the presentation.

If you don't believe that the city can find a final state that remains ideal forever, then you can also hardly assume that a building type can be repeated as a one-size-fits-all solution. Designs are always a customisation for place, programme, and time.

The academic track that always runs parallel to our work is crucial for this. As architects, we lead a kind of research existence, constantly trying new combinations, changing the perspective in the design process. The most important thing, which I, for one, learned at Foster: in the beginning there's never only one solution; you always have to work alternately on different paths. That's the case today in our office, too. With each project, we consider different concepts until one emerges as the most suitable solution.

Through teaching, but also as curators for the Architecture Biennial and in our work on publications, we reflect – beyond the project work – our own approach again and again. For this book, for example, we invited two very different artists to have their own look at our work: the painter Asmund Havsteen-Mikkelsen and the photographer Heji Shin. This change in perspective has surprised and fascinated us in many regards. Alienation and new discoveries are superimposed on our own perceptions and have created something quite new and autonomous.

Site prior to construction, 2005

Co-housing Auguststrasse, Berlin

The project site, on Auguststrasse, was a part of two neighbouring empty building lots that appeared as a large void in the fabric of the city. The objective was to fill this gap and to restore the urban form to its appropriate volume. Two new buildings were erected on these adjacent sites simultaneously. For us, the city's decision not to redevelop the triangular block between Gipsstrasse and Auguststrasse, but rather to preserve it as an open green space, was of central importance. Since our site was positioned directly opposite the park, this decision gave the site a quality it hadn't previously possessed.

This was a co-housing project, commissioned by a private building owners' association – in this case an alliance of friends and relatives. This meant that when we embarked on the project, we already knew who the building's tenants would be. The most challenging aspect of working for a co-housing group is that each party wants their own, entirely individual home – as the architect you're faced with needs and requirements for the spaces that don't always dovetail neatly.

For instance, everyone has an idea of where their bathroom should be located, but no one considers whether the installations are intelligently aligned with the other

baths in the building. In order to accommodate the diverse requirements of the users, the building needs to have a basic structure that is capable of accommodating complex spatial configurations.

Yes, and these considerations also had an impact on the building's exterior – although, of course as the architects, we maintain the final say in the design of the building's form. For instance, in order to be able to transform the terraces into interior spaces and to be able to shade them from the southern sun exposure, we originally planned to install a sliding, louvered, sun shading system across each double-height opening. One group member emphatically rejected these screens however, so, since two of them would have been installed in their apartment, we ultimately decided not to install them at all.

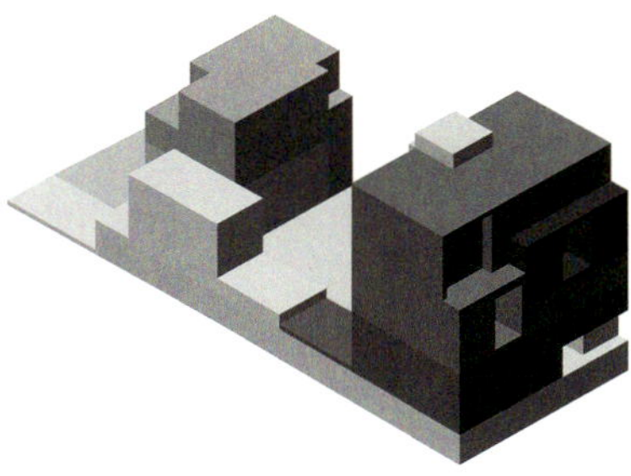

Configuration of the residential units

Actually, that's not entirely true. We did install rails for the sliding shades, so that it will be possible to install them at a later stage. This approach – planning for certain options that go beyond what's actually implemented – is a feature seen in many of our projects.

As it turned out, there was adequate protection from the sun even without the shades: the windows are triple-glazed, all of the apartments extend through from the street to courtyard, and each unit has a double-height space. These qualities ensure sufficient air circulation and preclude any heat build-up.

Each of the users, of course, had entirely different requirements for their spaces: working and living, exhibition space or workspace, a family home, an office, an apartment for elderly people...

For this reason, we organised the various units like pieces in a jigsaw puzzle. We organised the spatial sequences in layers. This organisational principle is revealed in the façade that faces the street.

The structural bands there, however, also serve another purpose: they relate the building to its neighbours. To maximise the connection between the apartments and the city around them, we incorporated large loggias and large-format windows

with no subdividing profiles. The urban environment is a visual extension of the living space: we see the city outside our window as a part of our home.

Where the rear of the building faces a courtyard, we were able to implement a whole different set of ideas. In the courtyard, there's a terraced building suitable for the elderly, with front and back gardens – a kind of suburban enclave within the city. Adjacent to it is an elevated villa, with a wide hall at ground level.

To ensure privacy, both the terraced house and the villa present a compact and enclosed profile to the fairly narrow courtyard. To compensate for this, they're significantly more open where they face the gardens and on their west sides.

What makes an apartment feel spacious is the alternatives it offers; if it lets me move from room to room in two or three different ways instead of just one. The same principle applies to an apartment's visual properties: an apartment with spatially complex views – across floors, for example – feels generously proportioned.

Hall beneath the villa

Visual links with the external environment as well as the lines of sight within the apartment are a factor in this. Each apartment achieves the desired visual effect in a different way: one example is the cascading line of sight from the roof apartment, via the loggia, into the park.

In the case of another apartment, we cut into the loggia to create rooms with both frontal and lateral vistas, creating a kind of bay window effect. Here, in addition to being able to look out onto the street, you can look across the loggia into another room of the apartment.

The same principle applies to the firm's office space. Originally, we planned to use the wide hall beneath the villa as exhibition space, but instead our firm's competitions team moved in. Originally, this was intended to be a provisional arrangement, but in the end it proved to be a long-term situation. This vis-à-vis configuration created a connection between the two parts of the firm across the courtyard.

Naturally, this spontaneous reprogramming of the hall rendered all our previous ideas about the floor plan moot. This shows how, ultimately, a space needs to be able to accommodate alternative scenarios, and how entirely new qualities can emerge through that process.

Foyer of the office

Co-housing Auguststrasse

Location
Auguststrasse 51, 10119 Berlin

Year
completion 2008

Team
Florian Fels, Olaf Menk, Volker Raatz, Jacob van Ommen, Thomas Ellinghaus, Arun Markus, Jon C. Ferrer, Jemima Retallack, Caroline Steinchen, Julia Wolter

Client
Auguststraße 51 GmbH & Co. KG

Technical planners
GTB-Berlin Gesellschaft für Technik am Bau mbH, Berlin (structural engineering)
Ingenieurgesellschaft Ridder und Meyn mbH, Berlin (building service)
Topotek 1 Gesellschaft von Landschafts-architekten mbH, Berlin (open space planning)

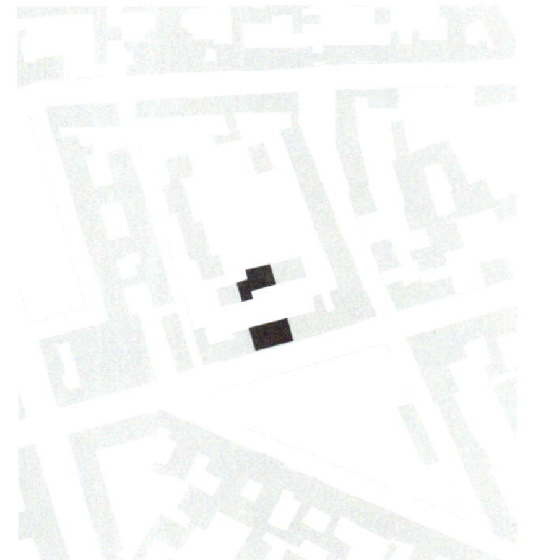

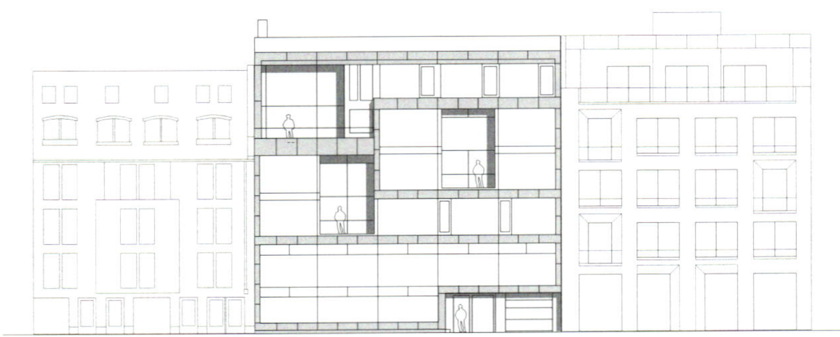

Street elevation

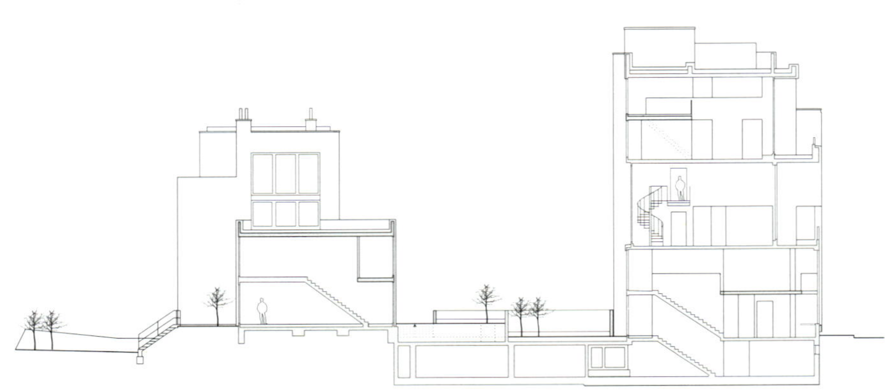

Section of the office and the garden house

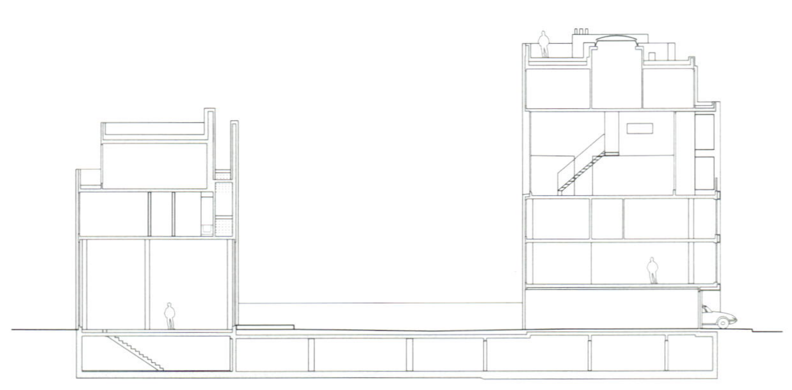

Section of the entryway and hall

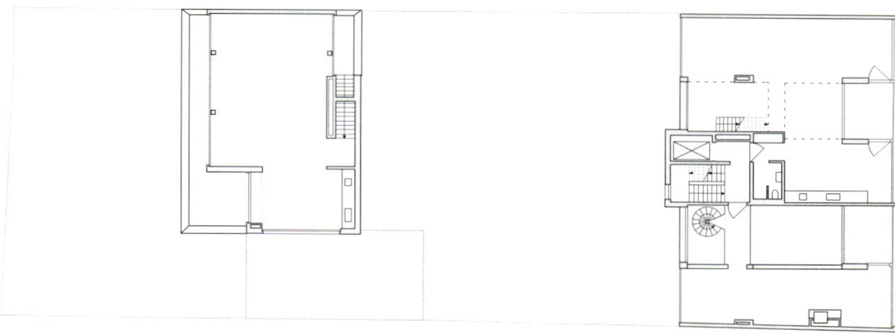

3rd floor

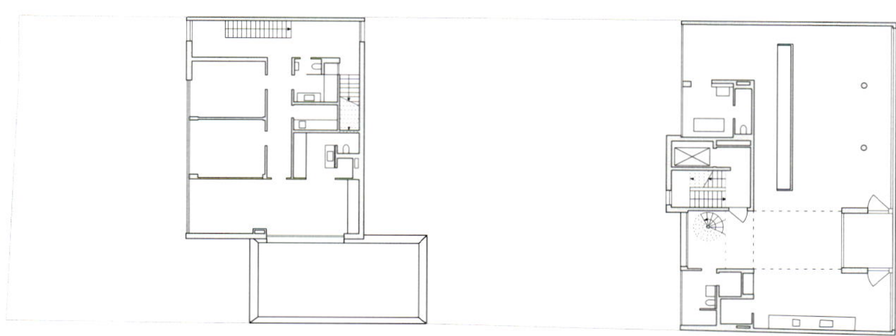

2nd floor

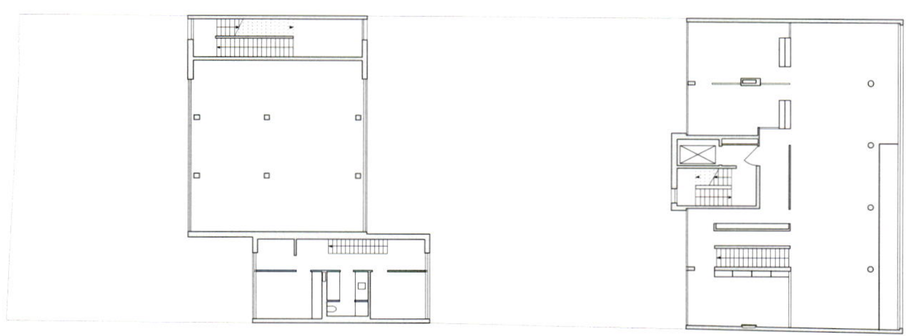

1st floor

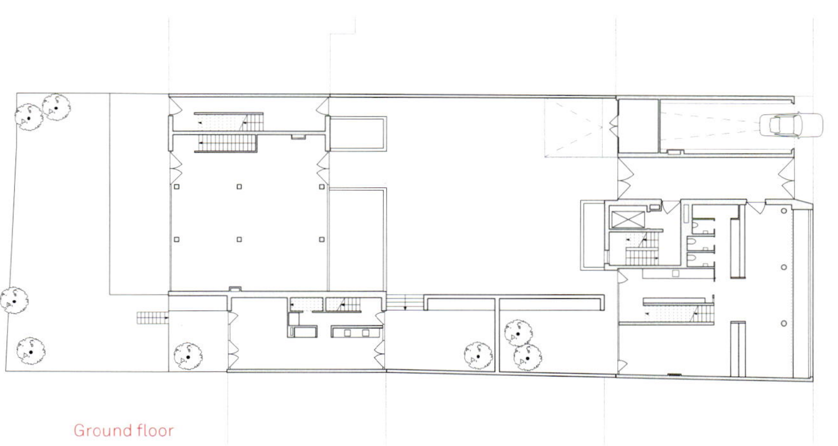

Ground floor

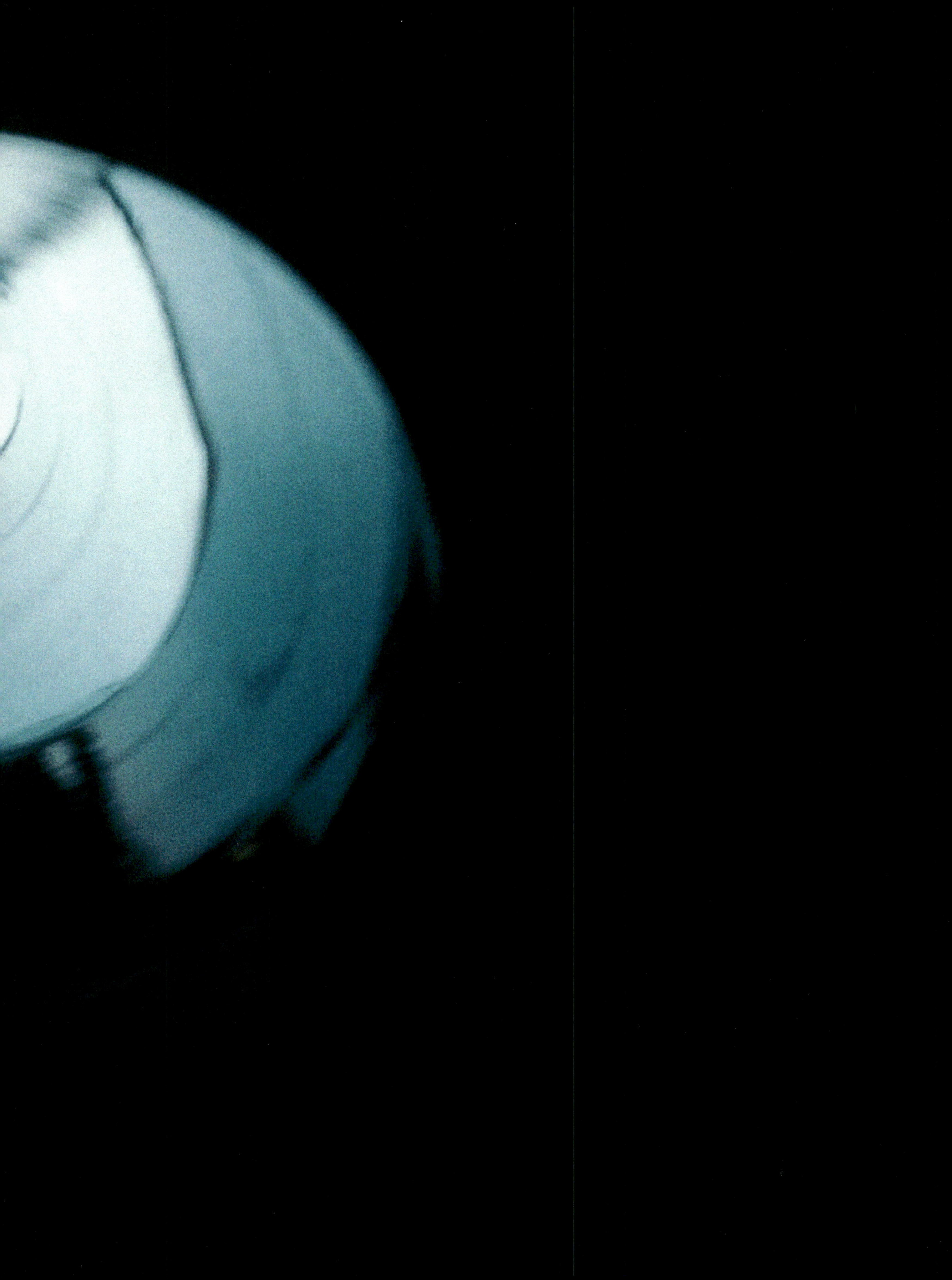

Ticket for the 1st Berlin Biennale

Center Peep at the Kunst-Werke, Berlin

Center Peep is the smallest project we've done so far. The first Berlin Art Biennial, curated by Hans Ulrich Obrist and Klaus Biesenbach, was held in 1998. A number of architects were invited to create work for this art festival.

As a matter of fact, our proposal was inspired by a previous design we did for the architecture initiative *Berlin und seine Zeit* ("Berlin and its Time"), in the context of a series of discussions entitled "Wohnen + X" ("Living + X"). "+ X" was a term we were using at the time to describe parasitic forms of housing placed on existing buildings. We took the Fernsehturm (the television tower at Alexanderplatz) as our central object – specifically, its prodigious shaft, which contains the lift and the emergency stairs. We wanted to put the exterior of this huge cylinder to use, and suggested colonising it with capsule units, like a coral reef.

Our choice of site was, of course, by no means random. The Fernsehturm is quite simply embedded in the subconscious of all Berliners – it's the central feature of our mental map of Berlin. You always think of your position in relation to the Fernsehturm. It marks the historic centre of the city – it stands at the city's point of origin, right near the former (and future) site of the Stadtschloss, Berlin's former royal palace. You might say that, in Berlin, all roads lead to the Fernsehturm.

Each of us constructs a mental map of the city in our own head, and that map governs our spatial perception and navigation. You don't orient yourself primarily using street names, but – often entirely unconsciously – with features of the urban landscape. As you recall places and think of your position in relation to certain buildings, you reconstruct the constructed environment as a personal spatial image.

When Klaus Biesenbach first approached us in connection with the Berlin Biennale, we went to have a closer look at the exhibition space "Kunst-Werke" in the Auguststrasse – we didn't know the place very well back then. It simply didn't register on our personal map of Berlin.

At the time, the Auguststrasse was not well known at all – the streetscape contained more voids and empty sites than buildings. Furthermore, the Kunst-Werke exhibition spaces were located in a courtyard where they essentially had no direct relationship to the surrounding city. We felt that it was the wrong place for such an important new art institution.

We had spent years living and working in London, and when we left for Berlin we took with us a feeling that architecture can move worlds. The Neue Nationalgalerie was our idea of a metropolitan space where people could properly engage with contemporary art. Instead, we found ourselves in a cramped little courtyard – in an unremarkable old building that had barely been given a lick of paint. And this was supposed to be the new home of contemporary art in Berlin?

Our aim was to give this site a new significance and to visually work it into the city's grid. So how would we do it? By placing a strong neighbour by its side that would help it stand out from its environment.

We wanted to create a connection between the Kunst-Werke and something really big, and, just as it had for the "Wohnen + X" project, the Fernsehturm immediately sprang to mind – in part because it stands close to the Kunst-Werke. We had the idea of creating a strong visual connection between the Kunst-Werke and the Fernsehturm.

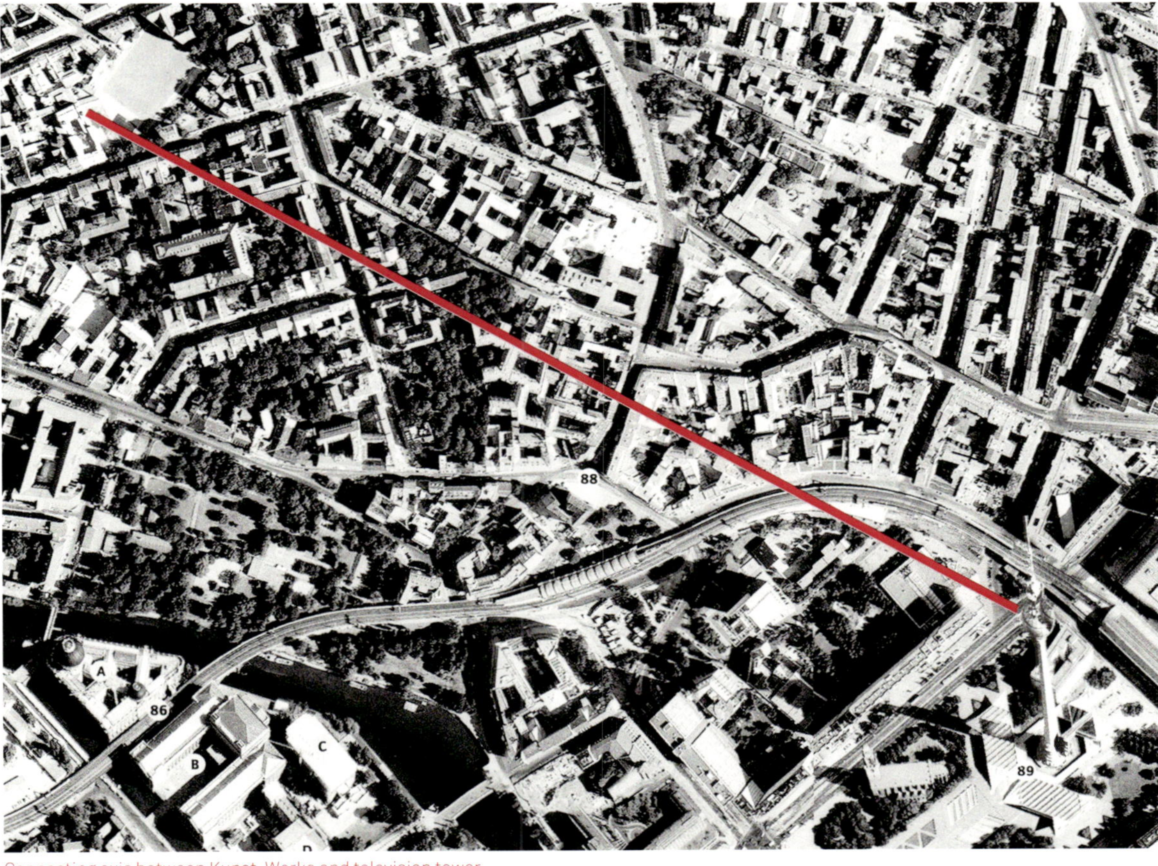

Connecting axis between Kunst-Werke and television tower

We didn't want to merely use a window to create a connection. Instead, we drilled a very small hole in the firewall. Through this hole we stuck a tube. If you looked through it, you saw the Fernsehturm – but not in the position where it actually stands. We created this visual confusion by means of mirrors and image deflection. Because you couldn't see the mirror, the image appeared to be a real view. The movement of the air against your eye made you aware that you were really looking through a hole in the wall into the space outside, and this made it all the more disconcerting to be seeing the Fernsehturm in a place where you knew it didn't really stand.

Schematic section and plan

This artwork creates a sense of unease. Viewers are left uncertain of what's real and what's unreal. They may at first believe that the image is a projection, but then they hear the sounds of the city and feel the movement of the air. You try to explain away these phenomena, thinking that the wind may be coming from a wind machine and that the sounds are a recording. It takes some time for you to notice that the image isn't a projection.

This artwork was a fixture at the Kunst-Werke for a number of years, until new construction work on the firewall meant that the hole had to be closed. We've returned to the subject of shifts in perception on a number of occasions – the Dallgow Marie-Curie-Gymnasium project, for instance, involved a periscope that allows you to stand in a dark hallway and look out at the playground and the surrounding landscape.

Yes, and this isn't the only project that uses the idea. We created another for Volker Diehl, a Berlin gallerist, to display at his stand at the first Art Forum event, held in Berlin's Messehallen (trade fair halls). We built a tower with two mirrors, angled to reflect the stands below and behind them. This resulted in a view of the exhibition that was quite simply turned on its head.

Themes such as alienation and shifts of perception have an abiding interest for us. They stimulate us and inspire all of our designs.

The temporary entrance to the Kunst-Werke, Berlin

Its concealed position in a courtyard off Auguststrasse makes the Kunst-Werke quite hard to find, and the situation isn't helped by its unprepossessing entrance or the low height of the building in front of it. Our submission to the temporary entrance design competition was similar to our Center Peep project – its aim was to make this cultural institution, the Kunst-Werke, a more visible part of the urban space.

At the time, we could already foresee that the adjacent property would be built higher, leaving the Kunst-Werke doomed to sag in between like some kind of dwarf. We wanted our project to give people on the street an idea of what was concealed behind the façade.

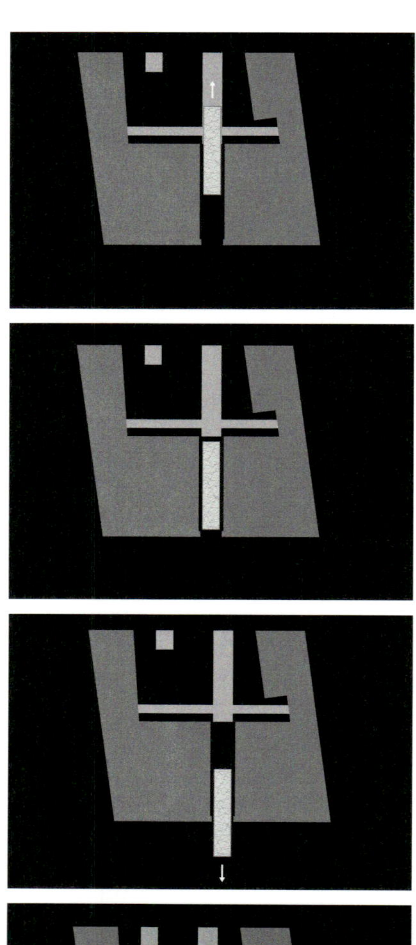

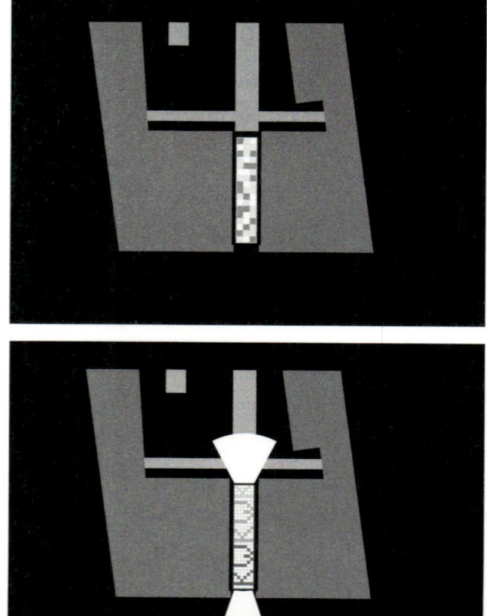

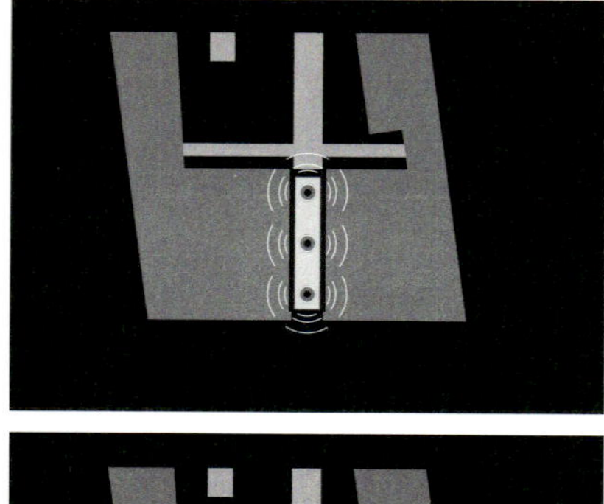

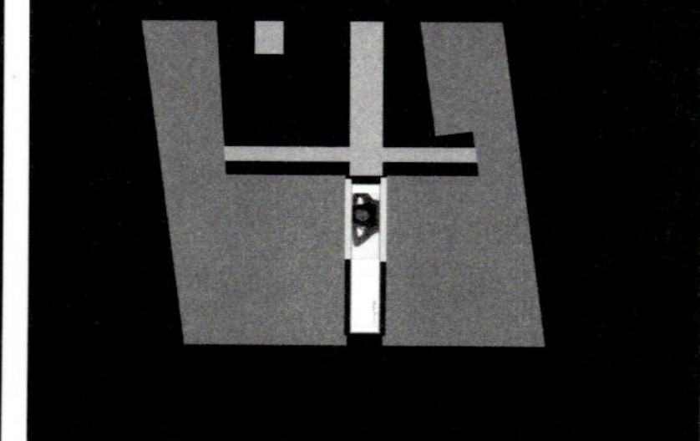

Dynamic communication tool for the curator

It was for precisely this reason that, for quite some time, we were unable to decide between two ideas – either to give the entrance a stronger emphasis, or to increase the building's sense of perceived volume. Ultimately, we submitted designs for both ideas.

The first scenario primarily concerned the problem of access. On the one hand, visitors to the Kunst-Werke had to be channelled through the entryway of the front building in order to reach the actual Kunst-Werke building in the courtyard. On the other hand, the residents of the front building would also have to pass through this passageway to reach their apartments.

We resolved this conflict by developing a kind of swathed object resembling a loom frame that could be parked in the courtyard's entryway to form a sort of tunnel leading into it. This moveable steel frame was fashioned with small notches, allowing its covering to be rearranged in a number of different ways. The first configuration we proposed was a wrapping of bands with circular openings, through which residents could pass into the side wings.

Additionally, we wanted to bring the ticket booth forward, so that anyone approaching through the passageway would recognise it as the entrance to the Kunst-Werke. This, however, would have involved moving one of the apartments. The conduit planned by us functioned as a ground-level tunnel, bridging the private space of the thoroughfare – through which the apartments are reached – to connect the public street space with the public courtyard space.

We also saw this framework as a tool for a curator who could constantly create new settings. The framework is constructed like a Vierendeel truss in order to provide the necessary rigidity, and it's on rollers, allowing it to be wheeled out into the street. In its default mode, the frame was to be located entirely within the entryway. On special occasions, however – such as the opening of an exhibition at the Kunst-Werke – we wanted to be able to make a statement by extending this object into the street space, perhaps even creating a roadblock.

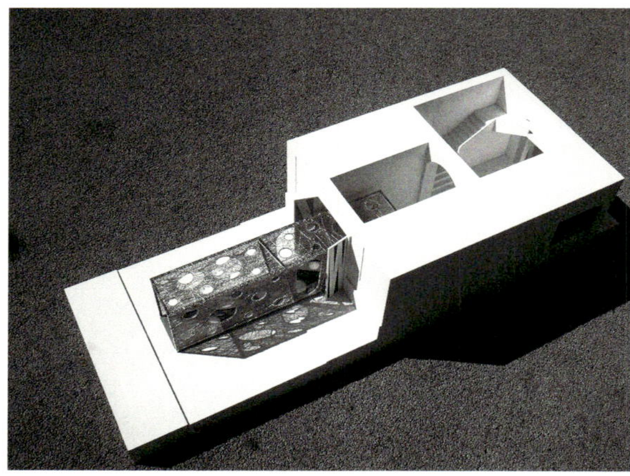

Incidentally, Auguststrasse has been blocked before – during the Berlin Biennale, when the street was transformed into a long pedestrian zone. People could hardly get through the crush – even without cars, it wasn't wide enough for all the people.

We wanted the installation to communicate that something special lay behind this building. It didn't, however, solve the problem of the building's height, so we came up with a second design to deal with that.

Cloth banners with KW logo above the entrance

We created a rendering of a taller building standing next door, in order to show the competition organiser how acute the contrast in building heights would be. We wanted to install a kind of festival architecture of cloth banners in the airspace above the Kunst-Werke and between the neighbouring houses, simultaneously giving the building additional height and offering a new view from below, one that would transform the Kunst-Werke logo. This, too, would have increased the Kunst-Werke's visibility.

Today, it's hard to believe that festival architecture was once a legitimate architectural genre. We're deluged with countless festival events, but their spatial settings are no longer created by architects. Yet festival architecture was once a significant laboratory for experimental architecture. In the 16th century, Andrea Palladio designed elaborate festival pageants, and in the French Revolutionary era, architects composed the spaces for triumphal processions. Our project was an attempt to reclaim the lost festival genre as part of the modern discipline of architecture.

At the same time, it was intended to be a light and unpretentious, yet definite, spatial presence – like the washing lines in Venice, which are so characteristic of the street spaces there and give them such a sculptural quality.

The effect would have been particularly dramatic at night, when fibre-optic cables integrated into the banners would have produced a swarm of glow-worms above the roof.

Although we weren't able to implement the design, this project remains important to us, because it showed us how architectural projects that restore the missing interface points between buildings and the wider urban space can achieve more for the city than autonomous objects can.

The fact that Berlin has been the location for most of our projects – with the majority in the city centre – helped us to realise this. We've created more than ten buildings in the Spandauer Vorstadt (a central quarter) alone. Over the years, this has allowed us to observe the transformative effect of architecture on the urban space and to see how a series of projects can change an entire civic district.

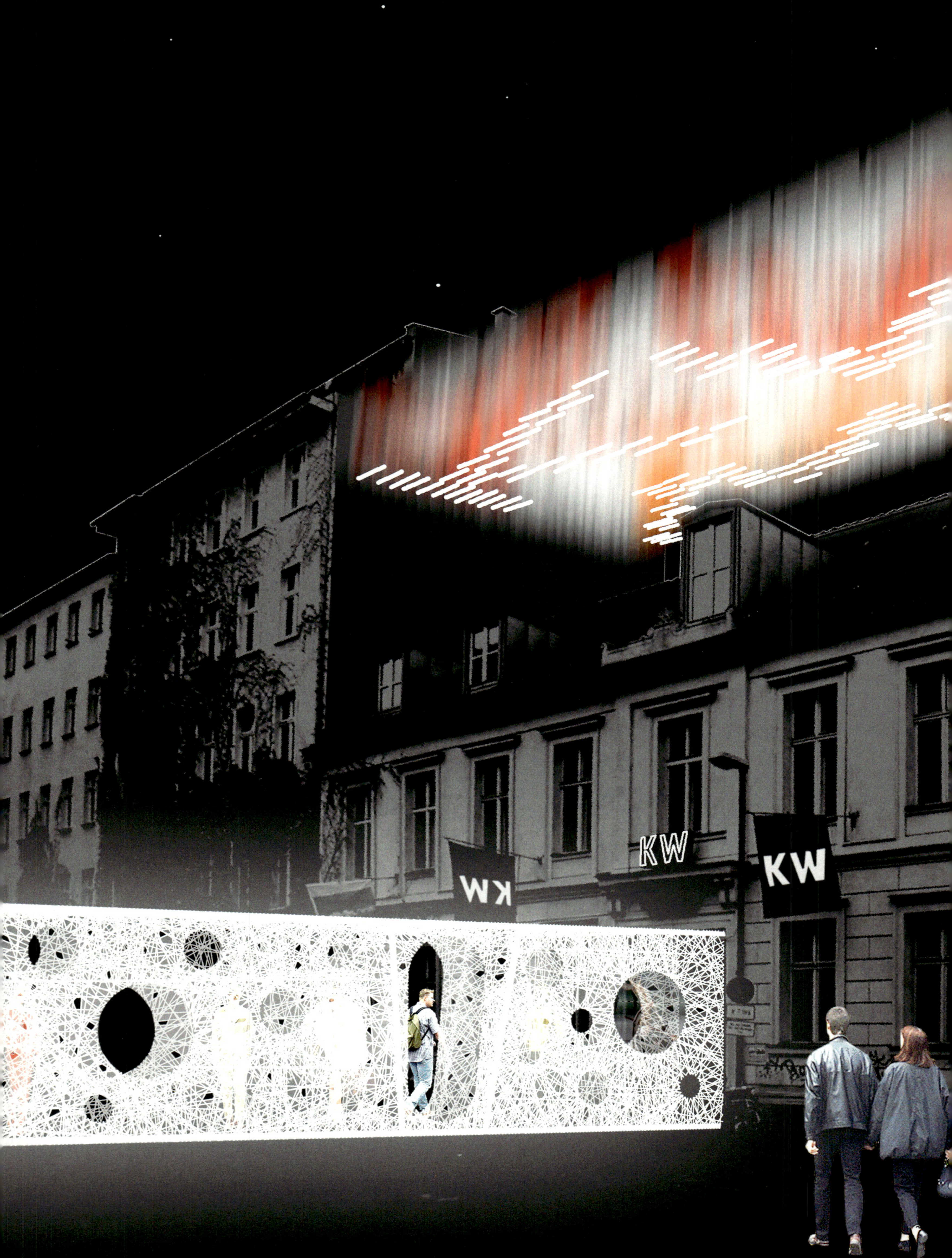
KW
KW

Temporary entrance Kunst-Werke

Location
Auguststrasse 69, 10117 Berlin

Year
competition 2004

Team
Erik Behrends, Jon C. Ferrer, Timotheus Kreidel, Arno Löbbecke, Peter Menken, Johannes Rueb

Client
KUNST-WERKE BERLIN e.V.

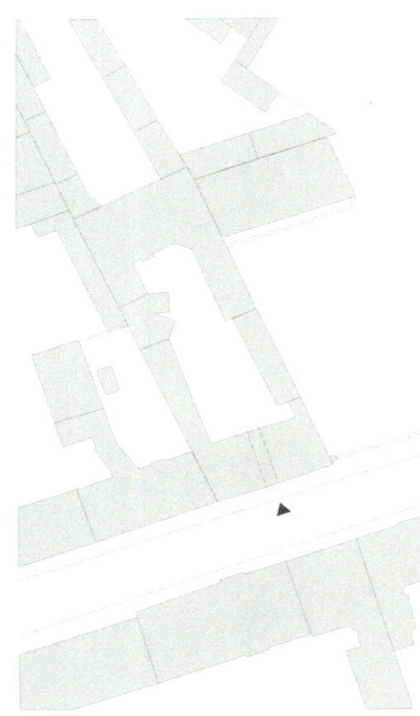

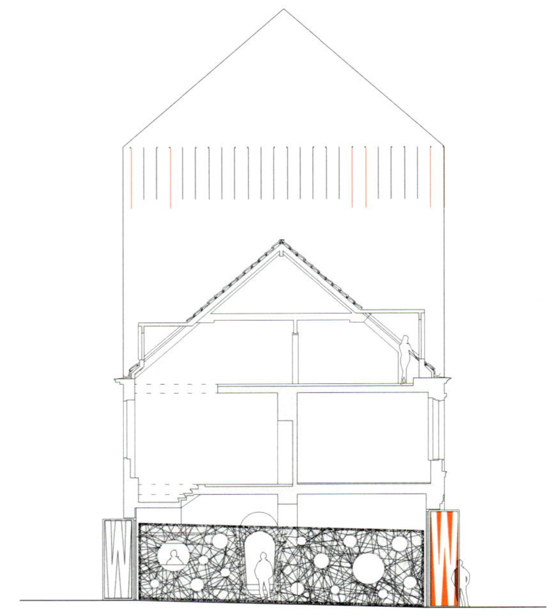

Section

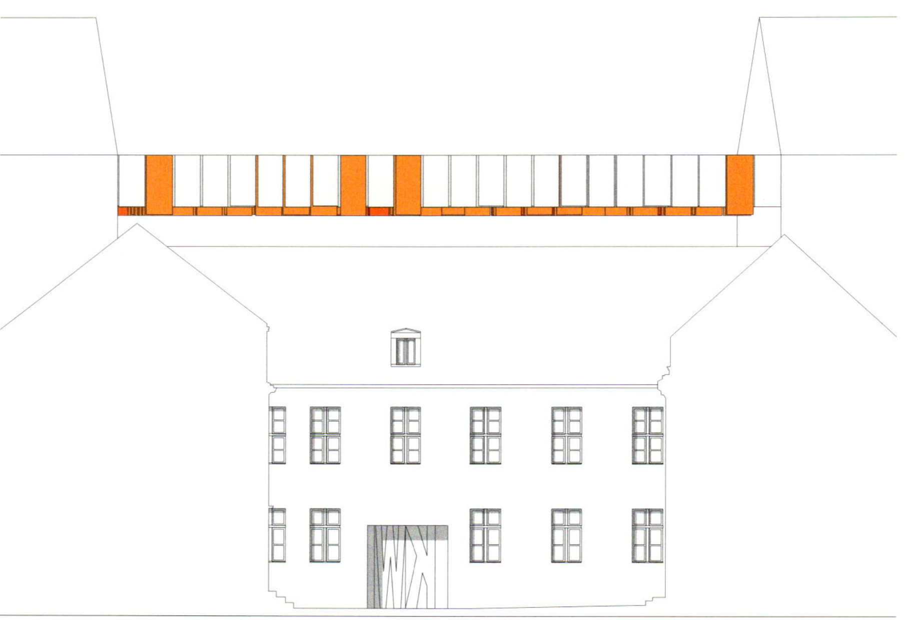

Courtyard elevation

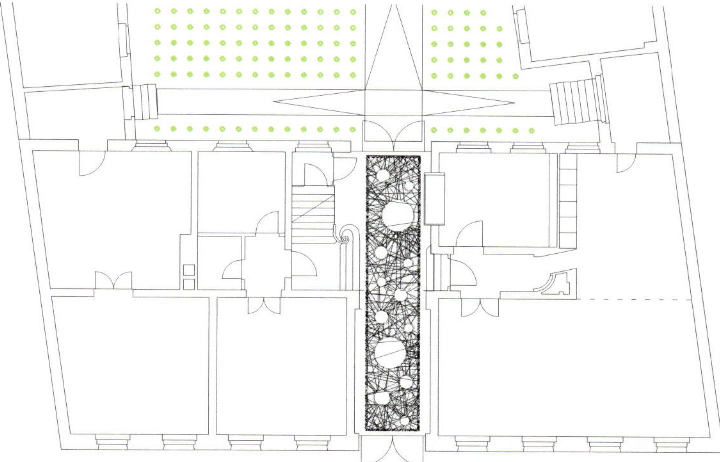

Ground floor

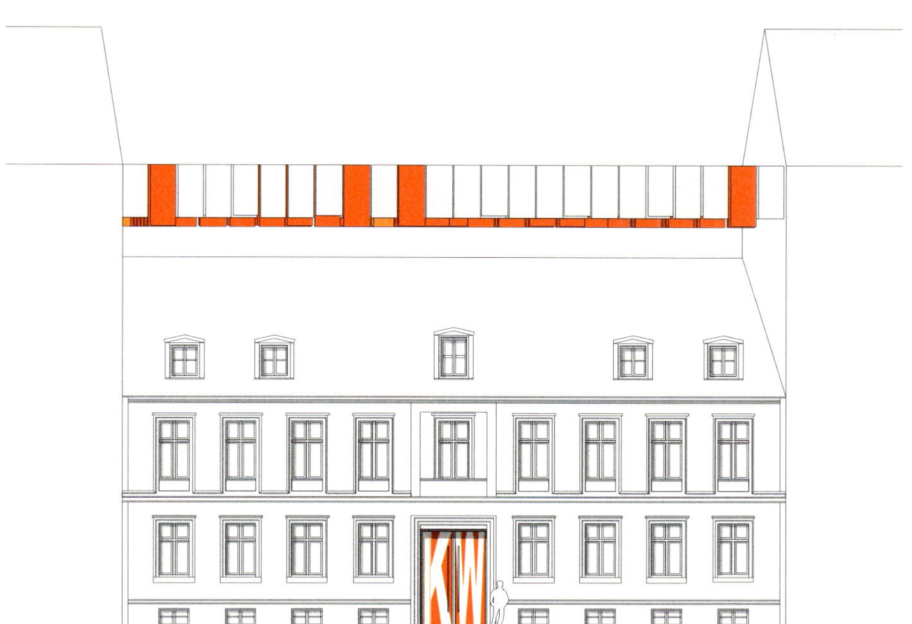

Street elevation

Courtyard view, 2011

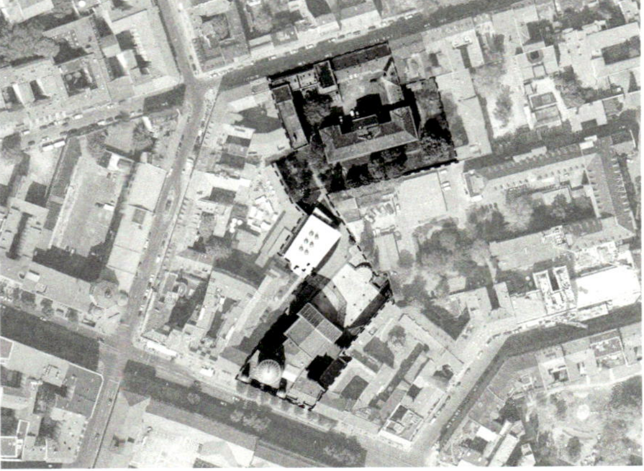
Connected buildings of the Jewish community

The Former Jewish Girls' School, Berlin

Our work at the former Jewish Girls' School involved the conversion and re-programming of an existing building. In many respects, however, it differed from a standard conversion project.

The building belongs to the Jüdische Gemeinde zu Berlin (Berlin's Jewish community organization), and was built by Alexander Beer on the community's land. It was one of the last buildings erected before the Second World War and in 1942, after the school had been shut down by the National Socialist government, the building was used as a makeshift hospital. Subsequently, it was used by a number of Berlin schools. It has remained largely vacant since 1996.

For many years, the school haunted Auguststrasse. Quite close to where we live stood this inaccessible building with boarded-up windows, past which pedestrians hurried.

It was a striking building, a sleeping beauty somehow removed from the passage of time.

A number of interested parties submitted concepts for putting the building to use. Many very courageous suggestions and architectonic visions were put forward that involved completely reshaping the building. We made a conscious decision to reveal the building's intrinsic qualities through minimal interventions, and worked to find suitable uses for its spaces.

This meant that for this project, we defined our role as architects differently. Beyond our role as designers, we wanted to act as mediators, bringing together the right programme, the right ideas and the right people to revitalize the site.

This led us to approach the conversion project as if it were a co-housing project. The result demonstrates that this approach, effective for private residential buildings, can also be used to bring together ideas for cultural spaces, creating a kind of co-culture project.

Interior views prior to conversion, 2009

With the gallerist Michael Fuchs, we deliberated on whom and what the building was suitable for, and how we could develop an idea capable of giving it a new identity. Fuchs took out a 30-year lease on the building and assumed the responsibility for maintaining it. Acting as the initiator of the group, he brought together a collective of diverse cultural players. The old school now houses restaurants and galleries, and has an apartment in its attic storey.

Of course, this conversion project posed challenges to us not only as co-initiators but as architects as well. We felt that it was important to preserve and strengthen the building's distinctive aura. For instance, we recreated the building's original façades and room divisions. When you look at images from the archives and see how the rooms used to be – they had since been plasterboarded – you realise how difficult it was to recover any elements of the building's original interior. After all, we also had to bear in mind all the modern-day requirements related to fire protection and so forth. In spite of this, parts of the building can now be experienced as they originally stood, most notably the generous stairwell.

or views prior to conversion, 2009

When we embarked on the project, we knew the interior of the building only from the Berlin Biennial, which was held there in 2006. Everything was in decay, with massive structural damage, and some of the building's spatial qualities had been altered by new installations.

There was, of course, historical documentation. Old images of the gymnasium being used by the girls, for instance, made a great impression on me. If one thinks about the fates of these girls: they are gone, but the building is still there, only the building just hasn't been able to tell its story – now this reality has a far greater importance than anything new one might integrate into the building.

An architect's task is to add things, but also to refrain from adding things – to minimise. As Mies van der Rohe put it: "You should make it as simple as possible, no matter what the cost." This spirit of reduction culminates in an attitude of self-restraint, making very few changes, knowing when to leave things be. And we wouldn't have done that if –

– if we hadn't already built so much around here, in the Spandauer Vorstadt?

Not so much that, but certainly we wouldn't have done it the same way ten years ago. In any case, the school project is important to us, not least because we'll be tenants of the building ourselves.

We've rented two classrooms for a potential expansion of our firm and as a potential site for holding exhibitions or workshops for students.

This is really the most interesting thing about urban development: creating spaces with potential, where something can emerge on its own. Not always defining everything precisely. That was the brilliant thing about the Palast der Republik – although, unfortunately, this was realised far too late.

The former girls' school also demonstrates the significance of architecture. I believe that the project wouldn't have been possible without our contribution as architects. In the end, everything also depends on the building. Someone has to say: It can be done this way. Even co-housing projects only function when someone contributes a high degree of architectural competence – and that quality is also necessary for the mediation process.

The Jewish community organization was extremely reluctant to lease the building. After all, 30 years is a long time. It meant that they were handing over the building for more than a generation. In return, however, they'll get a functioning building back. Leaving it to stand vacant was expensive, and, of course, a vacant building doesn't look good.

Ultimately, it was about finally getting the lights switched on again. The fundamental question was how to give such a building a vibrant sense of lightness and allow it to live in the present, but without trivialising its history.

Apartment in the former attic atelier

Former schoolyard on the roof of the side wing

Location
Auguststrasse 11–13, 10117 Berlin

Year
completion 2012

Team
Florian Fels, Ulrike Gardeler,
Anna Wolska, Daniel Strassburger,
Kerstin Thomsen

Client
Michael Fuchs Verwaltungs-GmbH, Berlin

Technical planners
Dr.-Ing. Jürgen Westphal, Zeuthen
(structural engineering)
service engineer Ingenieurbüro Weltzer,
Berlin (building services)

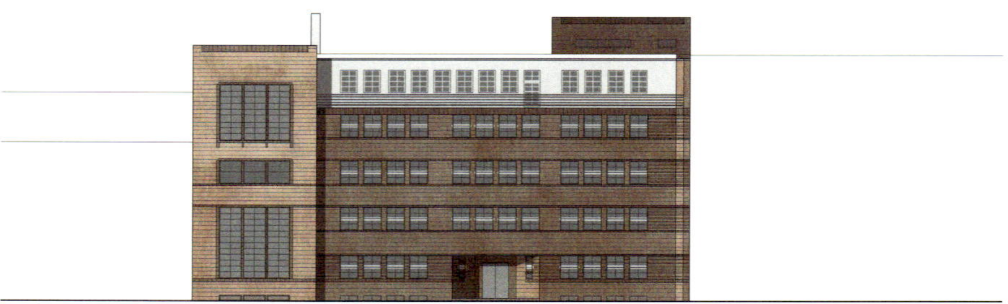

Street elevation

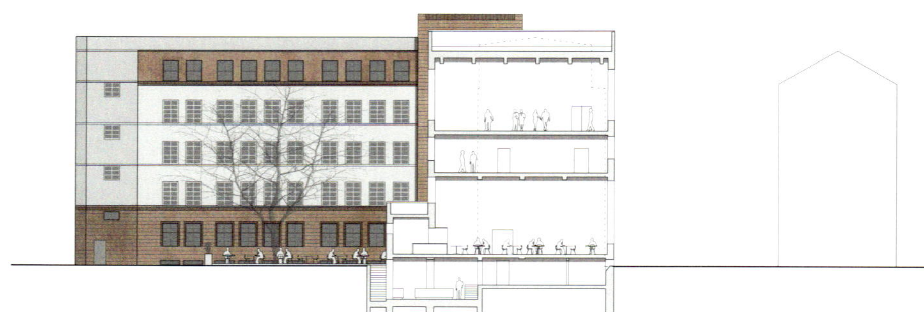

Section of the front building

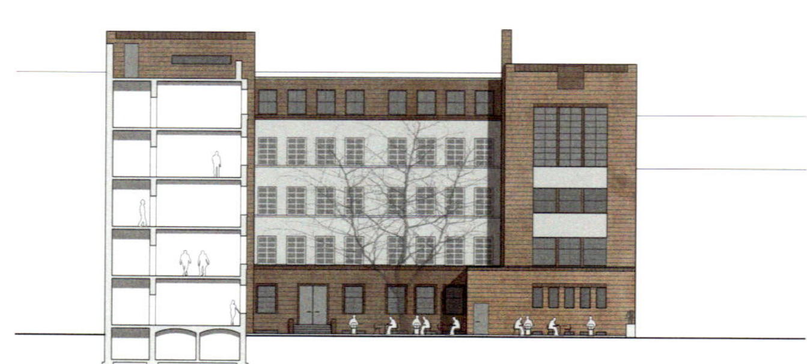

Section of the side wing

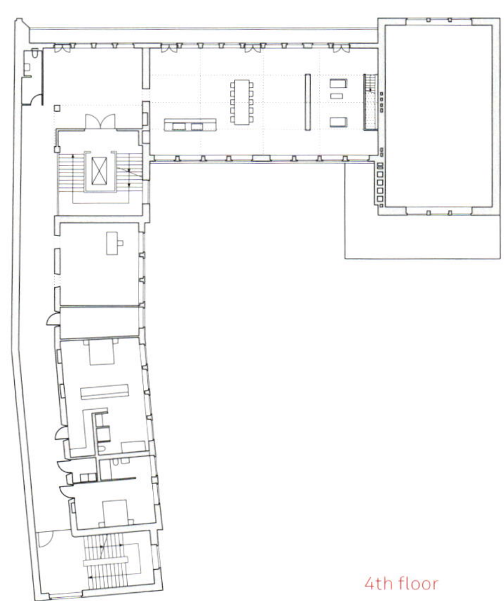

4th floor

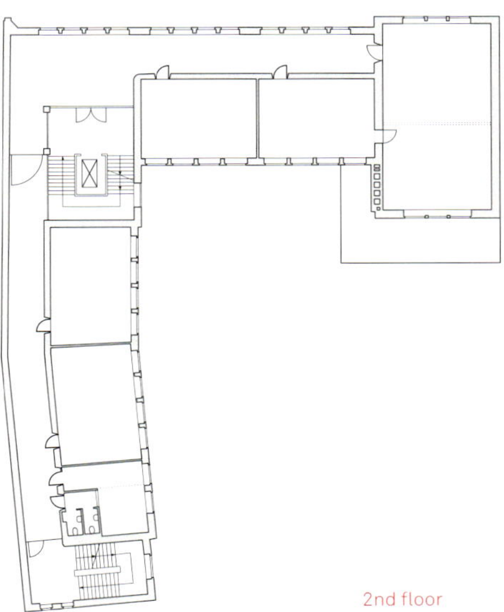

2nd floor

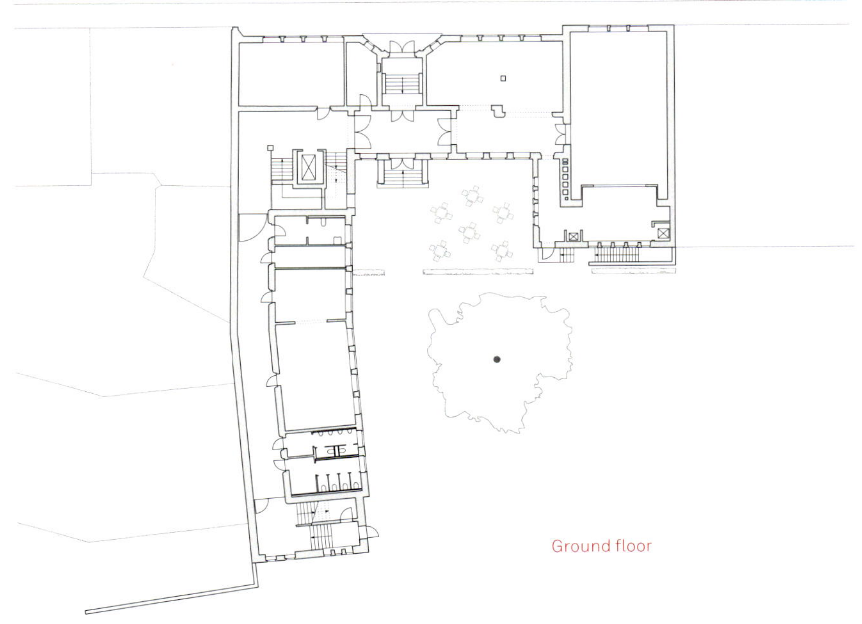

Ground floor

1.100 m²
SHOPFLÄCHE
FLÄCHE
BÜRO
BAUWERT
030/20 26 20

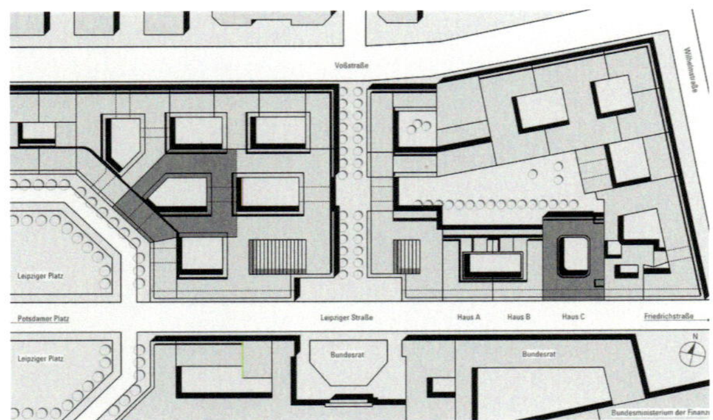

Competition site at Leipziger Platz and Leipziger Strasse 126

Leipziger Strasse office building, Berlin

The Leipziger Strasse building originated with an unsuccessful competition entry for a site at Leipziger Platz. The investor for the site was a developer with conservative values. In spite of that, we decided that, somehow, we'd have to win approval for something contemporary.

Our strategy was to employ the colour gold. In certain cities, for instance Moscow, there is a mysterious connection – which is ever more frequently noticeable – between the conservative architectural canon and the use of gold materials in façades. And because the client had just returned from Paris and was still in rapture over the city, we played on that, choosing the name "Palais d'Or" for our draft.

But we also meant for the gold to produce a further, entirely different reference. By setting a gold-coloured façade among natural stone façades, we wanted to create a counterpoint that would visually connect our work to the glittering buildings of Hans Scharoun's Kulturforum nearby.

We didn't win the Leipziger Platz competition. However, the client liked our concept so much that he commissioned us for a site a little further down Leipziger Strasse.

At the time, there were two managing directors at the firm backing the project, the younger of whom was receptive to contemporary architecture, and the older of whom had conservative tastes. They agreed to avoid a compromise solution: it should either look like an old building or like something else entirely. That's how we were able to build something truly contemporary.

On the plot directly adjacent to ours, the developer erected a new building with a façade in a historic style.

The neighbouring buildings, however, weren't the only significant factor: the Reichsluftfahrtgebäude (built to house the NSDAP-era Ministry of Aviation; now home to the Finance Ministry) was located on the opposite side of the street, and it represented an additional dialogue partner for our building.

It influenced our building in a number of respects, one of which were the proportions of the façade. A two-storey arcade design provided the basic structure, with the addition of a recessed upper storey. On top of that, the view of the former Reichsluftfahrtministerium from the office creates a sense of immediacy – you just feel its proximity. Our building should be emphatically open to the urban space around it.

Let's go back to the architectonic impression Paris made on our investors. You have to ask yourself: Why do they find Paris so beautiful?

A historical façade does have qualities that sometimes make modern glass façades appear lacking. Its recessed and projecting elements give it a high degree of plasticity and a varied structure. A façade of this type contains stories for the viewer to discover: it's not simply a one-liner.

For this reason, our façade's concept and sculptural form were both multi-layered in character. To the right of us, the real old building; to the left of us, the new "old building". Caught in the middle as we were, we wanted to respond to those who miss the old cityscape, but with contemporary strategies.

We therefore wanted a façade that was dynamic – one that could present a number of different faces. When people think of glass façades, they always think of a smooth skin, but the slats within our façade also create depth.

It's far harder to construct a good glass façade than it is to construct a stone building. There are five rules for working in stone, and if you keep to them, you can't go wrong –

– whereas when you're designing a glass construction, you always have to keep some kind of filter in mind, something to guarantee privacy and shade. Otherwise, you're stuck with the last resort of colourful curtains – which would, for us at least, be hard to bear.

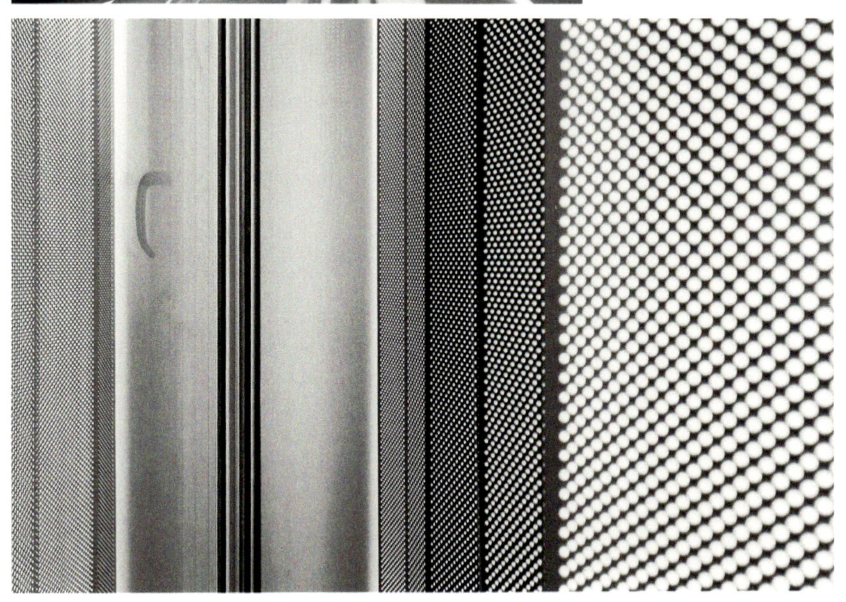

The shades have perforations, so that when they're closed, they obscure the view without blocking it completely. At the same time, you can't be seen from outside the building. You can rotate the elements and slide them to one side, creating a wide-open façade.

Another feature of our design was the double-skin façade. The distance between the two layers was relatively large: between 60 and 70 centimetres. There are really only two sensible areas of application for double façades – that is, only two areas in which they don't create more problems than they solve. One of these is noise protection, specifically protection from traffic noise (they allow you to work with the windows open), and the other is protection from the sun. External solar protection is essential for a sound climatic concept. In exposed positions, however, it'll constantly break down unless you place a second layer in front of it.

Air from outside flows into an interstitial space beneath each storey of our building. There, it's warmed by solar energy and then channelled out again at a higher level. In the winter, this creates a mild greenhouse effect, so that when you open the window, pre-warmed air streams in. In the summer, the building is so well ventilated that there's no significant overheating and the windows in all of its façades can be opened.

The construction of the double façade wasn't just a matter of technical performance, however – we also wanted to create a design with layered depth, and we accomplished this with variously coloured slats behind the storey-high glass panels.

The effect produced by the graduation of depth in the façade is heightened by the shifting vantage points of passers-by: as they move, the appearance of the building changes.

Leipziger Strasse office building

Location
Leipziger Strasse 126, 10117 Berlin

Year
completion 2008

Team
Volker Raatz, Olaf Menk, Jacob van Ommen, Dirk Zimmermann, Erik Behrends, Thomas Ellinghaus, Alessio Fossati

Client
apellasbauwert property group, Düsseldorf

Technical planners
GuD Planungsgesellschaft für Ingenieurbau mbH, Berlin (structural engineering)
Ingenieurbüro für Haustechnik KEM GmbH, Berlin (building services)
LA.BAR Landschaftsarchitekten bdla, Berlin (open space planning)

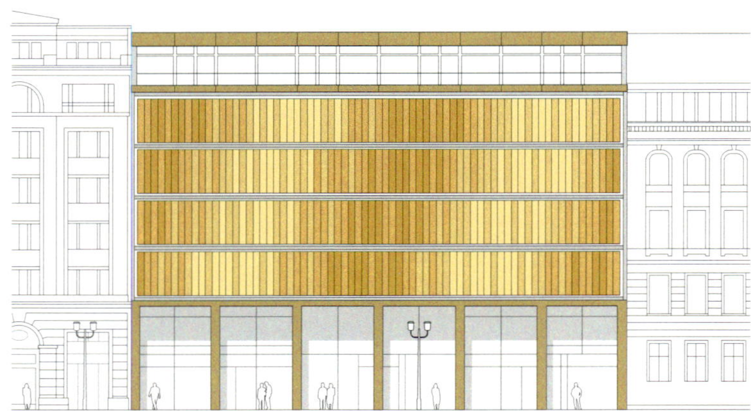

Street elevation

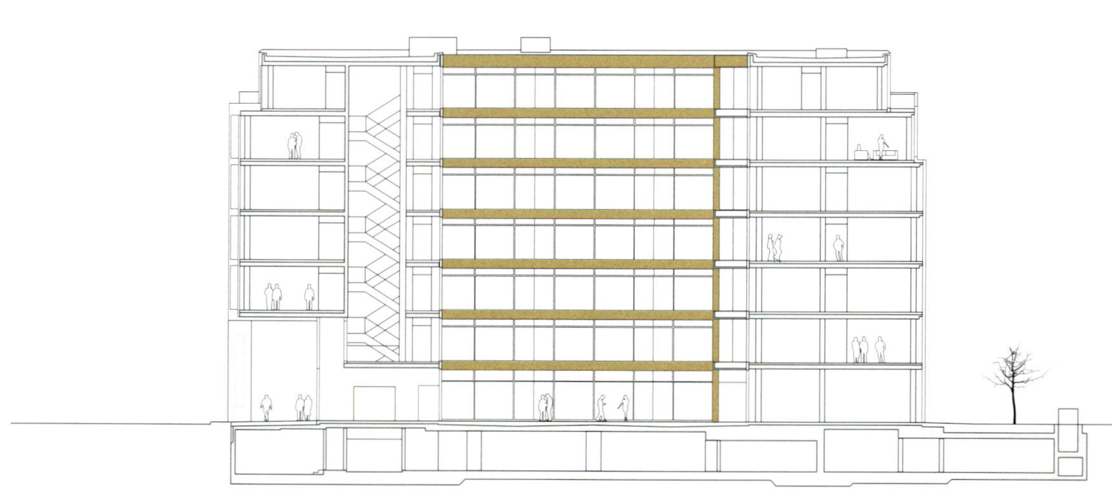

Section

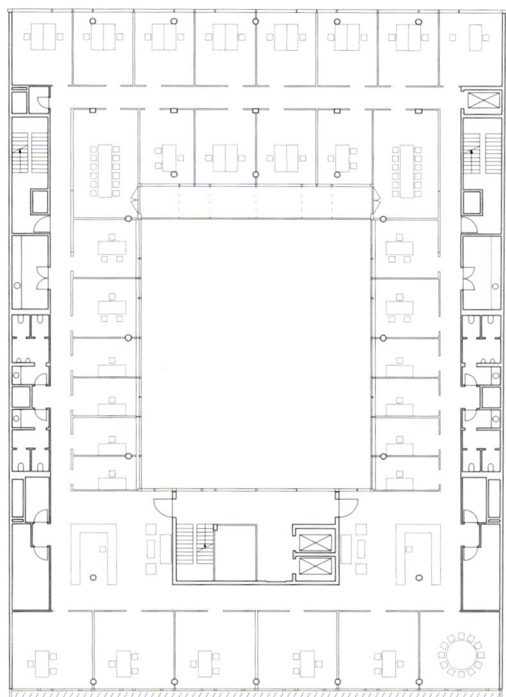
2nd floor

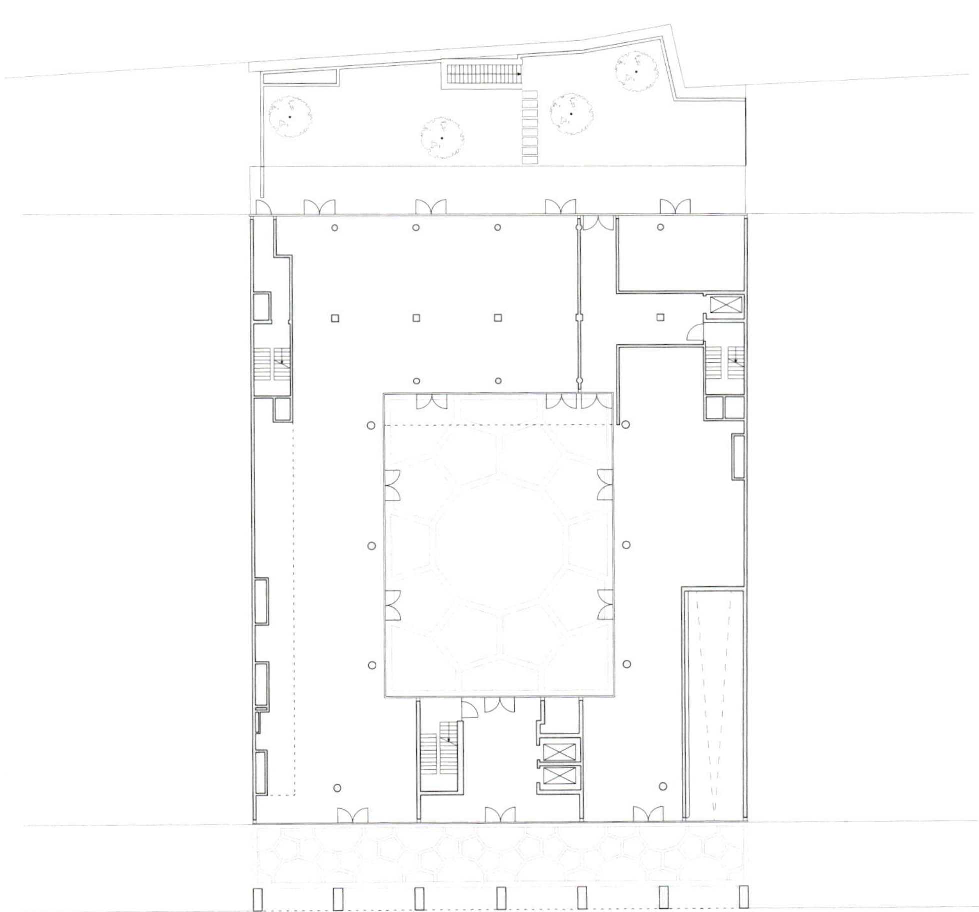
Ground floor

BODE-MUSEUM

The Hackesches Quartier, Berlin

For the new "Hackesches Quartier", we were commissioned to develop a quite small and inconspicuous site. The master plan for the Hackesches Quartier development was drawn up by the firm Müller Reimann Architekten, who also designed its new plaza and main street. Our plot, however, lay behind these new urban features. What I subsequently found remarkable was that our buildings, viewed across the Hackescher Markt station, had such a powerful presence. When we started out, I wouldn't have imagined it.

The project was to be a speculative new office block, which meant that we couldn't get around using a uniform grid of 1.35m. The challenge that faced us was to take this restriction and create something surprising – something that would have more impact on the city than some standard, anonymous office block façade.

The question was: How do you transform a 1.35-metre grid façade into an urban envelope? We solved this problem by turning the grid into a series of diagonals. Each of the diagonal bands corresponds to the diagonal on a 1.35-metre square, allowing the floors to be flexibly divided on a 1.35-metre grid by means of separating walls.

Yes, but that's not all. First and foremost, this approach created a sculptural architectural structure, positioned in front of the glass to serve as an external load-bearing shell. This structure covers the whole building, including the stepped storeys, giving it expression as a volume.

This structure makes our building stand out prominently from the rest of the district. The relatively crisp and hard rhythms of the neighbouring buildings are relieved by the playful elements of our building. Anyone passing the building has a very clear sense of this.

We'd previously used a design of this kind in a plan for an insurance company's headquarters in Lübeck. The floor plan for that project, however, was a full circle, and not a sector of a circle like the Berlin site. That project also offered more opportunities for placing large double-storey spaces between the office units.

At first glance, the Hackesches Quartier façade looks very simple, but when you take a closer look, you can see just how complex its geometry is. Because the upper storeys are recessed, the façade is inclined rather than vertical – this means that the diagonal supports are tilted on two planes.

In addition to this, the building has a rounded corner, meaning that in one area the diagonals actually had to be curved.

Concrete structure of the façade during construction

Constructing this feature using analogue methods wasn't exactly simple.

Our building is the only one in the new development that has a sloping roof. The other architects created stepped-back top floors – but, as in our Hackescher Markt building, our design consciously avoided this. When buildings stop at the eaves, stepped storeys on top often look as if they were added at a later stage, because they form no sculptural unity with the building.

As the vantage point of the viewer shifts, the combination of curves and inclined roof creates a very interesting Escher-like effect. There are places where the load-bearing structure appears to jump, places where it seems that something isn't quite right, that there is a kink – as if someone had traced the outline wrong.

GASAG

S-Bahnhof Hackescher Markt
Nails

Hackesches Quartier

Location
Henriette-Herz-Platz 3, 10178 Berlin

Year
competition 2006
completion 2011

Team
Olaf Menk, Dominik Queck

Client
Investitionsgesellschaft
Hackesches Quartier mbH & Co. KG, Berlin

Technical planners
Leonhardt, Andrä und Partner Beratende Ingenieure VBI, GmbH, Berlin (structural engineering)
Georg Mayer & Partner Beratende Ingenieure für Technische Gesamtplanung GmbH, Berlin (building services)
EGS-plan Ingenieurgesellschaft für Energie-, Gebäude- und Solartechnik mbH, Stuttgart (energy technology)

Elevation

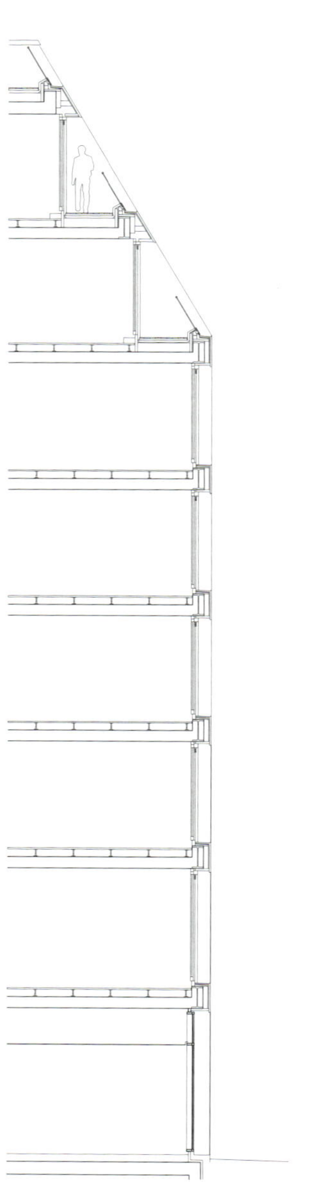

Façade section and elevation

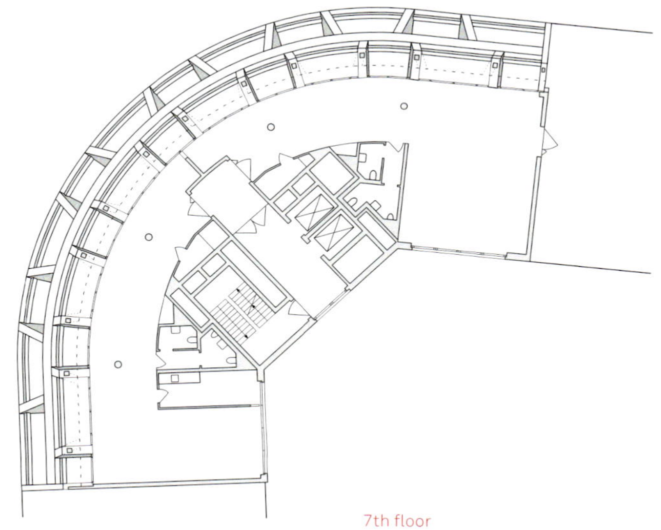
7th floor

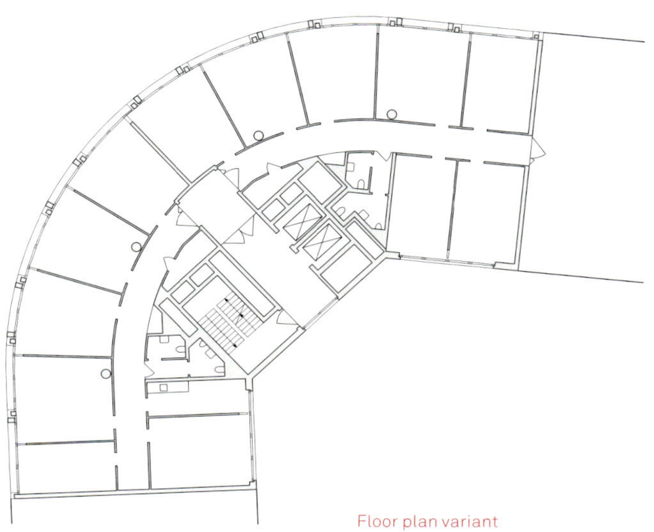
Floor plan variant

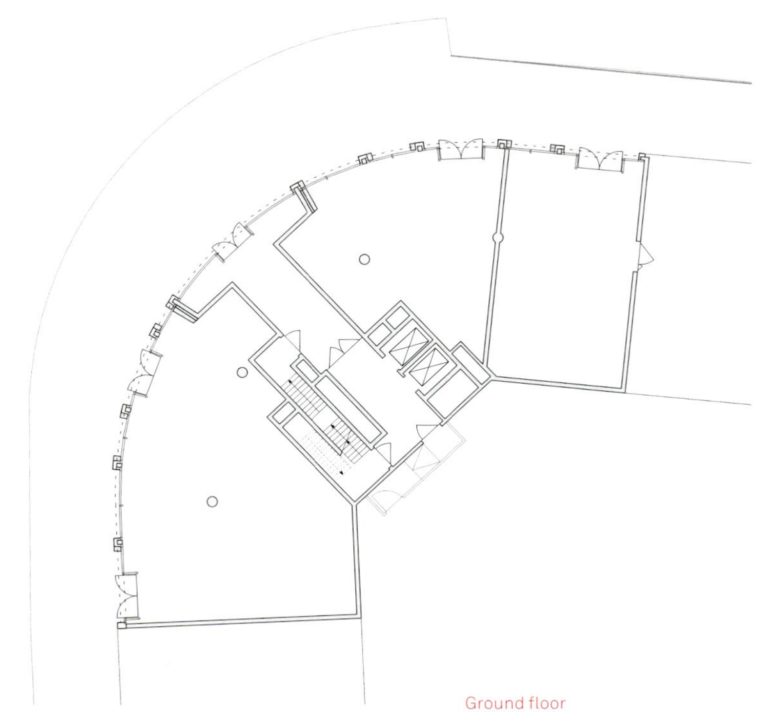
Ground floor

oxymoron
SOPHIENCLUB
Sparkasse

The building at Hackescher Markt, Berlin

The first time we saw Hackescher Markt, it made quite an impression on us. You don't often encounter this kind of situation: There was the plaza with the S-Bahn station, and then, right at the edge of the plaza, yawned an empty space with this humongous bare wall, stretching way back into the lot. This decades-old vacant site was unbelievably dramatic.

Yes – for that reason, we wanted this peculiarity to remain legible in some form even after the site had been developed. Our design achieved this through the use of what we've always called an "atrium joint", which serves as a passageway between the public space of the city and the semi-public area at the front of the building.

The flooring for the two-storey conference rooms does span this atrium, but the minimal construction still allows views of the deeper parts of the site.

The most fascinating thing about Berlin in the nineties was that the edges of blocks were so porous. These days, the deeper parts of a block are usually hidden from view – there are hardly any vacant lots left in the city centre – and so it's always a pleasure to get a sense of the worlds that open up beyond the perimeter.

Block prior to the reconstruction of the Hackesche Höfe, 1996

Roof terrace of the side wing

Another factor was important to us: Hackescher Markt is a historically and culturally significant place. For this reason, we wanted the contemporary building that we were inserting into it to respond to the rhythms of the adjacent façades. We therefore adopted their structure, on the vertical plane as well as the horizontal.

The façade that faces the street now consists of large-format glass panels, some of which are veiled by a screen-printed pattern of fine white lines or covered with a translucent film.

By alternating the façade's glass elements, we also wanted to create an effect of layered depth – the building changes significantly as the light changes, and the double façade develops an internal plasticity. However, this multi-layered construction was also chosen for acoustic reasons. After all, no one wants to hear every little squeal as the trains go by.

The glass panels are framed by bands of stone parapets, and there are also some areas where the walls are clad with stone.

We carried the theme established by this stone cladding deep into the interior. We continuously used stone inside and out across the building's entire height, giving certain areas a kind of foyer-like quality. This ambivalent feeling – the sense of standing at a threshold – can also be sensed in the two-storey conference rooms.

In the same spirit, incidentally, we also continued horizontal metal bands from the exterior into the building's interior, where they can be used as magnetic strips to hold drawings or notes.

The stone faces at the entrance have a particular significance: here the stones were chiselled to create a surface with expressly tactile qualities. We use stone tooled in this way on a regular basis – it's also a feature of our Auguststrasse building.

The building is located in a busy part of Berlin, and with its varied mix of tenants – shops, offices, and residential apartments – it's quite lively itself. We felt that it was imperative to give it contemplative spaces, too. The expanse

of water that we installed in the courtyard, for instance, creates a calm, quiet atmosphere.

This courtyard, however, is too dark for anyone to spend much time in. For this reason, we applied for permission to construct a children's play area on the roof of the side wing. Here, we created an amenity for all the building's tenants, with a spot for barbecues and benches where people can rest.

The side wing now contains seven apartments, with a terrace at the front for the maisonettes that form the uppermost group. In addition to windows facing the courtyard, all of the apartments in this part of the building have skylights facing the atrium. The overhead light provides an additional source of illumination, rather than just one-sided lighting from the courtyard. This creates a sense of place, opening two axes of orientation across each apartment.

We wanted to extend this concept to the electric lighting too, so we installed dynamic LED light strips in the atrium – an innovative feature for the time. The reflections from these lights draw the eye into a visual vortex, reinforcing the spatial impression of the atrium.

The lighting installations owed a great deal to our client, who worked in the lighting industry. It was fun for us to work with him, integrating special themes like this into the building.

We happily accepted his offer to lease parts of the building to us, and so, for seven years, our lives centred around this building, which contained both our offices and our home.

"Atrium-joint" with two-storey conference rooms

Terraces of the side wing

SISLEY
2-3

oxymoron
Heinrich Böll Stiftung
SOPHIENCLUB
Sparkasse
Sparkasse
HEINRICH BÖLL STIFTUNG
HEINRICH BÖLL STIFTUNG

Building at Hackescher Markt

Location
Hackescher Markt 2–3, 10178 Berlin

Year
completion 2000

Team
Olaf Menk, Jan Rützel

Client
Gantenbrink Grundstücksgesellschaft GbR, Menden

Technical planners
CBF Engineering GmbH, Berlin (structural engineering)
Amstein + Walthert AG, Zürich, Prof. Dr. Hansjürg Leibundgut, Zürich, KEP Klaus Engelhardt & Partner Beratende Ingenieure für Industrie- und Haustechnik, Berlin (building services)
Ludwig & Meyer, Berlin (façade consulting) Topotek 1 Gesellschaft von Landschaftsarchitekten mbH, Berlin (open space planning)

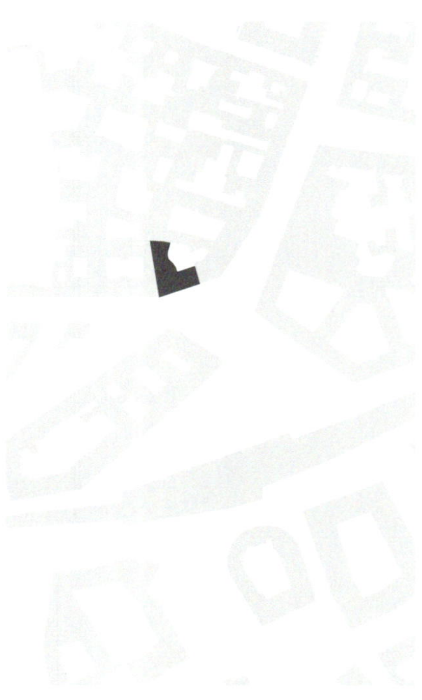

Street elevation

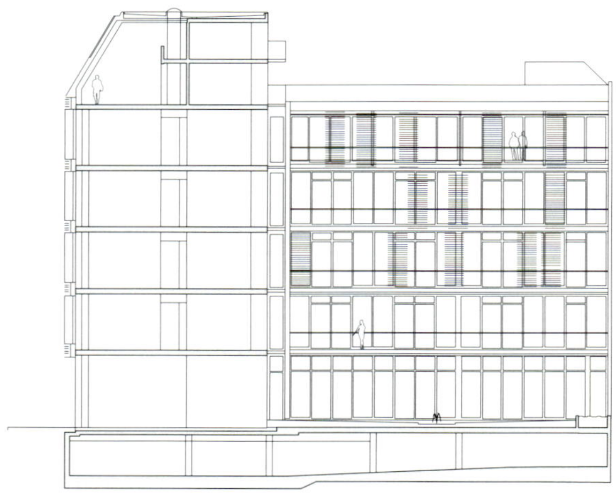

Section

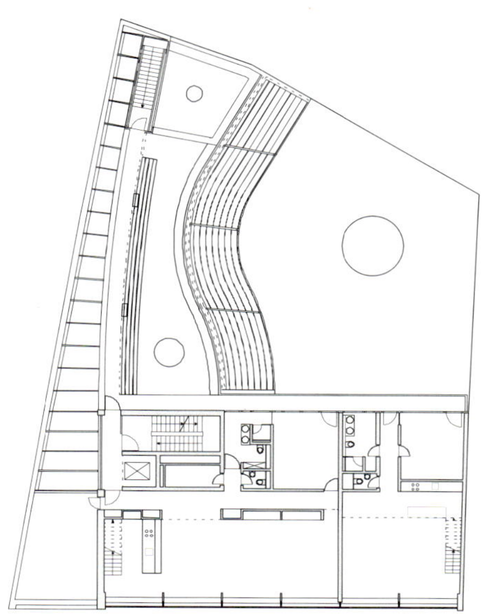

Attic

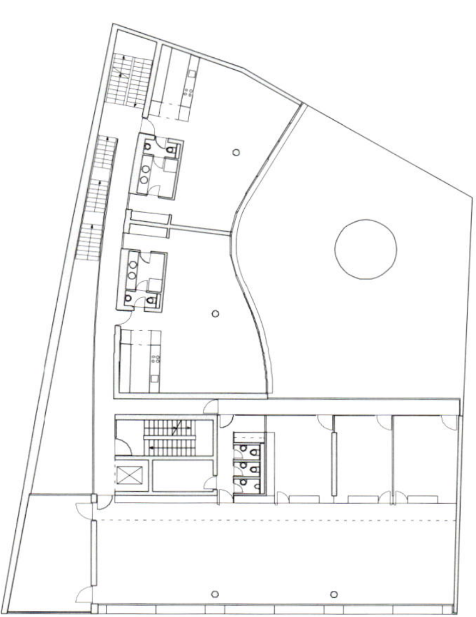

1st floor

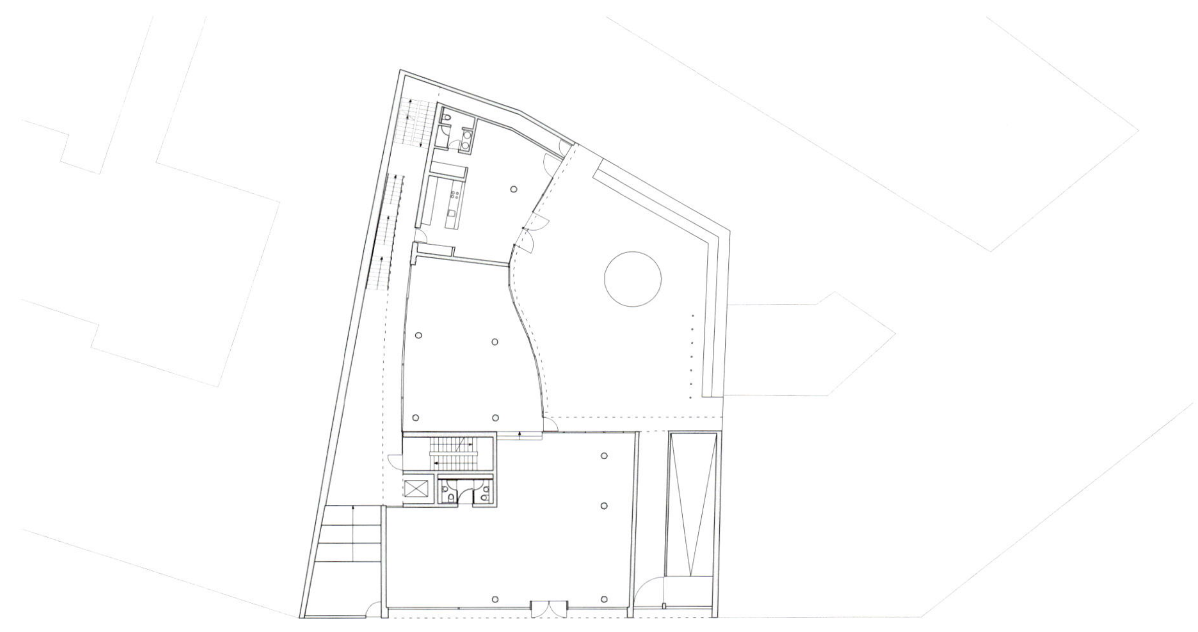

Ground floor

ZU VERMIET
0177/80188
21

On the brownfield site behind the Ministry of Foreign Affairs, 47 townhouses are being built simultaneously

Townhouse, Berlin

Our Townhouse project at Werderscher Markt thematised, in a much more direct way than the Floating Homes project, a common ideal living model: Many people dream of a house with a surrounding garden. We are concerned with finding alternatives to this space-intensive form of living that's hard to justify, given our limited amount of green space in the inner city.

The central question was how to unearth suburban qualities in our high-density urban developments, and how to develop spatial models that make them into fixed features of our cities.

This project was part of the Berlin Senate's "Townhouse" experiment, which involved selling parcels of land six metres wide to a number of developers. Each developer was then permitted to develop the plot more or less as they chose. On these urban sites, anyone could live out their suburban dreams. Tellingly, each developer employed a different architect. This meant that there was also a logistical problem to be solved: How would all the different cranes move unobstructedly over the construction site?

We always referred to it as the "not only but also" project, because it gave us a far greater degree of freedom than we'd normally have with an apartment building, and because the clients constantly had the feeling that they were getting a combination of things that you can't normally combine. This began with their being able to drive their car into the garage at ground level – not a standard feature of inner-city, single-family homes. They could then ascend to a split-level area that contained what was practically a two-storey dining room, extending via the terrace into the garden. From here, a single flight of stairs leads to the upper floors, which look as if they'd been suspended within this large, coherent space.

Various functions are distributed across the seven levels of the house, without doors or boundaries. The further up you go, the more private the space becomes. The only rooms that have doors are the bedroom and the bathroom. The rest of the house was conceived as, and is lived as, a continuum. The occupants have a garden *and* a penthouse with a view of the city.

This was an exciting experience: we were able to create a very coherent plan – for the overall concept, for the architectural details, and for the selection of materials.

The reason for this was that, at the same time, we were also converting a house at the Wannsee for the same clients. That house was an old building, meant to conjure up whole worlds of nostalgic emotions. There were flowered tapestry, chandeliers, and everything else the clients wanted.

Rather than having to cope with these two different sets of requirements in a single place, we were able to develop each of them in a pure form, with all their attendant attributes, in two separate projects.

I always thought of the house as a spatial sculpture that you could walk around in. The theme was exciting – tying everyday movements within a multi-perspectival space into a continuum.

The result of this experiment was a pretty accurate microcosm of our society. We simply have this desire for heterogeneity and individuality, and it extends to aesthetic tastes and the appearance of buildings.

What always happens in the suburbs also happened here. One guy's delighted to find blue tiles for sale, and thinks they'll look great on his roof. This upsets other people, because the resulting cocktail of materials, colours, and styles doesn't necessarily end up looking good. After all, the home is a form of self-expression, a way of saying who you are and what you can afford.

We designed one of these houses for a pair of friends. They wanted to live there, just the two of them. This gave us the freedom to develop a single apartment extending across the full height of the building.

Naturally, the narrowness of the six-metre property also represented a challenge. How do you create an access system for a building of this height? We had to find space for an elevator.

Normally, such a spatial continuum would conflict with the simple demands of comfort. Spaces with a pronounced flowing quality tend to have a certain elevated and remote aura.

Within them, a person often feels displaced and can't find a comfortable resting place.

That was my biggest problem with the house. Of course, I thought that the sculptural aspects were wonderful, but I was always asking myself: Will anybody actually find it pleasant to live here? Will it be cosy? Ultimately, I was really surprised to find that it's a perfectly cosy house.

I don't think that's really so surprising. The vertical access, of course, creates a certain energy flow, but there are "sedimentary" corners where that energy flow is gathered in again – the study, for instance, where you can sit with your back fully sheltered. The flow also slows down on the upper floors.

Ultimately, a home is always about the creation of special places. In this case, the particular challenge was to create defined places within a larger spatial continuum. This required us to think about niches and their qualities, about channelling an energy flow and slowing it down in places.

We didn't research this, but I think this house of ours would probably conform to the rules of Feng Shui. According to Feng Shui, you'd never want to place two doors straight across from one another, because then the energy there wouldn't be contained. Instead, the doors have to be offset, to create vortexes – places for stillness. This was also a key principle in our project – although we applied it on the vertical plane.

Ultimately, Feng Shui shares certain features with intelligent planning. After all, you can rationally compile and analyse data about how people behave within certain spatial configurations. Feng Shui is really about empirical values, which are then translated into concrete rules – in other words, it's a kind of intelligent planning.

DAVID LACHAPELLE

Townhouse

Location
Oberwallstrasse 21, 10117 Berlin

Year
completion 2008

Team
Florian Fels, Olaf Menk, Arno Löbbecke, Jacob van Ommen, Ingo Beckmann, Alessio Fossati

Client
private

Technical planners
IBT Ingenieurbüro für Tragwerksplanung GmbH & Co. KG, Mannheim (structural engineering)
RM Ingenieurgesellschaft Ridder und Meyn mbH, Berlin (building services)
Topotek 1 Gesellschaft von Landschafts-architekten mbH, Berlin (open space planning)

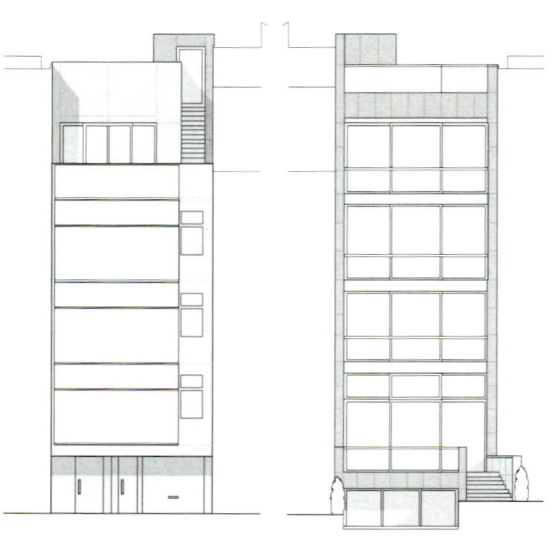

Street and courtyard elevations

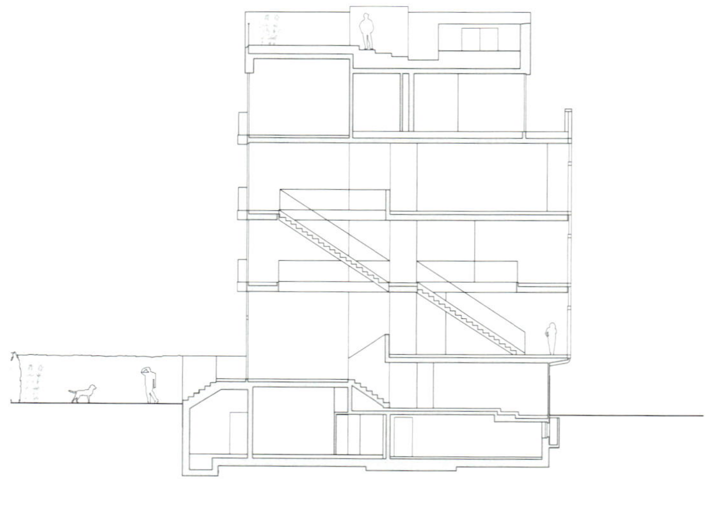

Section

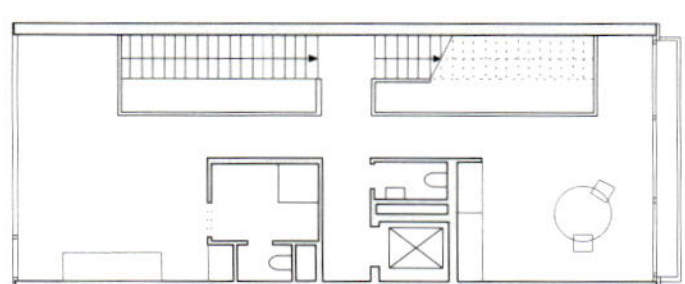
2nd floor

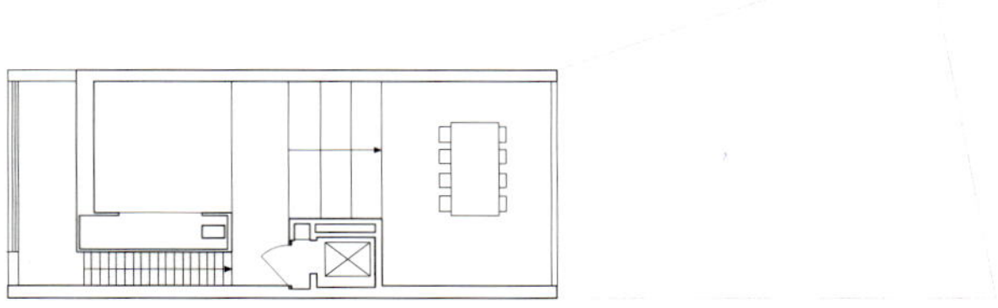
Roof

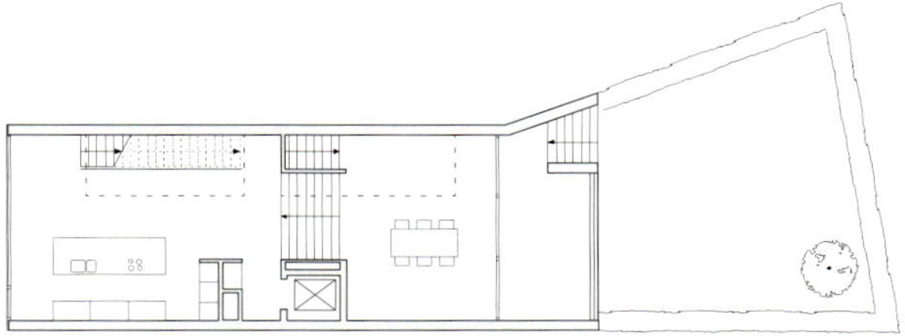
1st floor

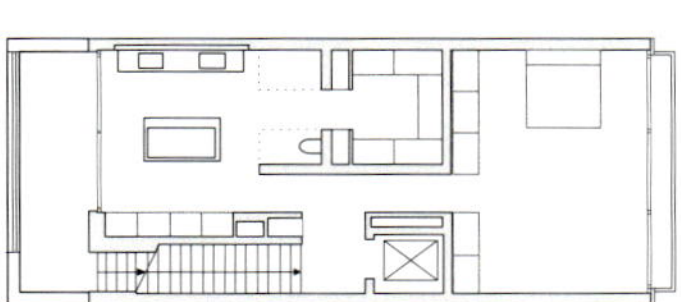
4th floor

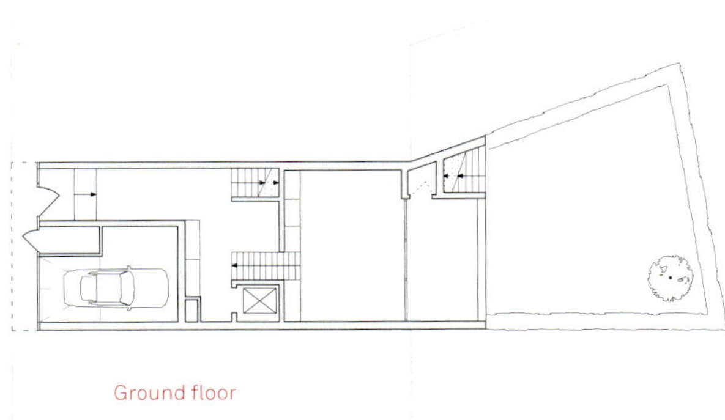
Ground floor

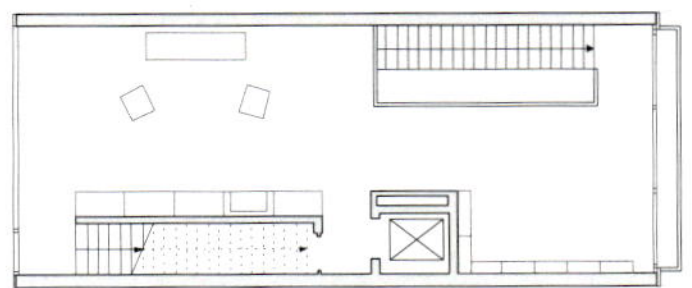
3rd floor

TEREX

Site facing the Kulturhaus

The Marthashof Residential Development, Berlin

Compared to our projects in the Spandauer Vorstadt, Marthashof was probably the largest empty lot we've ever worked with – a massive gap on Schwedter Strasse.

It was a textbook opportunity to fill in the block and create a lovely green courtyard at its centre – a classic urban villa development, the sort that's always being built in Berlin. Most of the competition entries proposed something along those lines.

We took the opposite approach. Thanks to its enormous size, this lot provided a space where alternative possibilities could be given free play. Additionally, a new building with all the new residents it brings into the district needs to add new qualities to the neighbourhood; it must be woven into the context created by the existing buildings.

View across Schwedter Strasse from the Kulturhaus into the courtyard of the new ensemble

As early as the competition phase the public character of the courtyard was discussed, and the building permit stipulated that it must be accessible to the public throughout the day.

We spent a good deal of time talking about the courtyard's accessibility. As an architect, you can only offer the community an idea about how to use such a space and then hope that its merits will be recognised.

Another question posed by this design was how to design a residential development of this size and still give it the same diversity and charm as a structure that has developed organically. Rather than repeatedly duplicating a single house type, we incorporated elements that provide contrasts and breaks.

The individual house types don't look as if they've all come from the same source – they suggest a variety of different attitudes.

Just over 140 new residential units were created, so that's perhaps 300 to 400 new residents. In order to compose one living organism from this diversity, we developed different user profiles beforehand, each with an associated living concept.

We gave a great deal of thought to the values we based our calculations on, and to what we wanted the use profile to look like. We aimed to achieve a well-mixed and vibrant occupancy profile by combining a variety of different home types. These included single-room apartments, maisonettes, townhouses and other types.

Our design had as its central theme the creation of a green centre – something that would give residents not just an address, but also an identity. The courtyard is surrounded on three sides by residential buildings and faces Schwedter Strasse on the fourth.

The Kulturhaus am Mauerpark, which is situated opposite our development, is an important part of the Marthashof ensemble; it represents the spatial ending point of the courtyard axis.

Two "gatehouses" on Schwedter Strasse form the entrance. The living spaces in the upper stories are organised here over single floors, while the ground storey is reserved for commercial tenants. The buildings that form the longitudinal axis are composed of stacked and terraced row houses – whereby, the individual homes can still be distinguished.

Every apartment has either a small garden, a spacious loggia, or a roof terrace. In this way, we created an attractive alternative to a freestanding, prefabricated house in the suburbs. All residents also have access to the large communal garden.

Aside from bringing new types of home into the city, the development of an inner-city site of this size offers an opportunity to enhance the city's core – an aim that goes beyond concerns related to individual residences. Of course, the project would be a drastic transformation of the neighbourhood one way or the other. After all, the site had been empty for 40 years!

After permission was granted, the terms were renegotiated – something we'd never experienced before. We had to reduce the absolute height of the buildings in order to reduce the amount of shade they cast on the windows in the firewalls of the neighbouring buildings.

To ensure that the garden courtyard would remain free of cars, we built an underground garage, which extends beneath the whole site. We created a green space above the underground garage, but not in the way it's usually done. Instead, we wanted big, stately trees. We therefore created large "tree rooms". These spaces perforate the garage's ceiling, which forms a collar around the trees, allowing them to grow deeper. Beneath the garage, the trees' roots can grow freely.

We physically separated the individual apartments from each other as much as possible. In the ground-storey apartments of the maisonettes, for instance, the living and dining areas face the garden, with the bedrooms positioned above them. On the upper levels, this arrangement is reversed, guaranteeing tenants complete privacy in the apartments' open spaces.

Incidentally, all our plans went out of the window as soon as the first buyer turned up! He'd actually sat down and planned out his entire life, and had decided to make himself a proper home in Marthashof. He got three apartments to house his future family. He'd already decided that his home would need bedrooms for three children, a room for an au pair, and an apartment for his in-laws.

I find it really crazy that we could plan so far ahead, consider so many possibilities, and then still be surprised by another person's ideas. But then, of course, some people will want to divide a maisonette apartment into two separate units.

By the way, fifteen percent of the buyers are architects – what do you make of that? I take it as a compliment – we must have gotten a few things right.

We thought it was interesting that more than half of our residents were locals – in fact, more than a third of our buyers didn't even change their postcode.

As architects, we found that the sales and distribution phase involved an awful lot of back and forth; sometimes the people in charge of sales would simply change the plans with their pens ...

Yes, but a good bit of that chaos is just part and parcel of the legitimate process of making something your own. The residents didn't want to be presented with a finished product – they wanted to influence the design of their homes. You could say that they bought their apartments off the peg and then had them tailored according to their wishes.

The basic structure provided room for special requests to be incorporated – bathroom decor and fittings, for instance.

We'd created a catalogue listing the various possible choices, but many of the residents had done some shopping on their own account and had discovered something for themselves – some lovely golden tiles, for instance. Then they wanted natural stone, too, and a bit of black in the bathroom – rather like gardeners who want to fit everything into their little gardens all at once.

One particular tenant springs to mind. He had the idea of giving his bathroom a classical design, with a row of columns and gates – all tiled. We went along with all this with gritted teeth. When it was all done, he stood there in his bathroom and said: "I'm going to be quite honest with you. It doesn't look the way I imagined it. Could you please rip this out and build it the way you wanted to?" I thought that was cool. Of course we photographed the bathroom before we tore it all out.

People making the property their own is a crucial part of creating a successful neighbourhood. With the Marthashof project, we felt like we were working with 140 clients all at once, all of whose wishes and idiosyncrasies had to be incorporated into the plan.

DIES KÖNNTE IHR LADEN SEIN!
Tel. 0172 66 555 37
www.lukoor.com
mail@lukoor.com
LUKOOR
Einbauschränke
Schiebetrennwände
Renovierungsarbeiten
KOMANDOR
B DM 808

Marthashof residential development

Location
Schwedter Strasse 37–40, 10435 Berlin

Year
1st prize competition 2006
completion 2012

Team
Erik Behrends, Florian Fels, Arno Löbbecke, Olaf Menk, Jens Schoppe, Thomas Birk, Janine Burdack, Kristin Bussenius, Alessio Fossati, Jost von Fritschen, Claudia Große-Hartlage, Götz Hinrichsen, Stefan John, Kai Arne Löper, Arun Markus, Dirk Nachtsheim, Jemima Retallack, Roland Schreiber, Kerstin Thomsen, Anna Wolska, Hagen Brandt

Client
Stofanel Investment AG, Berlin

Technical planners
city.bauten (project development)
Dr.-Ing. Pelle Ingenieurgesellschaft mbH, Berlin (structural engineering)
Ingenieurbüro für Energie- und Haustechnik Andreas Duba GmbH, Tröbnitz (building services)
Levin Monsigny Landschaftsarchitekten, Berlin (open space planning)
Mull und Partner Ingenieurgesellschaft mbH, Berlin (geothermal system)

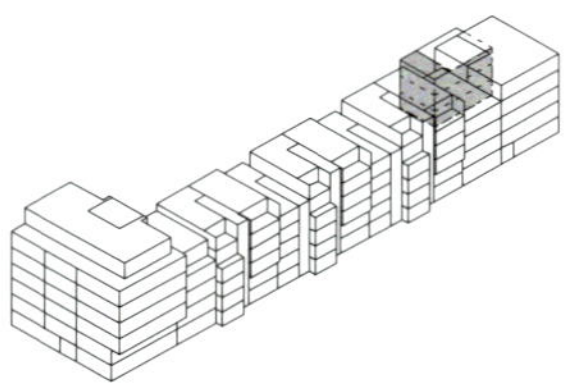

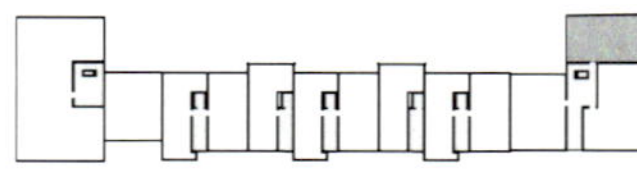

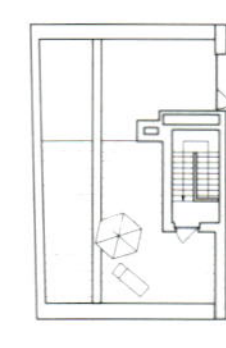

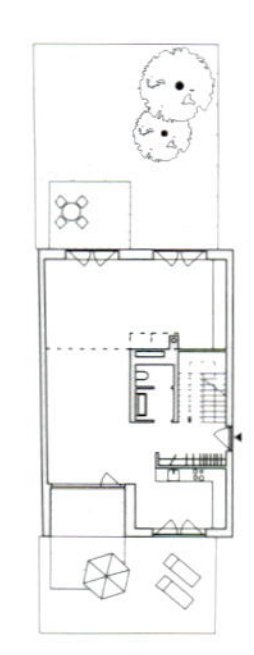

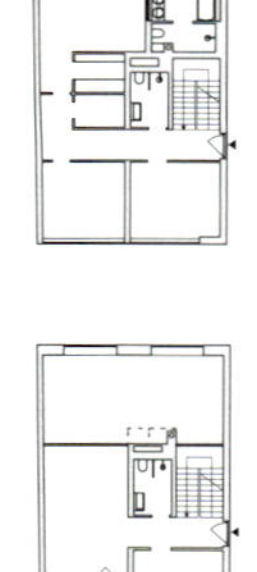

Townhouse with garden

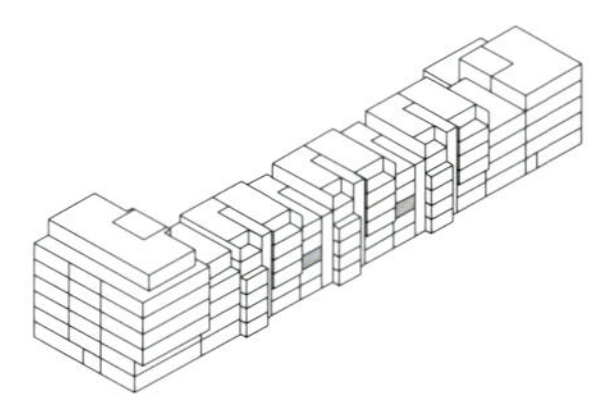

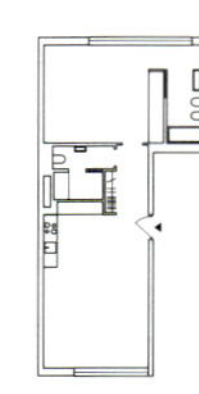

Studio apartment

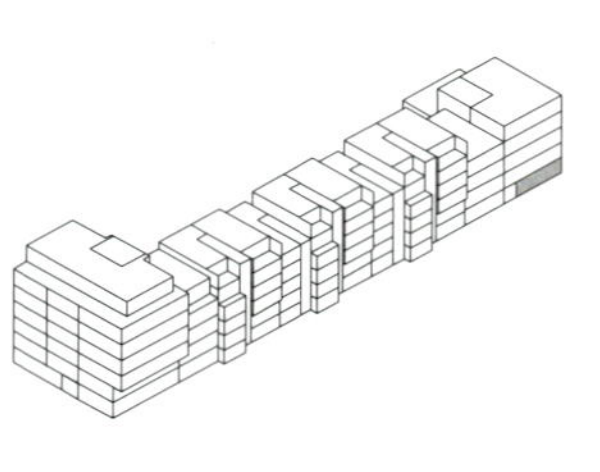

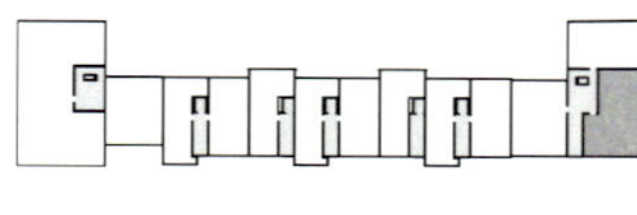

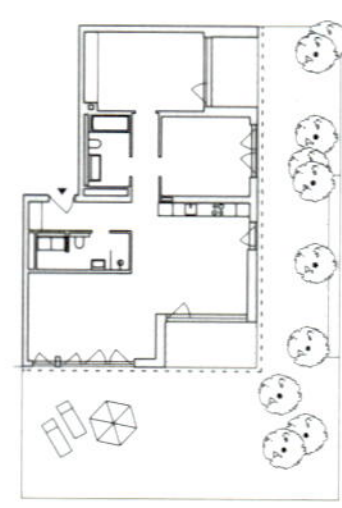

Garden apartment

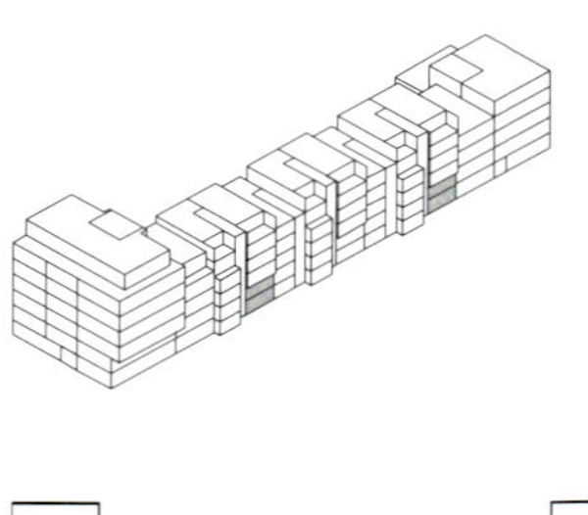

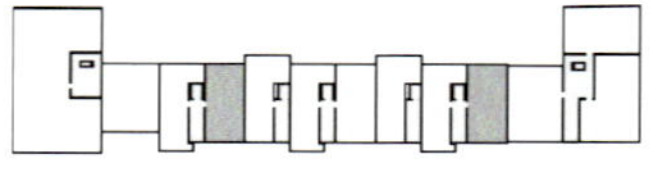

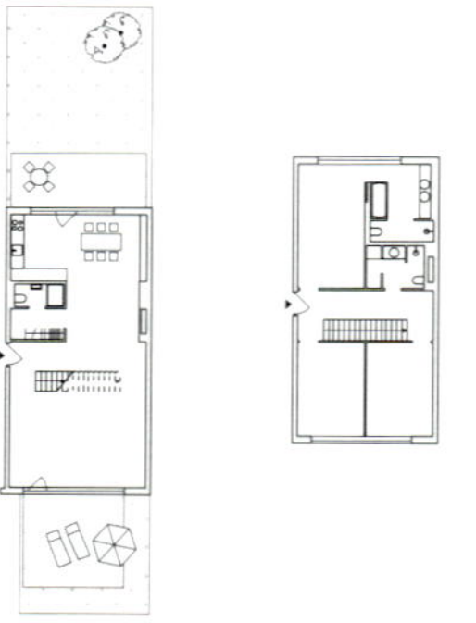

Garden maisonette

Ground-floor plan of the ensemble on Schwedter Strasse

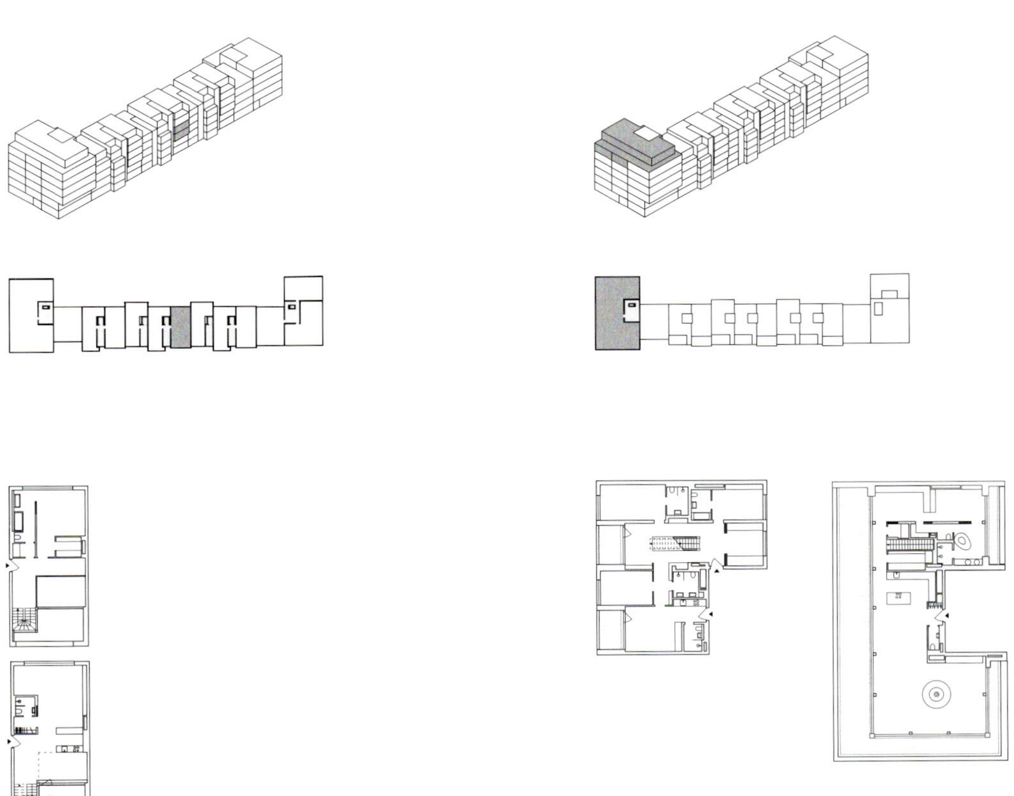

Maisonette with duplex loggia

Penthouse

Berliner Zeitung · Nummer 297 · Freitag, 20. Dezember 2002 17

Berlin

NACHRICHTEN

Im Norden Berlins fehlen 350 Polizisten

Im Norden Berlins fehlen nach Angaben der Deutschen Polizeigewerkschaft 350 Polizisten. „Den Bürgern ist die Polizei abhanden gekommen", sagte der Landesvorsitzende Rolf Taßler. Die Zahl der Funkwagen sei wegen der Sparmaßnahmen drastisch reduziert worden, was die Anfahrtswege bei Notfällen unzumutbar verlängere. *(kop.)*

Berlinerin als Drogenhändlerin verurteilt

Eine 27-jährige Bankkauffrau aus Berlin wurde gestern als Mitglied einer internationel operierenden Rauschgiftbande zu sieben Jahren und sechs Monaten Haft verurteilt. Die Frau sei auf hoher Ebene in die Bande eingegliedert gewesen, sagte Richter Joseph Hoch. Die zweifache Mutter hatte zugegeben, im Frühjahr 2000 selbst mindestens zwei Kilogramm Heroin transportiert und andere Frauen als Kuriere angeworben zu haben. *(dpa)*

Mit der Bahn zum Weihnachtsbaumschlagen

Die Deutsche Bahn (DB) und Dannenwalde im Kreis Oberhavel laden die Berliner für Sonntag zum Weihnachtsbaumschlagen ein. Gemeindevertreter erwarten die Fahrgäste und führen sie in den Forst. Sie übernehmen auch den Transport der Fichten zum Bahnhof. Die Anreise erfolgt mit dem Regionalexpress 5. Abfahrt am Ostbahnhof ist um 9.13 und 11.13, am Zoo um 9.29 und 11.29 Uhr. *(pn.)*

BKK Berlin erhöht Beitrag auf 15,7 Prozent

Die Betriebskrankenkasse BKK Berlin mit 118 000 Mitgliedern wird zum 1. Januar kommenden Jahres ihren Beitragssatz um 1,3 Prozentpunkte auf 15,7 Prozent erhöhen. Die seien 0,1 Punkte mehr als zunächst geplant, sagte der BKK-Chef Jochem Schulz gestern. *(dpa)*

Auf Wasser gebaut

Wasserstadt geht mit schwimmenden Häusern in Stralau und Spandau neue Wege im Wohnungsbau

WASSERSTADT GMBH/FÖRSTER-TRABITZSCH ARCHITEKTEN

Haus an Haus auf dem Wasser – so könnte es am Spandauer See einmal aussehen.

VON MARCEL GÄDING

Sie wirken wie aus einer anderen Welt, ähneln teilweise unbekannten Flugobjekten. Doch mit der Raumfahrt haben die „Floating Homes" der Wasserstadt GmbH nichts zu tun. Die landeseigene Projektentwicklerin will mit den schwimmenden Häusern Leute begeistern, die schon immer mal auf dem Wasser wohnen wollten. „Mit diesem Projekt setzen wir neue Akzente im Wohnungsbau", sagt Wasserstadt-Geschäftsführer Uli Hellweg. Im Herbst kommenden Jahres soll mit der Realisierung begonnen werden.

Zwei Standorte hat die Wasserstadt ausgewählt. Zunächst sind 24 schwimmende Häuser an der Insel Eiswerder im Spandauer See sowie auf der Stralauer Seite der Rummelsburger Bucht geplant. Dort entstanden nach der Wende bereits neue Viertel – auf märkischem Sand. Die Wasserhäuser sind aber teurer als eine Wohnung in den neuen Stadtquartieren. Zwischen 320 000 und 540 000 Euro pro Haus müssen kalkuliert werden.

Ein Architekten-Wettbewerb für die „Floating Homes" ist inzwischen beendet. Aus neun eingereichten Entwürfen kommen für jeden Standort jeweils drei in die engere Auswahl. Herman Hertzberger, ein Architekt aus Amsterdam, leitete die Gutachterkommission. „Ich bin sehr froh, dass ein solches Experiment nun auch in Berlin stattfindet." In Holland gebe es solche Häuser schon seit Jahren. Wasser bedeute Freiheit: „Wem der Standort nicht mehr gefällt, der legt irgendwo anders an."

Die Entwürfe der Architekten reichen von futuristisch bis klassisch: Alle Häuser stehen auf Pontons, erstrecken sich über mehrere Etagen, haben Terrassen und in einigen Fällen sogar einen schwimmenden Garten. Für jeden Entwurf gibt es bereits Investoren, die die Häuser vermarkten wollen. Die meisten „Floating Homes" verfügen über große Fensterfronten, die Zimmer sind großzügig gestaltet.

Die Senatsverwaltung für Stadtentwicklung steht dem Projekt wohl wollend gegenüber, sagt deren Sprecherin Petra Rohland. Allerdings gebe es noch Bedenken. „Der Seegrund darf nicht verschattet werden." Die Bezirke, in denen die Projekte realisiert werden sollen, haben indes keine oder kaum Bedenken. „Das könnte für uns ein Imagegewinn sein", sagt der Spandauer Baustadtrat Carsten-Michael Röding (CDU). In Berlin gebe es nichts Vergleichbares. Sein bündnisgrüner Amtskollege Franz Schulz aus Friedrichshain-Kreuzberg spricht von sehr ergiebigen Ergebnissen. Einige Entwürfe scheinen ihm aber zu futuristisch. „Die Diskussion wird sicher noch nicht zu Ende sein."

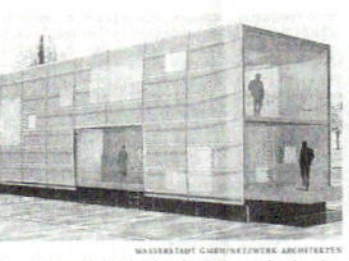

WASSERSTADT GMBH/NETZWERK ARCHITEKTEN

Dieser Entwurf zeigt ein über dem Wasser schwebendes, zweigeschossiges und röhrenförmiges Haus.

WASSERSTADT GMBH/FÖRSTER-TRABITZSCH ARCHITEKTEN

Zweigeschossig ist auch dieses Hausmodell. Es hat sogar einen kleinen Dachaufbau.

Erneut wurden zwei Kneipen überfallen

Vermummte Täter verletzten Gäste

Erneut sind am Donnerstagmorgen in Berlin zwei Lokale überfallen worden. Damit erhöhte sich die Zahl der seit Oktober überfallenen Kneipen auf 21. Kurz vor halb zwei stürmten drei mit Skimasken Vermummte in eine Kneipe am Eichhorster Weg in Reinickendorf. Sie bedrohten einen Angestellten und vier Gäste mit Pistolen. Der Angestellte musste seine Kasse öffnen, die Gäste mussten ihre Portmonees herausgeben. Bevor die Räuber das Lokal verließen schlug einer einem 45-jährigen Gast mit dem Pistolengriff auf den Kopf, so dass dieser vom Barhocker stürzte. Die Polizei vermutet, dass es sich um dieselbe Bande handelt, die für die Überfallserie verantwortlich ist. Dafür sprächen Bewaffnung und Vorgehensweise, sagte Chefermittler Manfred Schmandra.

Zwei Stunden später jedoch waren möglicherweise Trittbrettfahrer am Werk: In Tempelhof überfielen drei mit Skimasken vermummte Männer ein Lokal in der Werderstraße. Eine 29-jährige Angestellte musste die Einnahmen, zwei Gäste ihr Geld herausgeben. Einer 47-jährigen Frau sprühten die Räuber Reizgas ins Gesicht. Zeugen gaben an, dass die Täter mit grünen Bomberjacken bekleidet waren. Die Täter in Reinickendorf sollen dagegen dunkel gekleidet gewesen sein. „Deshalb sind wir nicht ganz sicher, ob es sich um dieselben Täter handelt oder um eine andere Gruppe", sagte Schmandra. Allerdings seien auch dieses Mal die Zeugenaussagen nur unzureichend gewesen.

Wegen der Überfälle wurden Polizisten auf den Abschnitten angewiesen, verstärkt Streife zu fahren und auf Bierlokale in den Kiezen zu achten. Ganz im Dunkeln scheint die Kripo jedoch nicht zu tappen. „Wir haben einige Anhaltspunkte, denen wir nachgehen", sagte Schmandra. *(kop.)*

Floating Homes

The Floating Homes design began with a competition for a small-scale waterfront property in Berlin. Although we didn't produce much material for this competition, the project suddenly developed an unbelievable degree of momentum and was publicised far beyond the usual channels. It appeared in the daily papers in Italy and in lifestyle magazines in Abu Dhabi. The exposure was so intense that I think we still aren't aware of everything that was written about the project.

When you think of houseboats and their inhabitants, your head is immediately filled with "alternative lifestyle" clichés: people who want to escape from our hectic world to live with an herb garden and three cats. But why not take it in another direction? If you designed a houseboat for James Bond, it'd be a different animal entirely.

Ultimately, a home isn't a question of engineering – it's an emotional world. It's about creating a lifestyle that someone can identify with. By shifting the home's location from land to water, you create a sense of a special kind of lifestyle, because water and boats, in our imagination, are always associated with freedom and leisure time.

That idea was our starting point. Our design was an attempt to combine two seemingly irreconcilable things – first the dream of a "happy little home" –

– which is something that architects have a problem with; it's given us this unceasing sprawl of freestanding suburban houses. Architects prefer to develop alternatives for high-density areas.

Still, there's this yearning for a family house. We wanted to respond to that dream in our own way, and to combine it with the sense of freedom that comes from being on the water. In theory, at least, this would allow any homeowner to change their surroundings and neighbours whenever they wished.

"Community" is the big buzzword today when we talk about the idea of home. When people think about places to live, they ask themselves, for instance: In what environment do I want to grow old, and with whom? Family ties are less dependable, making the freedom to choose extremely important.

The separation of work and leisure time is beginning to break down, and people don't put down roots the way they used to. Given our increasingly nomadic lifestyles and the increasing fragmentation of our daily routines, a floating house suddenly makes a lot of sense. The challenge was figuring out whether a house could float and still be the central space in someone's life. Could it be a place where you really put down emotional roots?

You start thinking about the essential qualities of a house, and where those qualities come from. The German language has the untranslatable word *Heimat* (homeland, spiritual home), which speaks to those elusive qualities. Can there be such a thing as a "*Heimat* to go", a home that you can take with you? There are plenty of nice pleasure craft with cabins like little houses, but they're not "Floating Homes" in the sense we intend. They are second, third or fourth homes.

The idea of "home", that's what's truly central. With that in mind, we adopted the attributes of a single-family home for our Floating Home. There's a veranda-like zone at the front of the boat, something like a front yard – this serves as an interface between the public area, which is

Τα ποταμίσια σπίτια δεν πρέπει να είναι ψηλότερα από 4,4

Στην καρδιά της Βενετίας

Πλωτό σπιτικό

Σπίτια πάνω στο νερό

Im Mai sollen die Häuser schwimmen

Ein Investor sucht Käufer und eine Werft für die ersten Berliner Floating-Homes

FRIEDRICHSHAIN-KREUZBERG. An der Rummelsburger Bucht sollen im Mai kommenden Jahres die ersten schwimmenden Häuser ankern. Die acht Schiffe, auch Floating Homes genannt, werden demnächst in einer Werft gebaut. Wo genau, steht noch nicht fest. Investorin ist die Kunkat Holding aus Lüneburg.

Anfang des Jahres hatte die landeseigene Wasserstadt ihre Pläne für die schwimmenden Häuser am Spandauer See und an der Rummelsburger Bucht vorgestellt. „Die Resonanz ist überwältigend", sagt Wasserstadt-Geschäftsführer Uli Hellweg. Bislang lägen 200 Anfragen vor. Neben dem Projekt an der Rummelsburger Bucht sei man auch an der Insel Eiswerder schon weit: Dort sind zwölf Floating Homes geplant. Wann es dort und am Spandauer See losgeht, steht noch nicht fest. An der Halbinsel Stralau sollen zweigeschossige Schiffe mit einer Wohnfläche von 170 Quadratmeter, einer Terrasse und einem schwimmenden Garten entstehen. Billig sind sie mit 400 000 Euro nicht. Hinzu kommen die Pacht für die Wasserfläche und Kosten für Abwasser und Wasser. „Noch haben wir keines verkauft", räumt der Investor Olaf Kunkat ein. Doch Interessanten gebe es: „Das sind Menschen, die individuelle Wohnformen bevorzugen. *(gäd.)*

WASSERSTADT

Die ersten Floating Homes sind von den Architekten Grüntuch + Ernst.

Über Floating Homes informiert bis 29. August eine Ausstellung im Ludwig-Erhard-Haus, Fasanenstraße 85.

IMMOBILIEN

11/03 Essenz

IMMOBILIEN

Anlegen ohne Kapital

Bei dem Wort HAUSBOOT denkt man an Verwahrlosung (Hippies in Holland) oder an Verfilmung (Sophia Loren in den USA). Neuerdings jedoch auch an Verwirklichung: mit einem preiswerten Eigenheim in Deutschland

18 NEWS — FEBRUARY 2, 2003 · THE SUNDAY TIMES

Testing the water

Making waves: how the German scheme could look

Berlin hopes its ingenious new floating homes will solve its housing shortage. If they do, Britain could be next, says Clare Chapman

The white, futuristic-looking homes, designed by renowned Berlin-based architects, look like giant breadbins

Water world: homes like these will soon be floating on Berlin's lake

26 Domenica 20 Marzo 2005 — LA GAZZETTA DEL MEZZOGIORNO

CULTURA & SPETTACOLI

Le radici dell'arte nel castello dei dischi volanti

Dove abiteremo domani / 1

L'architettura dei luoghi nomadi

Se il futuro viene ormeggiato nelle città anfibie

Natalia e il gusto di scrivere

fully exposed to view, and the private space inside the "building" proper. There's a large living and dining area with a curved roof overhead. There's a sun terrace, so you can spend time outside. And then there are private and intimate bedrooms below, with small windows –

– a kind of cabin concept. We purposefully put the upper edge of the mattress beneath the surface level of the surrounding water, in order to create the feeling of being sheltered underwater.

There's approximately 120 square metres of floor space aboard a Floating Home, including the outdoor areas – about the same as a terraced house. The Floating Home also has a similar number of rooms. The whole thing was secured to four pontoons so the residents wouldn't constantly be disturbed by the boat's rocking. This also would've allowed the Home to react if the river froze over, preventing it from being crushed. It'd be possible to dock a number of additions onto the Floating Home, such as an outdoor pool, a garden, or a play area, allowing you to expand your Floating Home to suit the time of year and context.

Ninety-nine percent of houseboats are constructed by building a normal house on top of a pontoon. They're basically just floating plots of land. Personally, I think I'd just as soon build my house next door, on solid ground. We were more interested in a true hybrid of boat and house. Because it has no means of propulsion, you can't really call it a boat – it has to be towed. However, it can change location. It's designed to be able to pass under bridges and through locks.

There was a fixed location for our Floating Homes in Berlin – the Rummelsberger Bucht. For the *Einwohnermeldeamt* (the residency registration office) to accept it as a permanent residence, you'd have to buy a piece of Berlin along with your Floating Home: somewhere for the bins, the mailbox, the car, and so forth. There had to be a fixed address.

Of course, the concept also has financial implications. People buying these houseboats couldn't secure the usual loans, as they wouldn't have any actual land to mortgage. Our investor had negotiated a lease agreement for the water with the city, which was to run for a maximum of 30 to 40 years.

After we won the competition, we received an incredible number of enquiries – one of which came from an investor based in Egypt. He wanted to create a kind of divers' paradise out on the water in order to establish himself near a waterfront property that hadn't yet been opened up for development, but which would hopefully be developed in 20, 30 or 40 years.

There was also a government agency in Abu Dhabi that wanted to start a Floating Homes pilot project. However, it didn't really interest us – in that context, the project would've become a gadget, a lifestyle accessory. We wanted to categorically change people's perspectives on homes and living.

We were also contacted by a number of private individuals who wished to order Floating Homes right away. As the project hadn't yet been turned into a product, it wasn't that simple.

There were plenty of interesting misunderstandings. An article on Floating Homes appeared in a London tabloid – it presented them as an answer to overcrowding. Apparently, the writers thought that Floating Homes were a way of squeezing still more people into densely populated areas. That had never been the idea. Rather, we wanted to create an unusual new living option for areas that were already fully developed.

When Hamburg bid to host the Olympics, we briefly considered the idea of housing the athletes in Floating Homes on the Outer Alster Lake. The Floating Homes could've been moved elsewhere once the Olympics were over – a clear demonstration of how urban spaces can be temporarily occupied. It would've been great!

The competition was actually backed by investors who intended to build the winning design. It was just before the end of the dotcom bubble, though, and when the bubble burst, the possibility of implementing the project went with it.

We would've needed a certain amount of venture capital, as prototype development would only have made sense if someone wanted at least twelve units. And, of course, the first house is always the most expensive.

For the sake of comparison, a yacht costs, on average, a million euros per metre. So if Abramovich has a 100-metre yacht, it costs 100 million euros. The advantage of a houseboat is that it's not in that price range; you're working with relatively manageable prices. We calculated that, at 13 to 15 metres in length, our houseboats would cost approximately 700,000 euros apiece – that's about 50,000 euros per metre.

We've researched this project in great detail, with the assistance of the engineering firm Arup, because the large number of enquiries has caused us to return to it time and again over the years. We spoke to a number of manufacturers about what the houseboat would look like, what kind of materials we'd need for the bulkheads, how to get the counterweighting right, and so forth. A house of this kind has certain technical peculiarities that also have a bearing on the cost.

When the investor jumped ship, we briefly considered finding a replacement, but we really just didn't have the time or energy. Bringing together the right people for something like this requires a certain amount of energy – developing a new type of home from scratch is a real research project. There are so many technical issues that have to be resolved. For instance, how would the lapping of the water or the creaking of ice affect the desired homely atmosphere?

Virtual journey of a floating home through collaged imagery

We also needed part of the boat – 1.1 metres – to remain submerged, which meant that we needed a certain amount of weight. This led us to give the boat an eggcup-like construction. There would be a lower shell of concrete – a very conventional and economical material. In Holland, for instance, you can get affordable, prefabricated pontoons. This solves a number of problems. It provides enough weight to keep the boat riding low in the water and gives it a certain inertia, reducing rocking.

But there are still other issues to be resolved, such as the need for an independent energy supply, water supply, and wastewater removal.

We just didn't have a precedent for implementing a project like this one. All the questions that, in a normal construction project, have routine, well-practiced solutions had to be answered here on a case-by-case basis. To implement the project in Berlin, for instance, we'd have had to apply for a building permit and for a boat licence.

Of course, a boatyard would be an ideal partner for such a project. Such a company would have the necessary experience and would also be able to provide solutions to some of our more unconventional problems.

On the other hand, that was precisely the problem, as it'd cause costs to skyrocket – meaning that we'd be faced with yacht prices. We'd have to listen to what the yacht experts said and then "transcribe" it for the building process. Or, in other words: we'd have to develop everything from scratch in order to bring the prices down to something approaching those of a normal house.

Even so, a Floating Home would always be more expensive than a normal family home. And as long as property prices here in Berlin remain low, nobody's going to want to move out onto the water.

In Hamburg, on the other hand, the whole Floating Homes project spawned a political movement, a push for homes on the water. In fact, a few floating houses have already been built in Hamburg.

Even though we weren't able to create *our* Floating Homes, this was a really important project for us. We found the radical approach to design incredibly stimulating, and we were able to channel it to bring new energy into our work.

Floating Homes

Location
e.g. Rummelsburger Bucht, 10245 Berlin

Year
1st prize competition 2002

Team
Olaf Menk, Dennis Hawner

Client
Wasserstadt Berlin GmbH

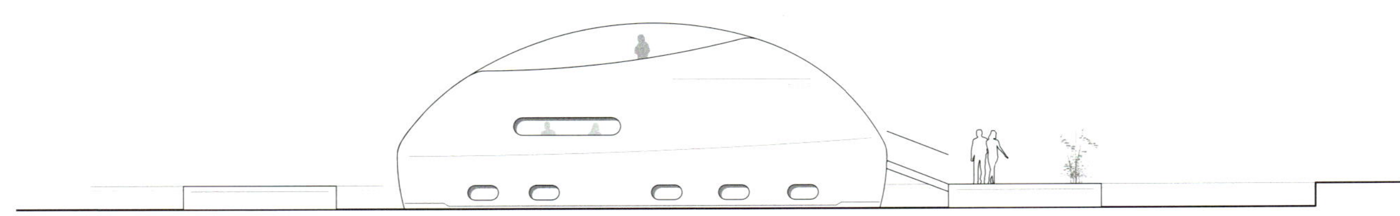

Side elevation

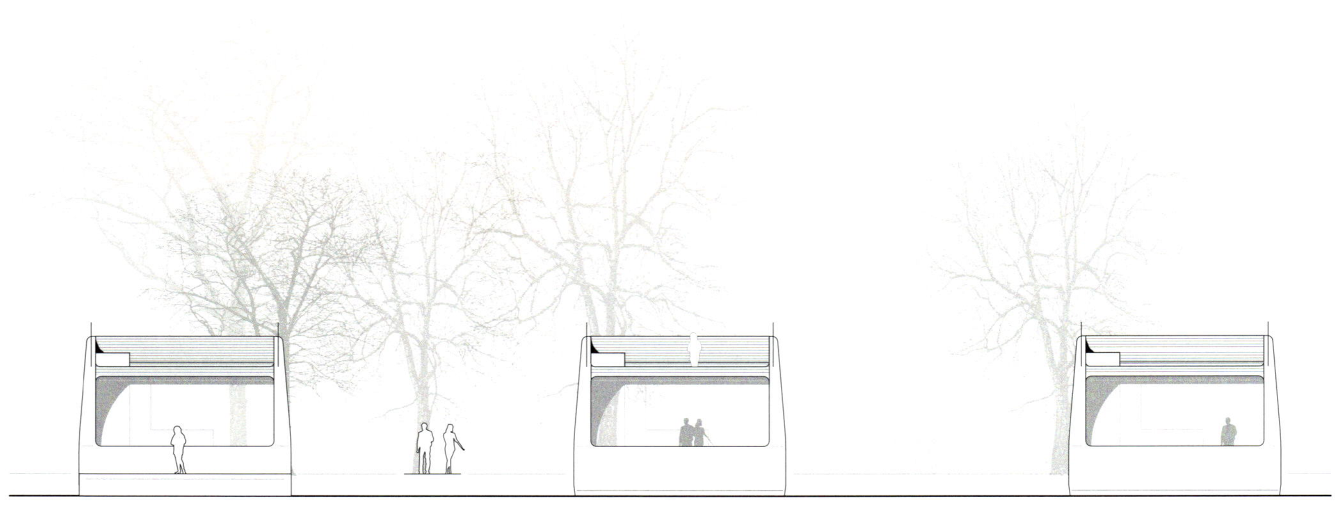

Elevation

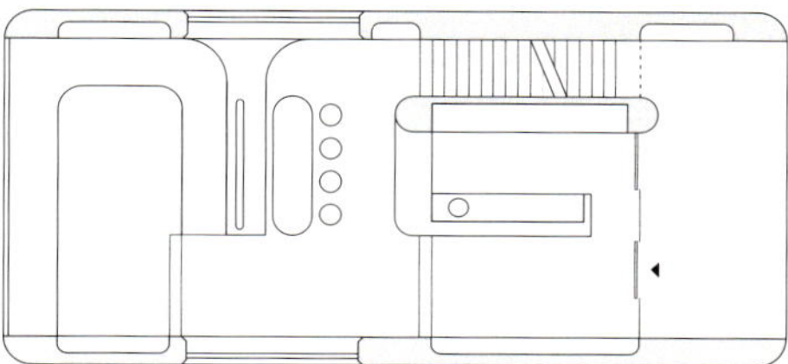

Floor plan, upper deck

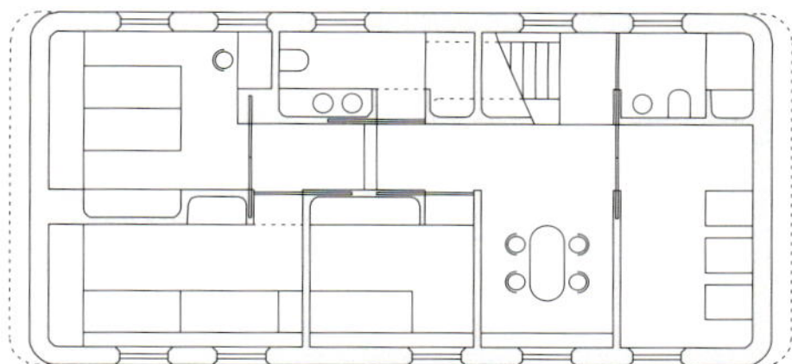

Floor plan, lower deck

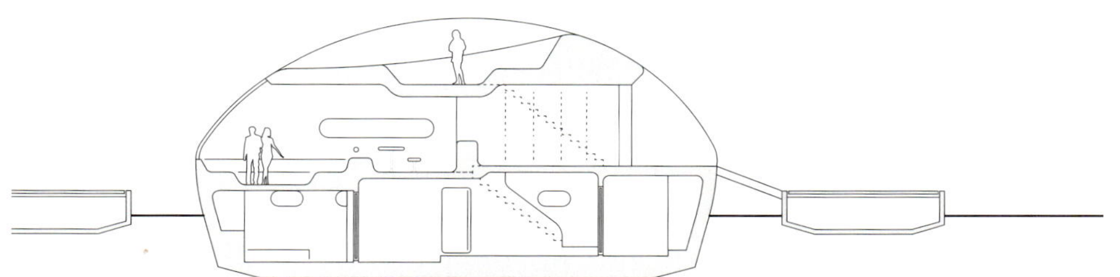

Longitudinal section

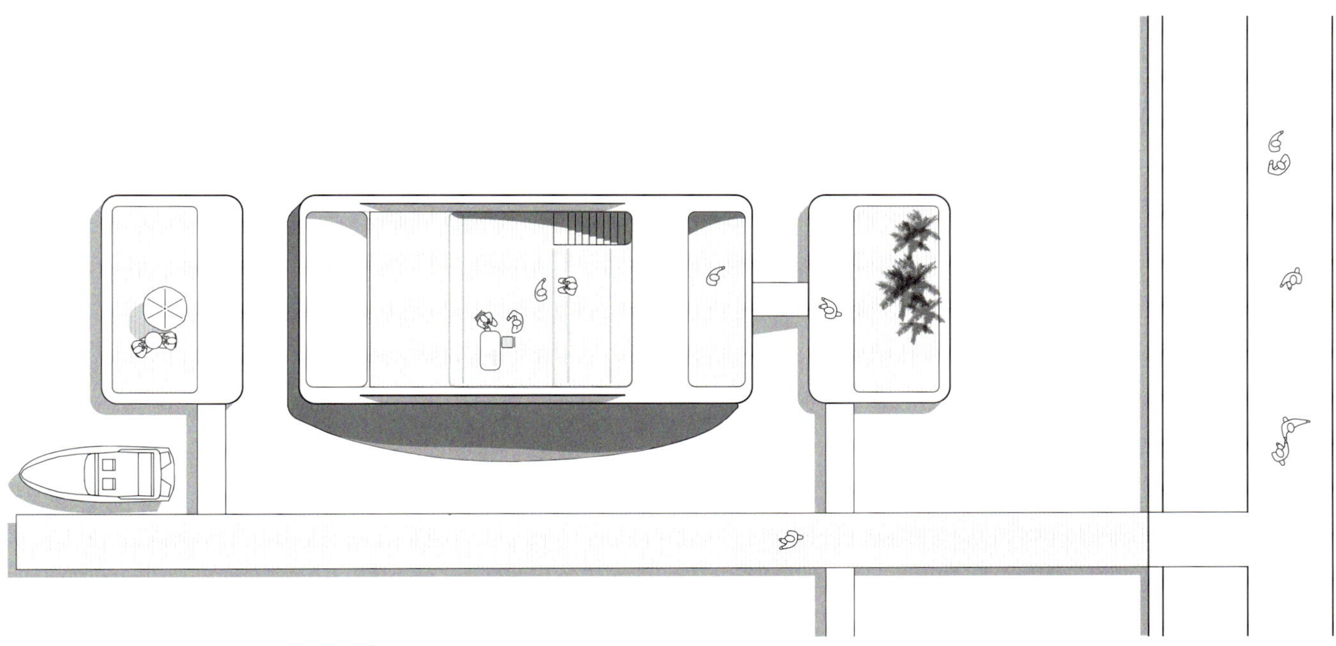

Upper deck

The Stuttgart 21 residential highrise

In the summer of 2008, we were invited to take part in a competition to build in the Stuttgart 21 development area. At the time, of course, we didn't know that Stuttgart 21 would provoke such massive protests. The projected transformation of the city has made locals deeply uneasy, and this has inspired a new culture of debate and a drive for political participation. However, because our project lies at the edge of the area under development, it wasn't attacked; most of the protests' energy has been directed at the central railway station.

For us, a bigger problem was that high-rise apartment blocks have such a bad reputation in Germany. Berlin's Hansaviertel is a rarity, an example of post-war modernism that's been accepted by mainstream society. In general, the public treats such developments with hostility.

We asked ourselves: Is high-rise living appropriate to the times? What are the opportunities and risks associated with this typology? Globally, increased urbanisation – whether in South America or in Asia – has produced multifarious forms of high-density development and led to a revival of the High-rise apartment block. For instance, the firm WOHA won the 2010 International Highrise Award for their high-rise apartments in Bangkok.

When high-rise developments of this type are built in megacities, they're primarily the product of growth pressures, and they appear en masse. In Europe, conditions are different: residential towers are an exception. They are integrated into an existing fabric of the city as a singular building block.

This theme fascinates us – we recently took part in a competition for high-rise apartments on the Spree river, and at the University in Braunschweig, I issued a project on the subject of high-rises for the master's thesis. The fact that a high-rise building is such a prominent feature of a city forces architects to take their design responsibilities seriously. This was particularly true of our site in Stuttgart, which stood in an exposed position at a busy intersection.

What's more, Stuttgart is located in a large valley. The site therefore presented us with an opportunity to re-imagine the high-rise building, particularly because it would be possible to look at this high-rise from a number of different angles. For this reason, we didn't want to create a building that could be understood at first glance, one that would always present the same appearance. Instead, we wanted to create a building that would offer anyone looking at its exterior a dynamic visual experience. It's a familiar quality of sculpture: if you walk around one of the sculptures in the Glyptothek in Munich, you might see a sad expression from one side, but a smile from the other.

The idea was that the building should look different from different angles. We wanted to give it a sculptural appearance suited to our understanding of the high-rise model. Instead of a typical high-rise with a pedestal, a shaft, and a roof, we see the design as a continuum of staggered levels that look different from all sides. It is, in fact, an urban sculpture.

The recesses and protuberances created by these various staggered levels give residents the sense that they're living in a kind of penthouse.

If you have an apartment in this building, rather than simply an anonymous window somewhere, you have a home whose unique character is expressed by the building's exterior.

This also means that the building's interior has a wide variety of apartments to offer. One apartment may have a large exterior terrace, while another, on the opposite side of the building, has a loggia. This approach produces many individual spaces; the different floors don't all look the same.

An important design theme for us is a transition from indoors to outdoors that crosses no perceptible threshold. At X-Haus, designed for the Truman Plaza residential project, and at the Spreetower high-rise, we similarly used projecting and staggered levels to create an exciting interplay between interior and exterior.

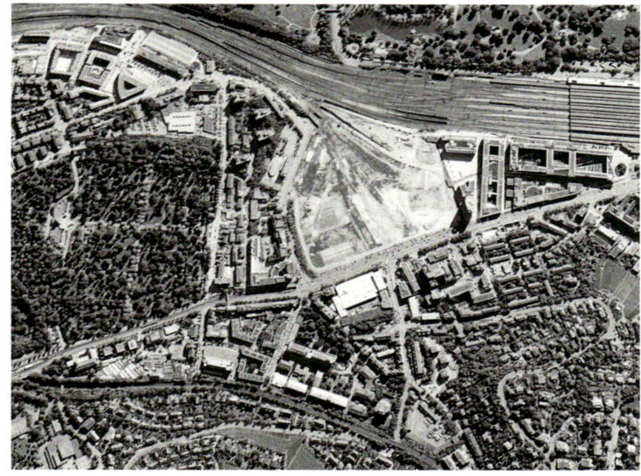

Aerial view of Europaviertel A1 Stuttgart 21 (top) and façade element with phase change material (bottom)

Energy issues, admittedly, dictate that a building should be as compact as possible. This is a fundamental balancing act that we, as architects, must negotiate. On the one hand, we want to minimize the building's surface area in order to save energy. On the other hand are all the demands of a contemporary living space and the desire for attractive outdoor areas – for bays, balconies, loggias and roof terraces. In short, the need for everything that makes the city an agreeable place to live.

And that's exactly where we see our responsibility as architects. Ultimately, political decisions about development policy have more impact on the environment than something like the cubic volume of a building. It's crucial that people don't all move to little houses in the suburbs, but they need new options in the city. We believe that the quest for high-quality urban living and the desire to live close to nature, combined with the current paradigm shift in energy policy, demand new residential high-rises. It's an exciting subject for design to address.

It was more important for us to create beautiful outdoor spaces, and make living in the city more attractive to potential residents, than to design a building with a minimised outer shell where no one would want to live.

Proximity to the town centre and vertical access, both standard features of high-rises, are also requirements of elderly-friendly housing. The demographic changes taking place in German society today mean that we can no longer build apartments that are unsuitable for people with disabilities.

And in Stuttgart, this poses a real problem. This is a city where the good residential areas are on sloping ground, not always easy to reach on foot.

I always think of my grandmother, who lived in Stuttgart: she used to place chairs on the stair landings so she could rest between floors.

At the beginning of the competition, we made a thorough study of the various basic demands on housing – partly because at the time it wasn't clear whether we'd be building a hotel or an apartment block.

We were caught between these two possibilities. For a hotel, we would've had to efficiently stack many rooms of minimal size atop one another. On the other hand, we still wanted to create the flowing spaces and connection with the outdoors that we considered to be essential features for modern homes.

In a residential structure, the building envelope has an additional role, serving as a filter that separates public space from private.

Because we'd dispensed with the idea of a compact building envelope in order to improve the quality of residents' homes, we wanted our building envelope to be highly energy-efficient. Unlike our project office building in Hamburg-Neumühlen, another fully glass-clad building into which we incorporated building component activation, we wanted to utilize the façade of the building as an energy production site, with the help of innovative products derived from research into phase change materials.

Sustainable buildings shouldn't just consume energy, they should be capable of producing and storing it as well – especially high-rises.

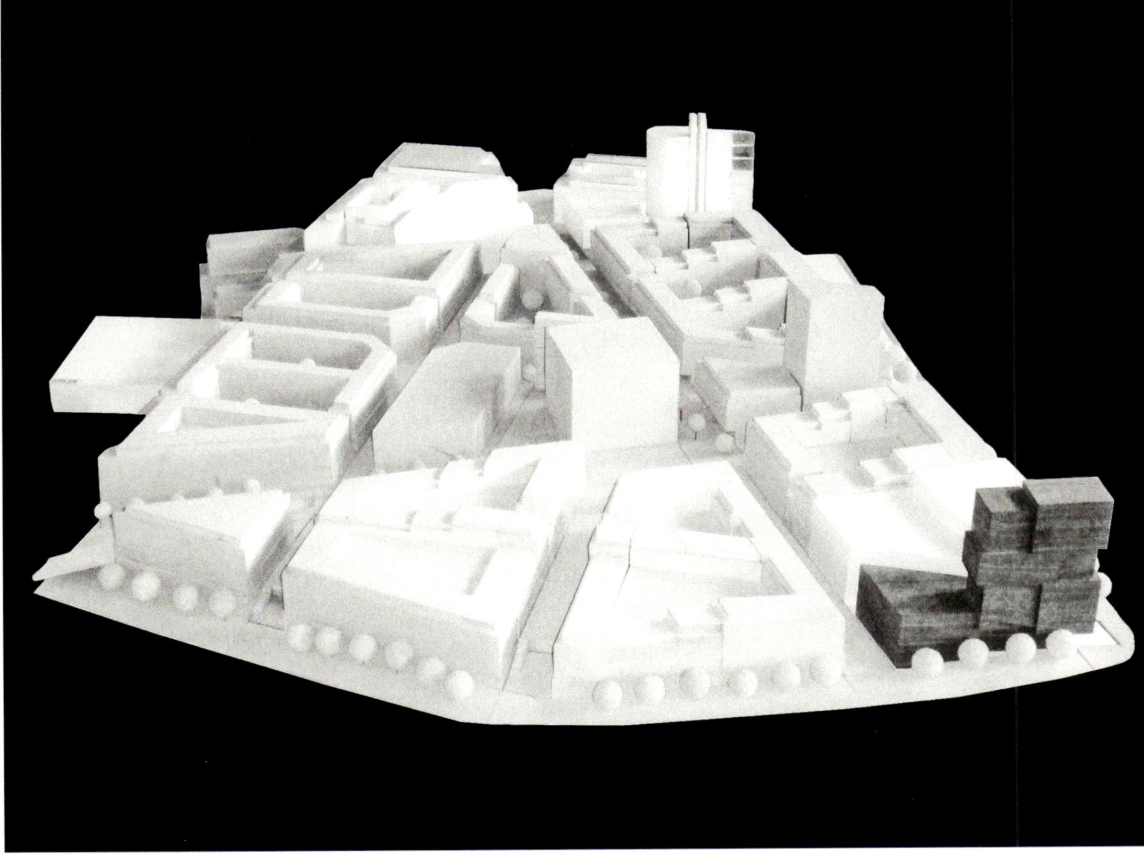

Stuttgart 21 residential highrise

Location
Heilbronner Strasse / Wolframstrasse, 70191 Stuttgart

Year
1st prize competition 2008

Team
Olaf Menk, Henning Wiethaus, Kai Hansen, Benjamin Bühs, Arno Löbbecke, Thiele Nickau, Dominik Queck, Stefan Rützel

Client
Baufeld 7 Grundstücksgesellschaft mbH

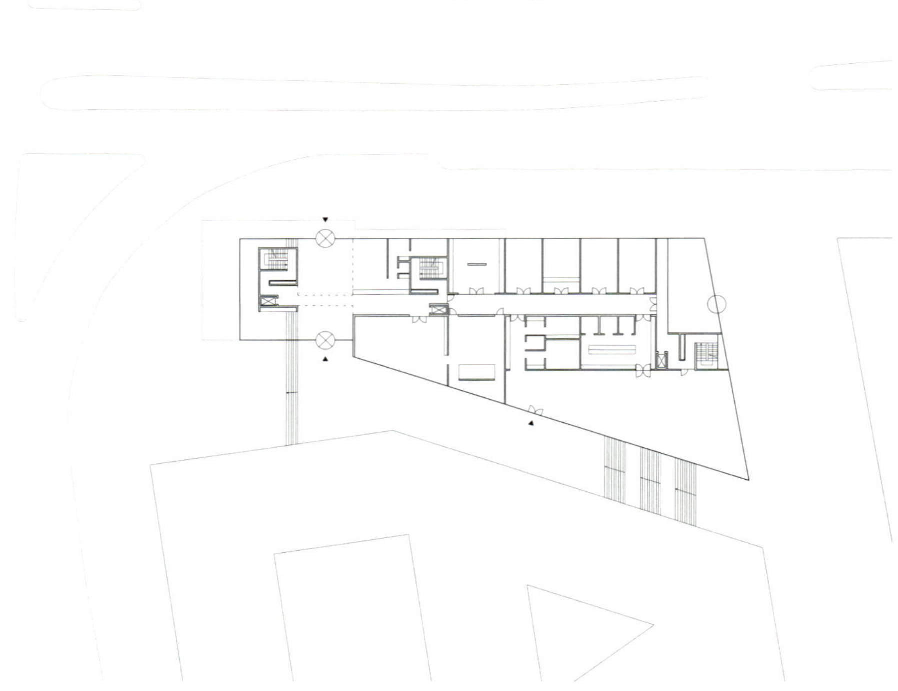

Ground floor with surroundings

South elevation

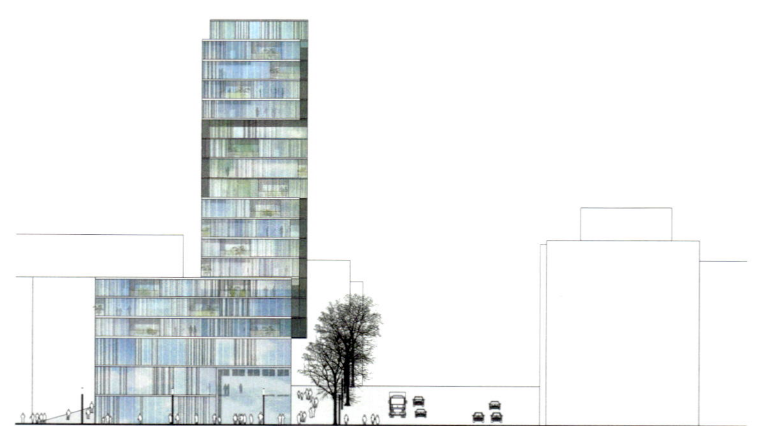

East elevation

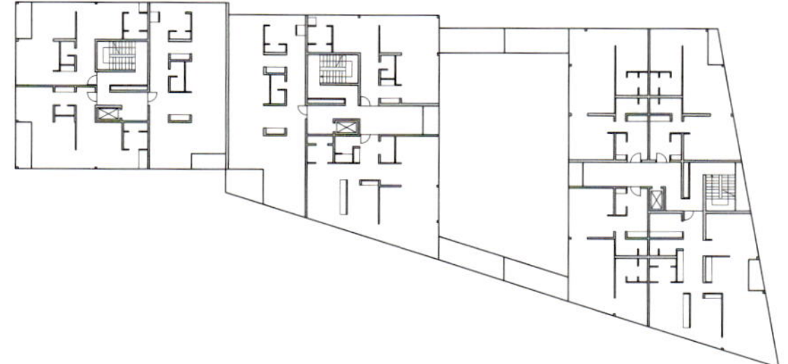

3rd–4th floors

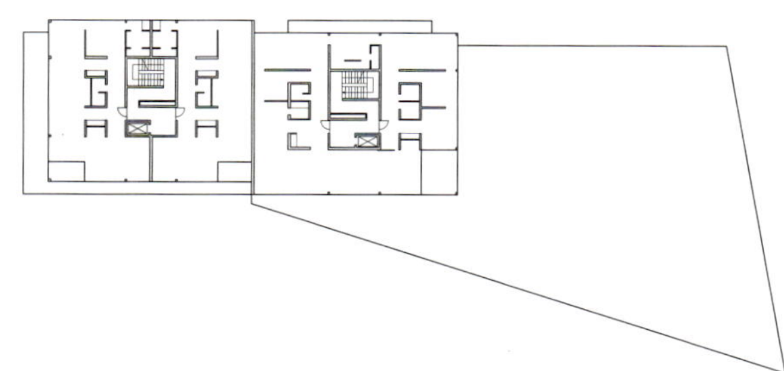

13th–16th floors

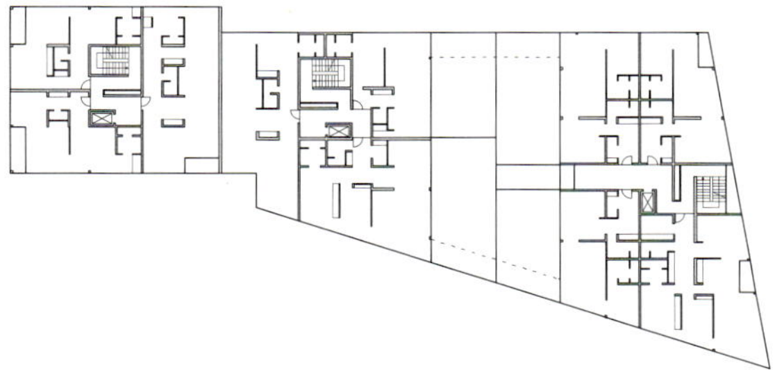

2nd floor

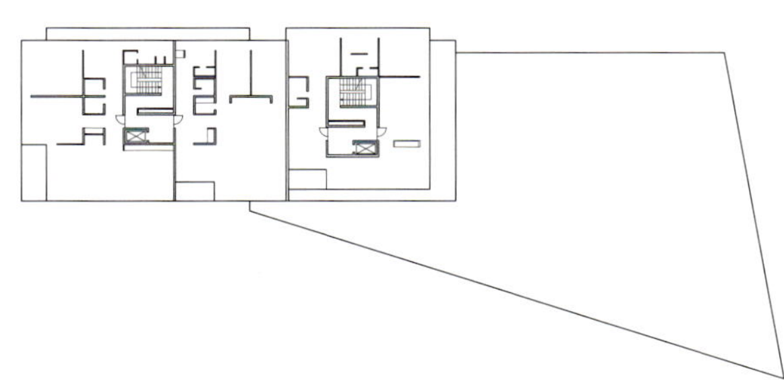

9th–12th floors

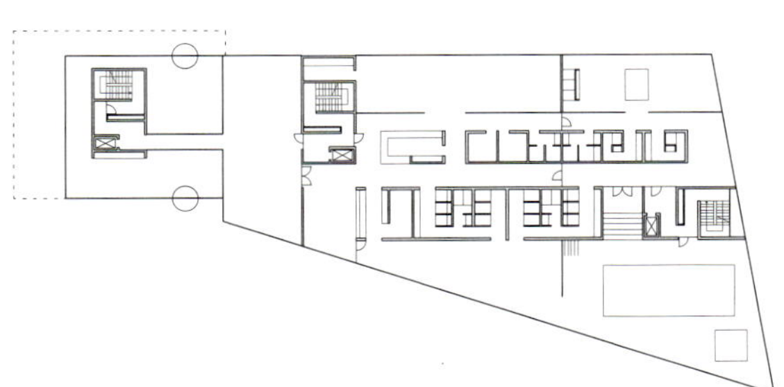

1st floor

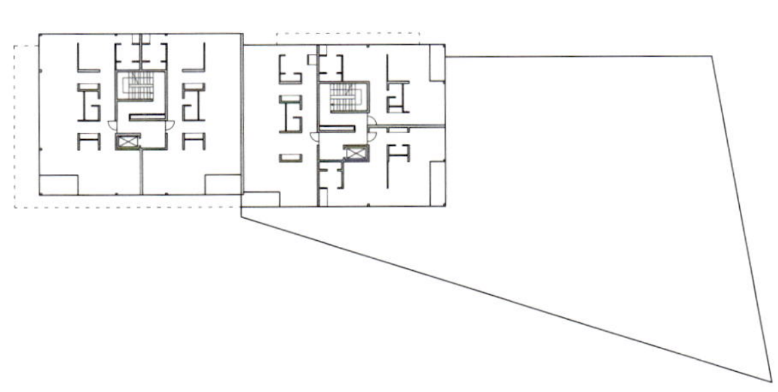

5th–8th floors

The Spreedreieck office building, Berlin

Taken together, our projects look quite heterogeneous. The question is: what do they have in common? One theme we've returned to time and time again is the search for a suitably sculptural architectural solution – the architect as a sculptor working in the urban space. Many of our projects are motivated by this question, even though the end result of each might look very different.

One such project was for an office building on Friedrichstrasse. There was a competition in 1921 for this very property; Mies van der Rohe and Hugo Häring, among others, submitted entries. Today, even though they were never built, those designs are famous; Mies' glass tower is particularly well-known. You could say that, in our heads, the property was already occupied.

Unlike Mies van der Rohe, we started out with a height restriction, meaning that we wouldn't be able to achieve sculptural power through verticality as he did. Still, the city's silhouette was important to us – what kind of skyline would we be creating?

And, above all: what kind of places would we be creating?

Competition entries of Hugo Häring (left) and Ludwig Mies van der Rohe (right), 1921

Building site at the former border crossing station, with Tränenpalast (Palace of Tears), 2004

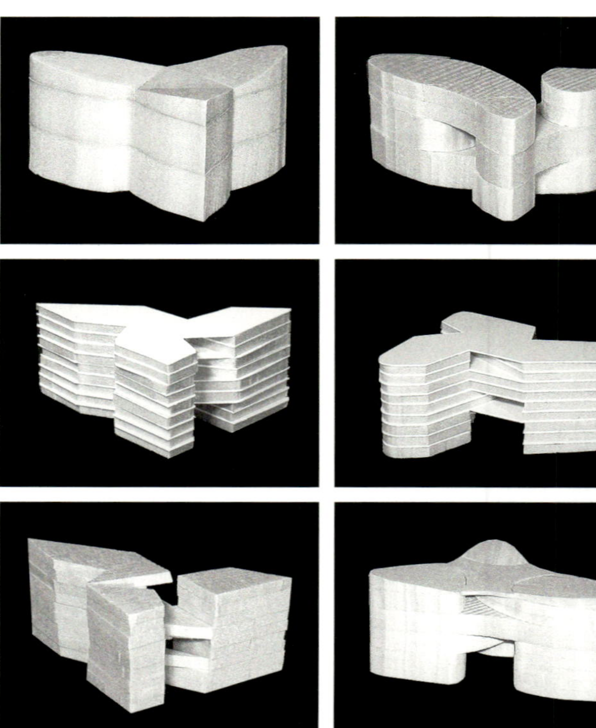

Model studies on the cubature of the design

There are few places in a city that can be viewed from a distance and, simultaneously, seen in the context of their surroundings. Those that do exist are always special places, visible across the waterfront or through a park.

Sites that are exposed to view from all sides are totally atypical of Berlin, and ours was in such a prominent location, too. That's what made this assignment so fascinating.

Starting with our thoughts about the city's silhouette, we gave a great deal of thought to the top of this building.

Here, we worked with a motif that frequently appears in our projects: a curved silhouette combined with a curved base.

The highest points of a building always suggest movement – either a recess that produces a sense of reduced scale, or the kind of dynamization you see here.

At least as important as the silhouette, however, is the functionality of the roof. In the third-place design, which has since been realised, the roof is crowded with building services – which, unfortunately, is almost always the case with office buildings. We, on the other hand, saw the roof as a key location in the new building's working environment. We wanted the roof to function as an extension of the common areas inside the building. Its shape would've suggested a rolling dune landscape, creating a unique urban experience.

The somewhat simply phrased plea "roof gardens instead of solar panels!" was also our motto for projects like the Marthashof development and our Biennale contribution, "convertible city". In order to combat suburban sprawl, we need to use roof surfaces in a way that makes the city more attractive, rather than packing them with boring solar panels. Solar panels are fine for the Sahara, but not for the city's most valuable spaces – and the roof is an absolutely precious one.

Of course, the geometry of inclined roofs already in place makes it hard to build roof terraces on extant buildings. Under normal conditions, an inclined roof and a roof terrace are mutually exclusive. There are exceptions, like the Altana Terraces of Venice, which are simply level platforms atop an inclined roof.

For new buildings, the picture is different: every new structure subtracts a certain amount of space from the city, and the roof is a logical place to return that space to the city. Le Corbusier was absolutely right about that.

Apart from the roof, the most significant feature of the floor plan was a large atrium, criss-crossed by transverse bridges that connected the various levels. The façade would've consisted of two layers of glass folded into each other. This created a multi-layered sculptural effect that gave the building's glass-clad envelope a sense of depth – it was rather like a fashionably pleated skirt, complete with undulations.

Of course, these folded surfaces also had cost implications – curved glazing is simply very expensive. For this reason, we proposed a façade constructed from an array of mini-bay windows, which would replace the rounded shape with a pleated form. The foremost layer would've been glass, and those behind it composed of polished, highly reflective stainless steel panels.

This is another theme that we revisit frequently: how much depth can a building's skin have? For our competition entry for Weimar's Neue Bauhaus-Museum, we worked on a similar solution, deploying a pleated metal façade with a ceramic coating. The front section is coloured white, whereas the rear section features colour fields from the canon of Johannes Itten. The outermost layer is given a harmonious structure of vertical lines by the matte white ceramic material. In combination with the colour sequences, this generates a subtle effect of reflected coloured light.

The intensity and sculptural depth of the colour effect changes depending on the angle of light and your vantage point, altering your spatial perception of the building – it has a poetic quality.

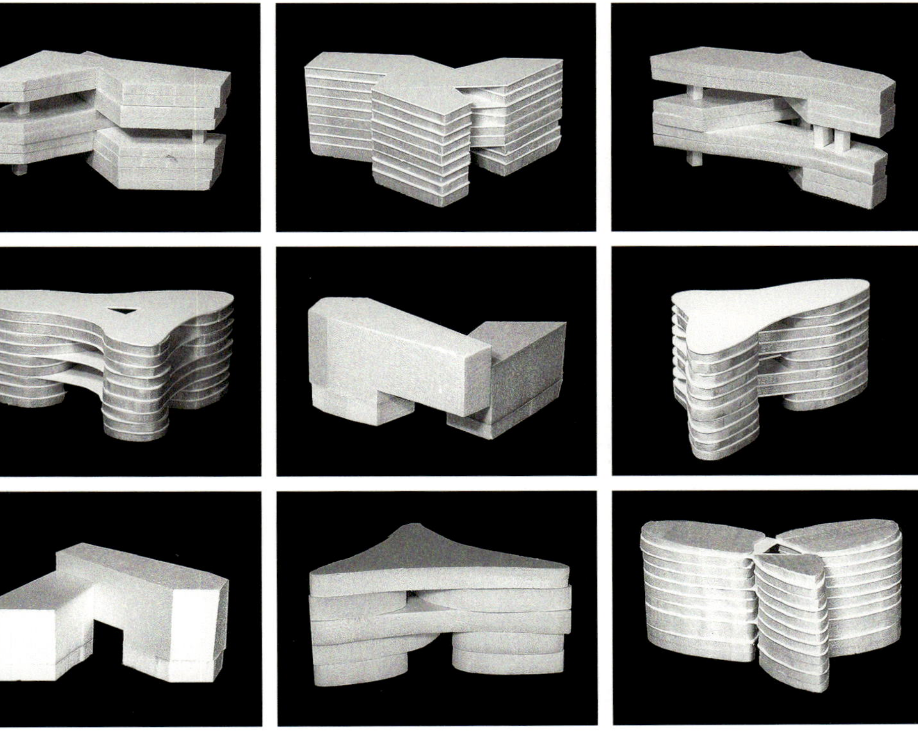

Location
Friedrichstrasse 140, 10117 Berlin

Year
2nd prize competition 2005

Team
Kai Hansen, Arno Löbbecke,
Dennis Hawner, Jon C. Ferrer

Client
Müller-Spreer & Co. Spreedreieck KG,
Berlin

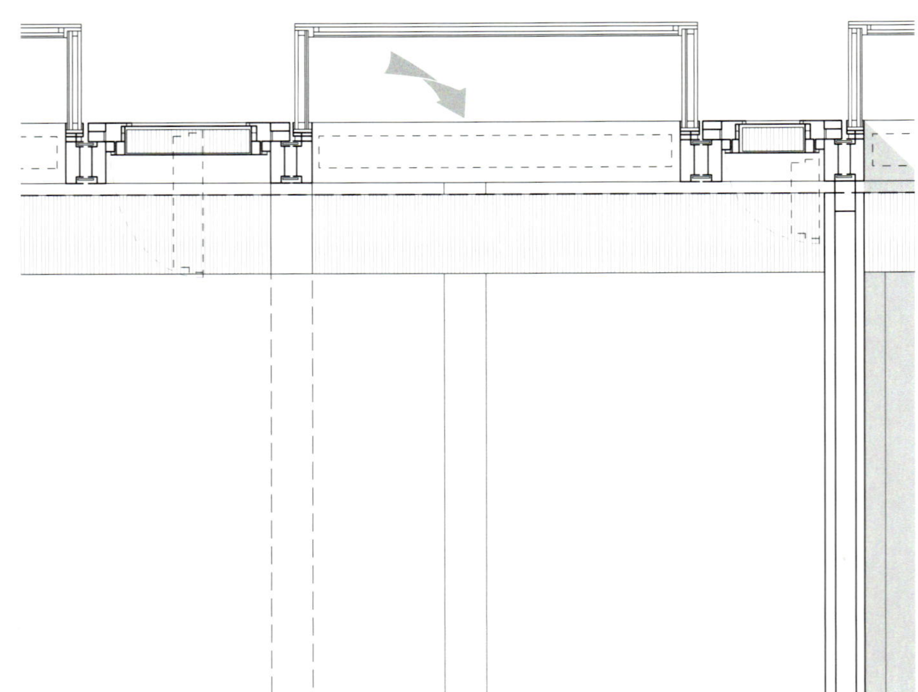

Façade detail

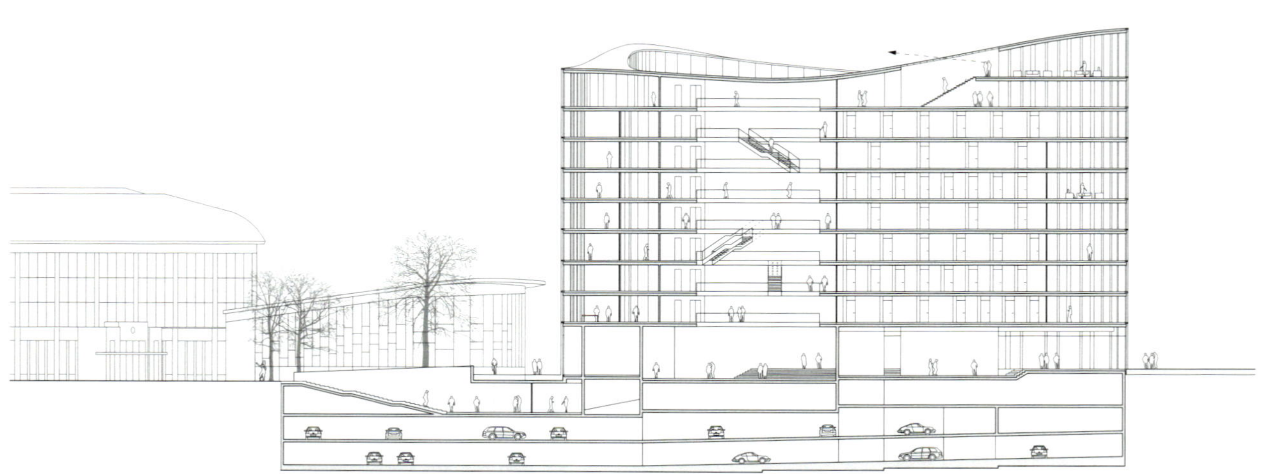

Section

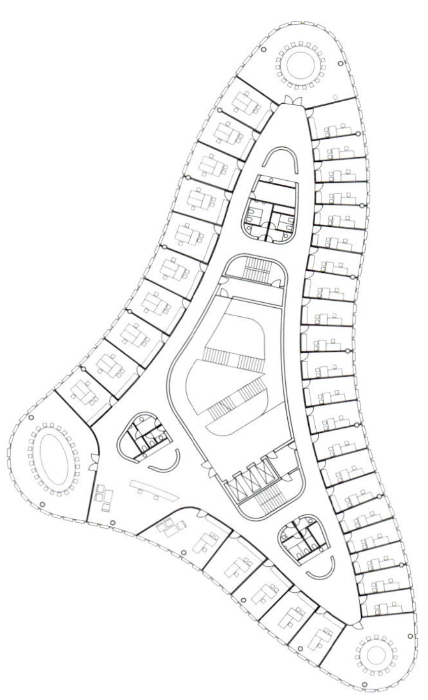

Floor plan variant

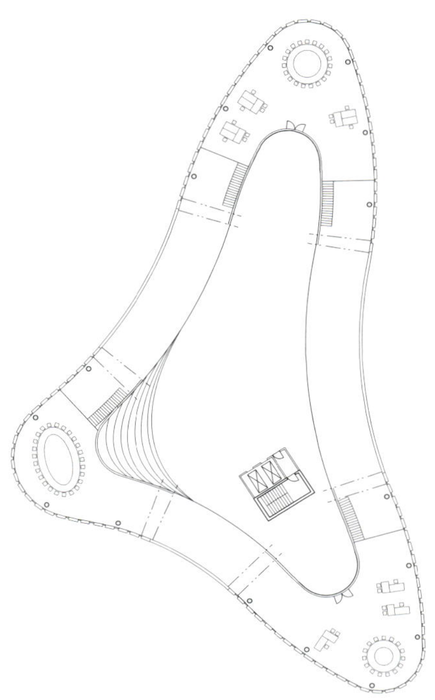

Gallery floor

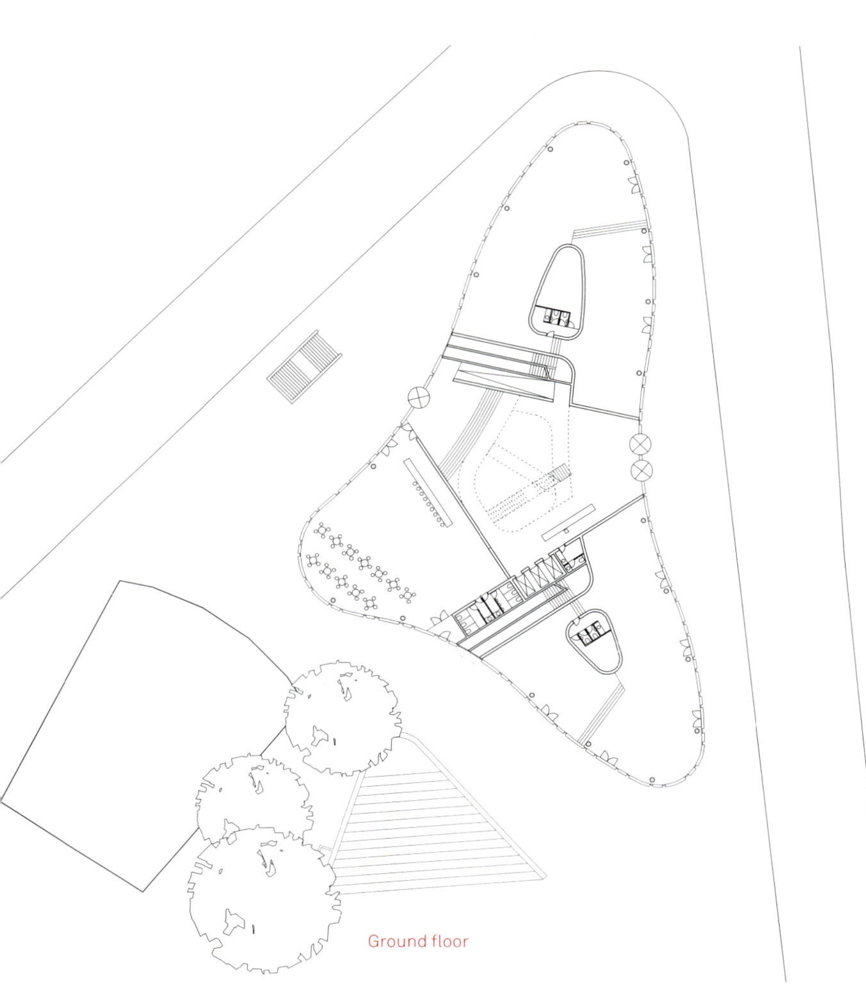

Ground floor

Top floor

Site prior to the competition

Rendering of the design without the pavilion

Department store, Lübeck

People often say that we make beautiful glass buildings, but the hotel in Flensburg and the department store in Lübeck were two projects that had nothing to do with glass. The Lübeck building is primarily constructed out of stone.

This department store is located in the centre of Lübeck's old city, on a corner at the beginning of the pedestrian zone. Lübeck is a very beautiful city, but contains a few architectural blemishes from the post-war period. But one of these, sadly, is located right here: somebody stuck this small pavilion out in the middle of the pedestrian zone. It's been leased for the next 20 years, so it's not going anywhere. A developer had bought the property on the corner behind it and demolished the existing five-storey building so he could build a new, one- or two-storey shopping centre. The plan really wouldn't have done justice to the site's exposed position.

The Lübeck city planning commission – which, by the way, is very ambitious in comparison to those in many other cities – held an architectural competition for this new building, but just to design the façade. Initially, we weren't sure we should take part in a competition solely concerned with designing a façade. Eventually, we decided not only to create an outer shell but developed a sculptural volume.

However, there were two fundamental problems. The first was the pavilion. It was a kind of cartographic eccentricity around which the design had to be cunningly arranged because of the awkward angles it produced. The other problem was the basic question of the building's height.

The civic pride of certain North German cities – like Flensburg, Bremen and Lübeck – is expressed in their architecture. There is a prevailing theme of heavily emphasised gables, for instance: everywhere you find verticality, buildings that strive upwards.

For this reason, we felt that a horizontal building with building services mounted on a flat roof would be unacceptable. We came up with an alternative. The original floor plan had, apart from the sales floors, only a few secondary spaces, such as a kitchenette and offices. We rearranged the plan, combining the building services with these smaller secondary spaces in order to produce a greater spatial volume.

To be able to respond to the neighbouring development, we developed a roof structure of folded triangular surfaces. We played on the conventional form of a gabled house, which our design transforms into something new.

The gables run around the corners, creating an unusual profile. Normally, roof gables are on the same level along their full length. This corner situation, however, creates slanting edges at the sides, where the gable connects between eaves and ridge.

At the edges, we performed a kind of seamless join, taking the lines of the neighbouring development and weaving them into our design.

And, of course, a building also needs windows. The client's original design requirements made no mention of them, but we felt that windows were important, even for a department store. However, the windows became smaller and smaller as our plans developed.

For us, as architects, this project represented a considerable struggle. The building had already been leased even before construction started, putting the developer under enormous time and financial pressures.

For instance, cost restrictions prevented us from using the large-format stone elements that we used on the façade on the roof as well, as we'd originally planned. Simple slate roofing was significantly cheaper, and so today the façade and the roof of the building use different types of stone. Architects sometimes have to live with these compromises, particularly when, as we did in this case, they only have responsibility for phases one through four. Specifically, this meant that we were only in charge of the design until the permits came through – everything after that was beyond our control.

We wanted to have the same kind of stone cladding on the roof as on the façade, in order to give the building the character of a monolithic sculpture. With this in mind, we'd selected a special kind of stone from Tuscany; in Italy, you often see houses roofed with stone slabs. This stone can be split like slate to create a good roofing surface, so it would have been particularly suitable for this project.

Department store

Location
Breite Strasse 36–42, 23552 Lübeck

Year
1st prize competition 2007
completion 2009

Team
Olaf Menk, Arno Löbbecke,
Alessio Fossati, Stefan John

Client
GbR Lübeck Breite Strasse 36–42

Technical planners
LSM Ingenieure für Tragwerksplanung,
Hannover (structural engineering)
Ingenieurbüro Gunder & Benz, Goslar
(building services)

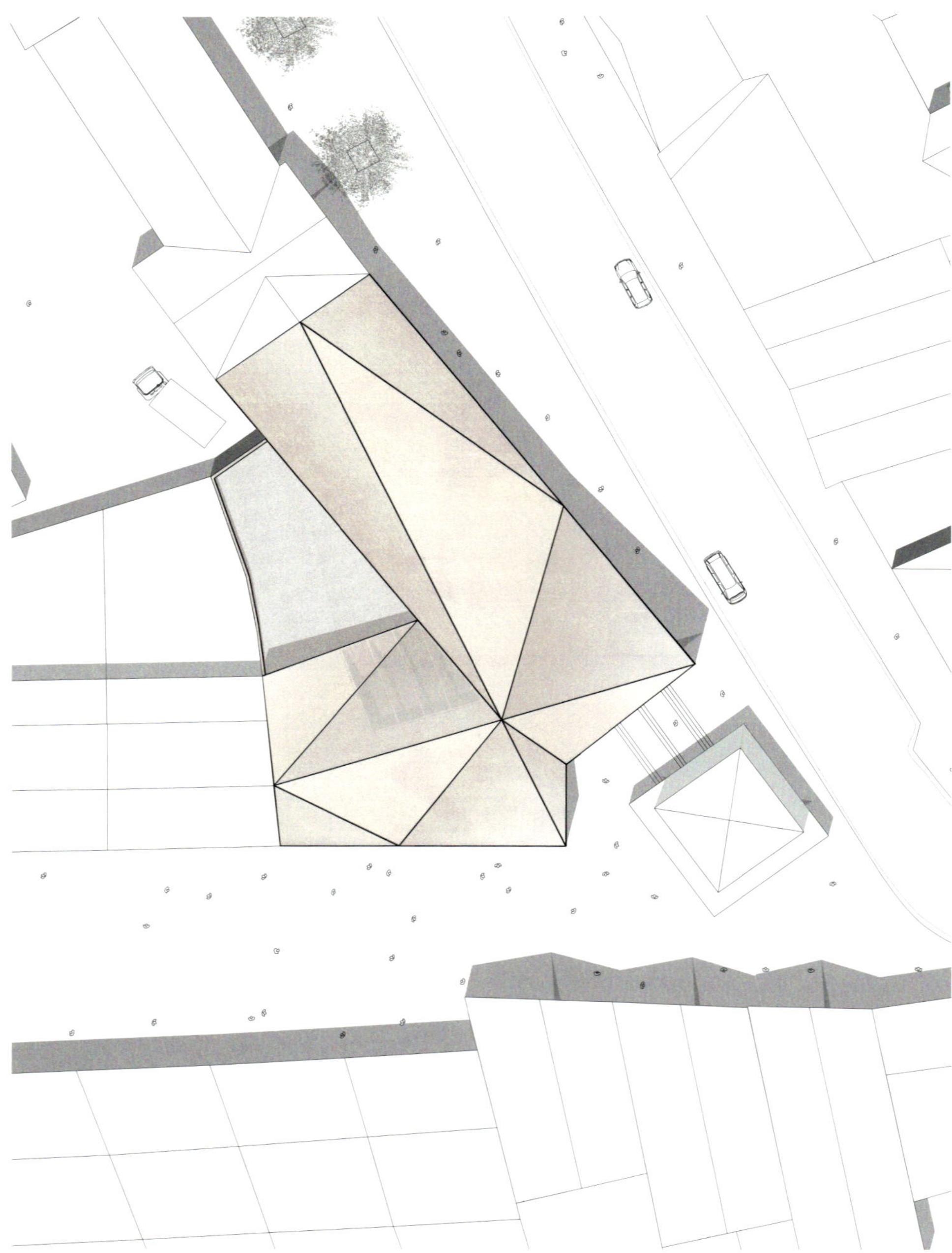

Roof plan with surroundings

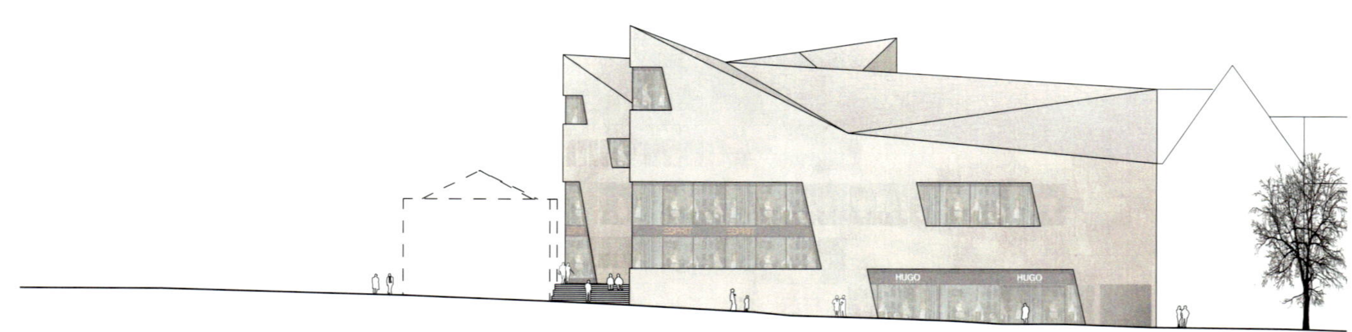

East elevation

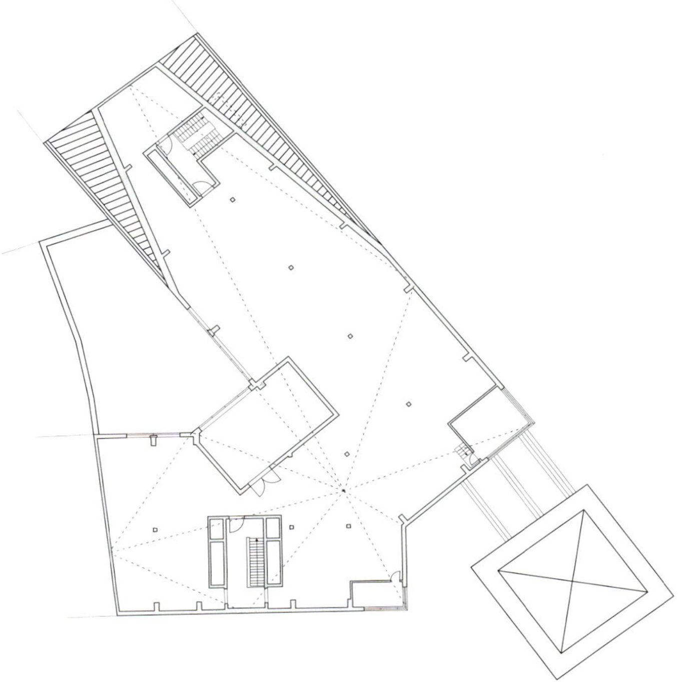

Top floor

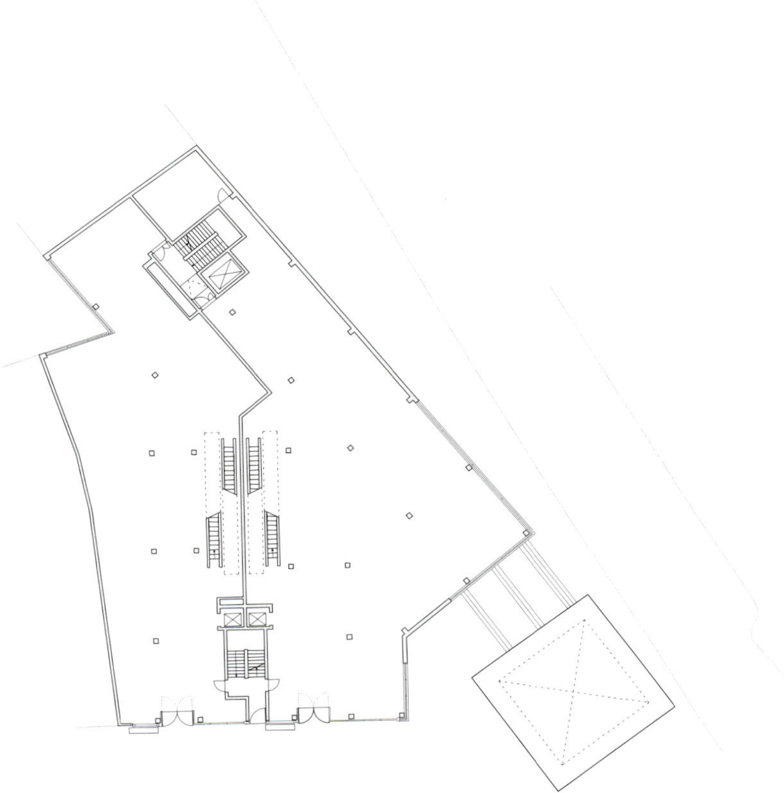

Ground floor

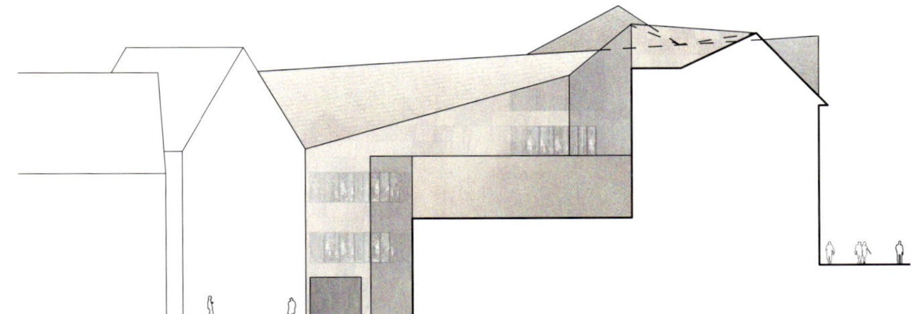

West elevation

South elevation

The Fördehotel Flensburg

The hotel in Flensburg is another project in which sculptural architectural techniques played a major role.

Flensburg is divided in two by a fjord: the west side of Flensburg is more beautiful, whereas the east side of town contains the former harbour district. The property was there, on the less attractive, industrial side of town.

When you look along the fjord, you see large storage buildings, a few unremarkable residential buildings, and some warehouses. The skyline, on the other hand, is characterised by the zigzag lines of church steeples and gables, which harmonise nicely with the occasional passing sailboat.

When we were looking for a shape for the building, we asked ourselves two questions. First, how could we break up the huge mass of the building to create some lines of sight all the way through, allowing people to sense something of the fjord that lies behind it? And, second, how could we tie our design into the city's historic urban form, built up over the generations, which is a source of strong civic pride?

We divided the volume into three prismatic bodies, run through with a series of gaps that offer specific views.

At the same time, these features formally reference the gabled houses in the historic city centre across the fjord. They also have the same sense of scale.

This idea won us the competition. Subsequently, however, the design was hotly discussed among the public and the press. This just goes to show that architecture can have a significant political dimension! As a general rule, it's always easier to mobilise people against something – that was the case for Stuttgart 21, and we experienced something similar during our project to redevelop the Brühl in Leipzig, where a man chained himself to the old building that was to be demolished. It was the same way here.

Ultimately, the building wasn't constructed. A development plan had been drawn up before the competition was held, but in the end the politicians lacked the courage to follow through with their decision. The competition was a way for the city to test the waters, to find out what the public would accept – and public interest in the project was enormous. Between 600 and 700 people attended the discussion forum.

Flensburger Nachrichten

Sonnabend, 28. Januar 2006

Wechsel im Vorstand

Flensburg/yv – Beim Verschönerungsverein Flensburg (VVF) hat es Veränderungen im Vorstand gegeben. Der langjährige stellvertretende Vorsitzende Karl-Wilhelm Lönnecker verzichtete auf eine erneute Kandidatur. Neue stellvertretende Vorsitzende wurde Cordelia Feuerhake. Susanne Braas gab ihren Posten als Schriftführerin ebenfalls auf. Sie wird sich als Projektleiterin für den Erhalt des Kollunder Waldes einsetzen. Als Nachfolgerin wählten die Mitglieder Carolin Iversen. Der erst im Herbst kommissarisch eingesetzte Schatzmeister Kai Petersen wurde bestätigt.

Einem Säurebad gleich sind Flensburgs Bürgeranhörungen, die in Planerkreisen einen nachgerade legendären Ruf genießen, findet Kim Schmidt.

Newspaper headlines in Flensburg a day prior to the public hearing, 2006

Flensburg's old town on the other side of the fjord

Flensburger Nachrichten

Sonnabend, 28. Januar 2006 FT Seite 9 – Jahrgang 200

Bürgerversammlung diskutiert Hotelprojekt am Hafen

Flensburg /ft — Am kommenden Dienstag, 31. Januar, um 19.30 Uhr gibt es in der Bürgerhalle des Rathauses Gelegenheit, sich über die Pläne für das Hotel am Hafen zu informieren. Mit dabei sind Vertreter der Stadt und der Investoren sowie Volkwin Marg, der dem Preisgericht angehörte. Moderiert wird der Abend von Stephan Menschel. Umstritten ist in der bisherigen Diskussion vor allem die Größe und Höhe des geplanten Gebäudes. In einem Internet-Diskussionsforum unter www.shz.de nahmen die Leser Stellung: „Das ist mal wieder (...) typisch Flensburg. Sobald jemand etwas verändern möchte, wird es von allen wieder mies gemacht", meinte Frank H., Teilnehmer des Forums. Er findet den Plan für das Hotel am Ballastkai „einfach klasse". Neben Frank H. nahmen 35 weitere Personen seit Dienstag an der Diskussion teil. „Superhässlich", „überdimensioniertes Etwas", „grenzt an Größenwahn", einfach eine dieser „utopischen Geschmacklosigkeiten", die die „schöne Altstadt" verschandele — bei einem großen Teil der Beiträge überwog indes die Kritik. Inhaltlicher Tenor der Diskussion: Das Hotel sei zu groß, zu hoch, passe nicht ins Stadtbild, die Bronze-Haut sei wenig „verlockend". Der Hafen sei a der Stelle zu schmal, verlier an Charme, „vor allen wenn die Gründerbaute nicht mehr zu sehen sind' Am Dienstag geht die Dis kussion weiter. Ab 19 Uh liegen die Pläne zur Einsich aus.

Nobody took issue with the building itself – the competition and the quality of the design were well-received.

Rather, the questions that came out of the public discussion were more along the lines of, "couldn't you find a better place for this building?"

The building was ultimately rejected not because of its architecture, but because of its function: a location that had previously been open to the public was to be put to private use, and this met with criticism. We, however, do see a clear connection between the design's striking, conspicuous form and the project's rejection. Our plot wasn't the only new development site in the area; right next door, for instance, residential houses were being built – another private-use project. But because they didn't stand out so much, nobody noticed them. The hotel, with its striking form, would've acted as a quasi-public building, but was built for a private developer.

In the case of a library or a museum, a distinct, sculptural look tends to be accepted, because it expresses the social significance of the building. However, a private use in this extremely public place, combined with such an exceptional appearance – somehow, they just didn't work together.

It also had something to do with the nature of the city of Flensburg, where the citizenry has always played an active role. Two years later, the small citizens' initiative to oppose the project had even formed its own political party, which received 30 percent of the vote.

The way I see it, the project was by no means a failure – at least not in this one respect. That architecture is capable of motivating people to this degree is a testament to its social relevance – even if its actual material realization, in the form of a building, doesn't come to pass (which, of course, is a hard thing for an architect to accept). Ultimately, architecture is about more than just the construction of buildings – it's also about the construction of society.

Fördehotel Flensburg

Location
Ballastkai 1, 24937 Flensburg

Year
1st prize competition 2005

Team
Kai Hansen, Olaf Menk, Thomas Ellinghaus, Alessio Fossati, Ingo Beckmann, Peter Menken and Dominik Queck

Client
Projektgesellschaft Ballastkai GmbH & Co. KG, Glücksburg

Technical planners
Topotek 1 Gesellschaft von Landschaftsarchitekten mbH, Berlin (open space planning)

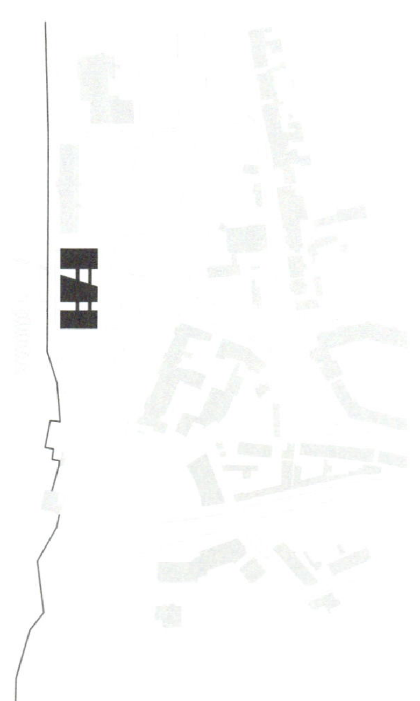

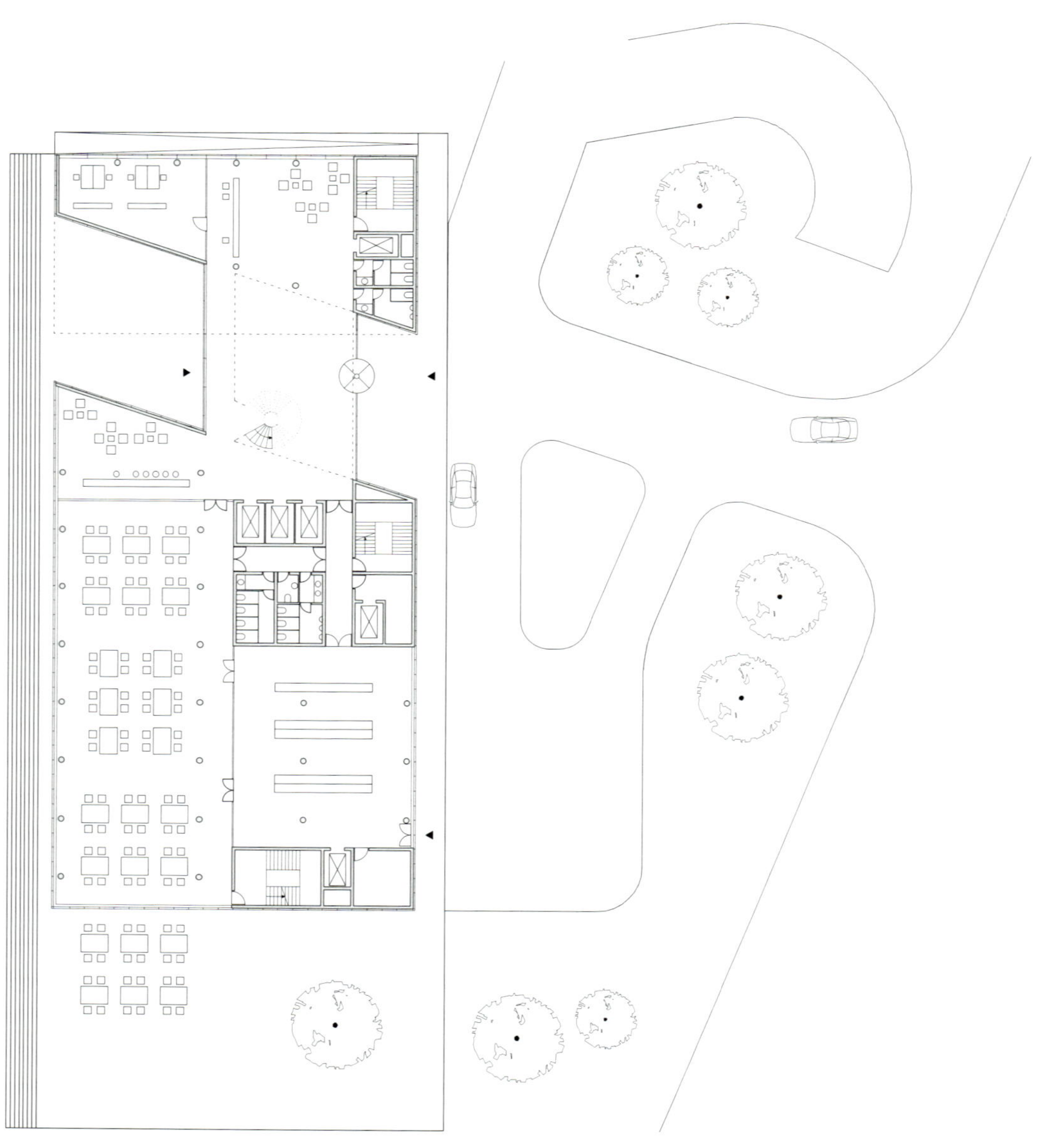

Ground floor

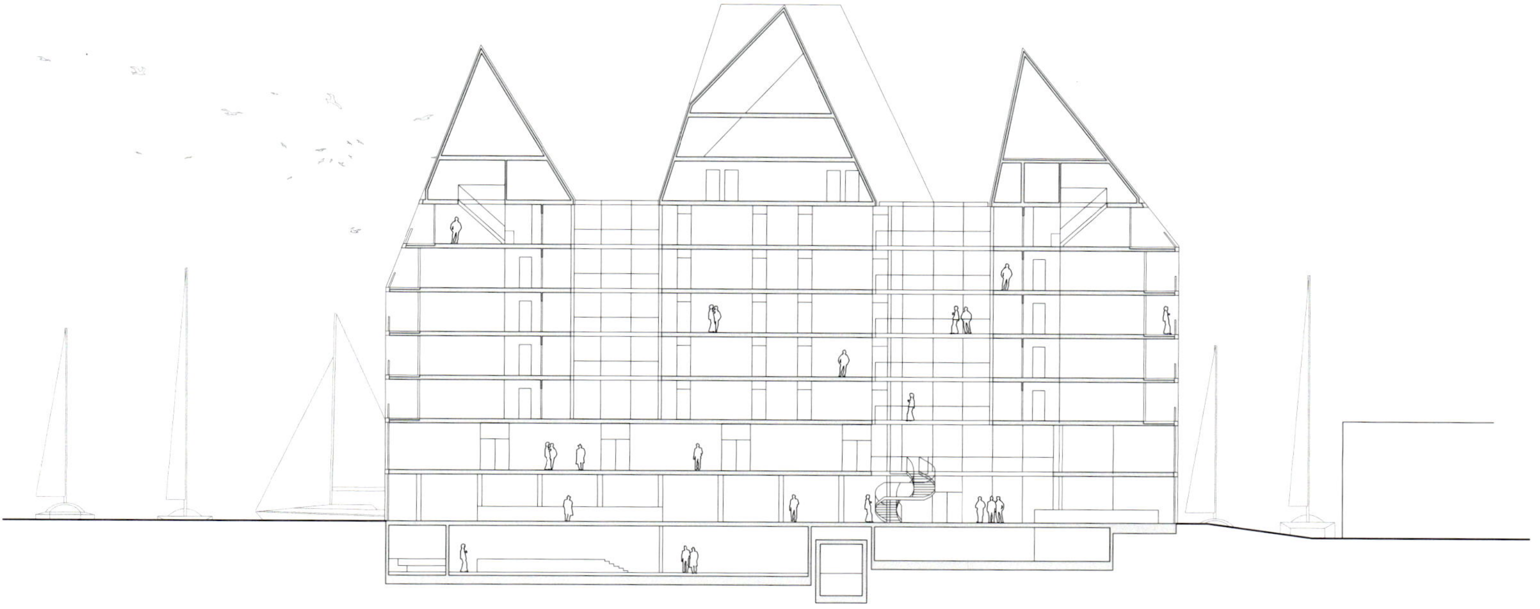

Section

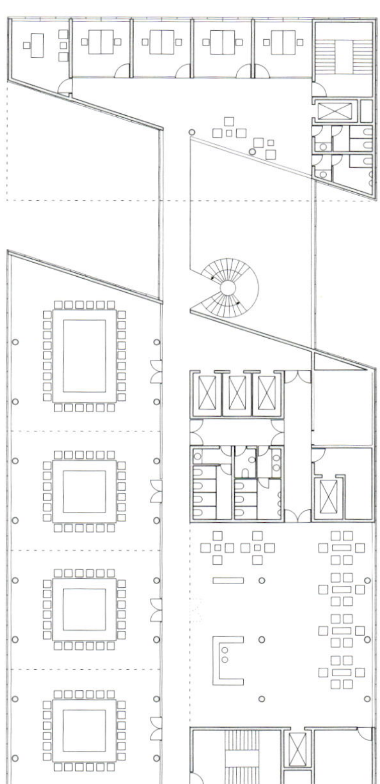

Floor plan variant

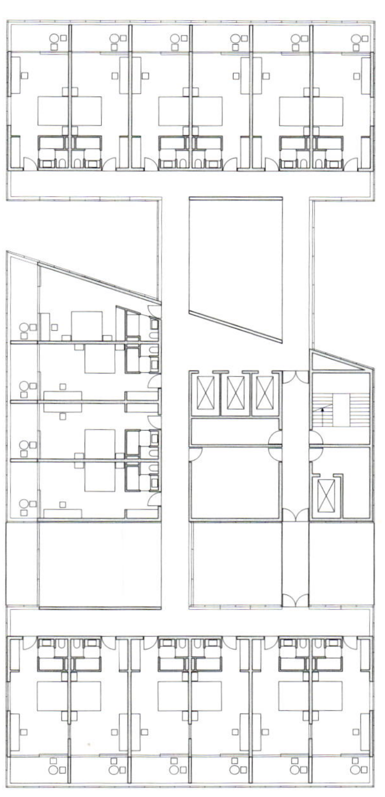

Floor plan variant

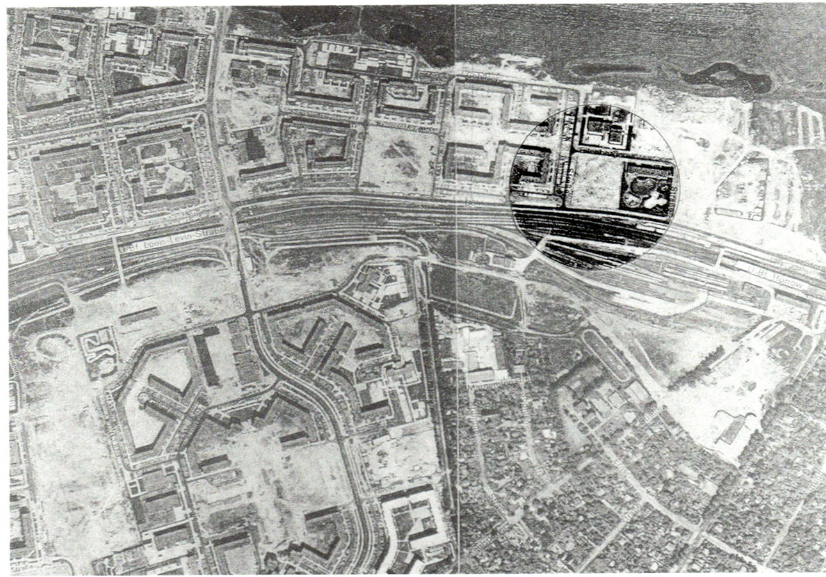

Site at the edge of a large-scale housing estate

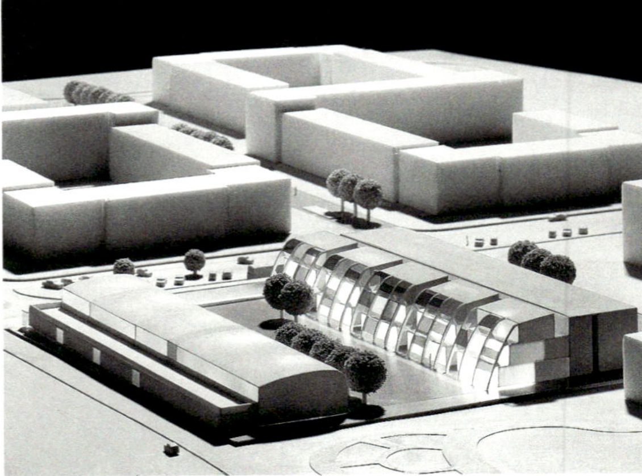

Urban context in 1993 (top) and competition model (bottom)

Berlin-Hellersdorf Special Needs School

This project is one of our school buildings. The Deutsche Schule Madrid, which we're currently working on, will be our fourth. The special needs school at Berlin-Hellersdorf, built in the early nineties, was our first.

This is a school for mentally handicapped children. Personally, I've never liked that term, and prefer "Förderschule" (special needs school; lit. "support school" or "advancement school").

We'd studied the subject in depth beforehand and compiled reports, which was why a young firm like ours was invited to take part in the competition in the first place.

You have to understand that the children who attend this school don't perceive the world the same way we do. As an architect, you have to approach a project like this differently – highly aware and with a great sensitivity.

We constantly had to perform a balancing act. On the one hand, the school needs to be a kind of "protected space" where the children can spend time safely. On the other hand, the children also need training to cope with everyday life in the outside world. This balancing act had to be borne in mind in every discussion, whether it was about the design of a certain space or the height of a railing.

This process wasn't made any easier by the fact that it was a very difficult plot. It's located near the Hönow rail terminus, so actually out in Brandenburg. The Hellersdorf housing estate was poised to expand across this area – the containers for the next construction site were already in place. The school site had been "baked into" the structure of the housing estate.

Aside from this, the plot is far too small – there wasn't space for open areas. When you consider that the children live in apartment buildings without immediate access to outdoor spaces, and that many of them have restricted mobility, it becomes clear that they spend the vast majority of their time indoors. That was why they needed a connection to the outside world so badly!

We therefore suggested that the classrooms be arranged one above the other so that each class could have its own south-facing terrace – compensation for the deficiencies of the children's living environments. Expansion of the inner areas into the outer space was a key element of the design; to facilitate this, the classrooms on the upper storeys open, with no intervening threshold, onto large roof terraces with easily accessible plant beds. These offer a substitute for the non-existent school garden. The graduation of the terraces correlates with the children's increasing autonomy – the students are organized not by age but by skill and degree of independence.

The small garden courtyard itself is enclosed by the two buildings. We wanted it to be experienced in every way possible. Towards the street, the buildings have distinct edges that reference the urban environment, but where they face the courtyard, the eaves dissolve into soft curves, making the courtyard seem bigger than it is. We took advantage of the introverted character imposed on the courtyard by the enclosing buildings, making the gym in the therapy centre completely open on its courtyard side.

Normally, windows that go right down to the ground are proscribed for gymnasia, so we redefined the space: today, it's not a gym fit for competitive sports, it's just a hall – although it has the dimensions of a regular gym.

Classroom units between the load-bearing bulkheads during construction

This allowed us to create a visual connection to the school building, which helps the students orient themselves and gives them an increased sense of security.

There's a glass-enclosed walkway leading from the therapy centre to the school building. This feature was discussed and debated for an incredibly long time. The local government felt that in order to be kept safe, the children had to be kept hidden. Some of the competitions entries hid the school behind a massive masonry wall. People worried that the glass walkway would attract vandals, that skinheads would stand in the street and throw stones ...

We countered these objections by saying that if it really proved necessary, the children could finger-paint the glass, rendering it opaque. However, we wanted to at least give our idea a try! As it turned out, there was no need for finger-paint. On the contrary, the whole glass façade is now used as a display window where the children can present their arts and crafts.

We were very lucky to have the support of the school director – she stood behind our design all the way from the competition on.

One reason for this was that the school had temporarily been housed in a modular kindergarten – a very unsatisfactory arrangement. After all, more than a quarter of the children were wheelchair users! The director was just happy that a school was to be built specifically for these children, and that she'd be able to participate in and contribute her experience to the tailoring of the design.

She was generally the deciding vote. What you have to understand is that in Germany, schools for disabled children are always unique, isolated designs. The architects simply learn project by project. There's little accumulation of experience, so every new building is a sort of prototype. Normally, for instance, you wouldn't include a big terrace in a design like this – that's the sort of thing people associate with a resort in the south of Spain. In spite of that, the school director fought for this design to be implemented.

I think that what she liked best about the design was that we tried to do as much as possible, under the circumstances, for the children. You have to keep in mind that the plot was extremely small; we could barely fit the necessary sports fields into it.

We developed many elements of the architectural plan in consultation with the school leadership, altering them from the original program. For instance, we wanted an auditorium that would be used regularly, not one that would be locked except at Christmas and Easter. The large, slightly outward-sweeping hallways were designed to allow an expansion where they join the central hall of the auditorium, allowing it to be turned into a playground on rainy days. The classrooms themselves are planned like small houses: you can walk around them on all sides, making them seem like independent units. This also helps students to orient themselves.

We designed the climate control systems jointly with Christopher McCarthy and Guy Battle, two veteran British designers of sustainable buildings. This was in 1993, and in those days there weren't many standard solutions for sustainability. For instance, it was a huge challenge to integrate the fire protection into the climate control systems.

Although it's 28 metres wide, the school building has natural light and ventilation, which was important to us. Multi-storey conservatories between the classroom units offer the possibility of opening the classroom doors in winter, allowing pre-warmed air to stream in. In summer, they perform the reverse function, acting as a chimney: a hatch at the top of the conservatory is opened and warm air is drawn upward by the resulting thermal induction.

Each classroom unit is installed between the building's bulkheads without supports, permitting the space to be flexibly divided into therapy and group-rooms. In future, more children with disabilities will be integrated into the mainstream school system and, as a result, the proportion of children with severe and multiple disabilities will rise at special needs schools. If the school got just five more students who use wheelchairs, a rigid arrangement of rooms would become unworkable. So it was important to us that the room boundaries be adjustable, not rigidly imposed by a static system.

We designed the classrooms to be bigger than requirements dictated, meaning that storage spaces had to be omitted. To compensate for this, we planned deep closet zones with sliding elements as part of the hallway wall, into which the kitchens were also integrated.

Small windows installed at varying heights offer a view from the classroom into the hallway. They're supplemented by a slit, making communication between inside and outside possible. This gives each classroom a façade that looks outwards. These windows also double as showcases.

We planned to use a special effect for the corridor walls: they'd be painted with heat-sensitive colour-changing paint, so that when the children touched them, their hands would leave a trace. At that time, there was a lack of experience in dealing with this kind of paint, and implementing a study to prove that it posed no health risks to this group of students would've been too difficult. Still, it would've been nice for the children to see the building responding to them.

Incidentally, demand for placement for disabled children in this district has since grown so much that the primary school across the street is now being used to provide additional space. The location is very popular, and there are plenty of applications. I believe that one of the reasons for this is that the building is easy for the children to intuitively understand and feel at home in.

That's surely one of the most important aspects of the project: a building like this must be intuitively understandable. We couldn't use a normal system of guidance and orientation based on signage. Instead, repeating modules and contrasting sequences of rooms were used to make navigation easier, underlined by a strong colour theme.

For instance, we used coloured filters to tint the sunlight as it falls into the rooms. There's yellow light in the stairwells and green light in the glass walkway. The children move through the colour fields, making the transition from the school to the therapy centre perceptible. The aperture that brings natural light into the auditorium has red-painted walls, which colour the incoming light and improve the auditorium's atmosphere.

We placed a great deal of importance on combining an ordered environment with possibilities for the students to try out new things. We wanted the children to feel comfortable and perhaps to open up in a way that would help them grow closer to others.

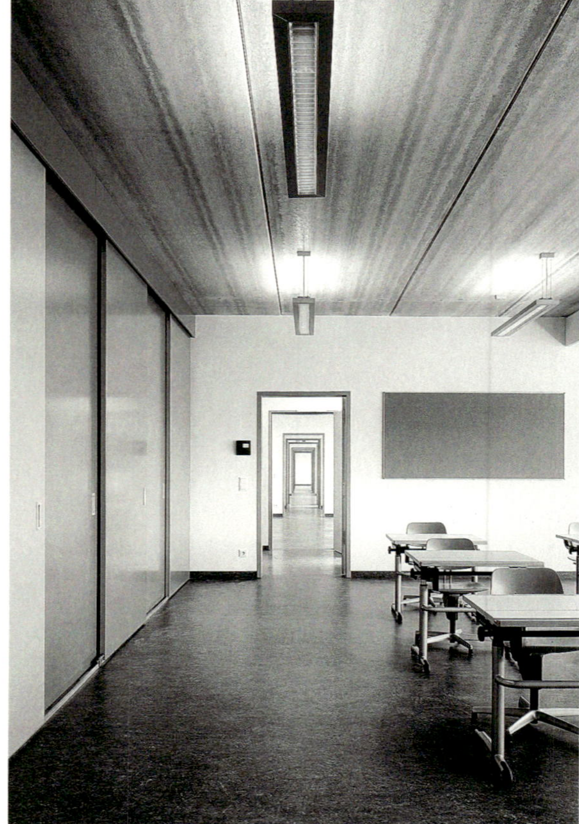

The auditorium is facing the kindergarden on the opposite side of the street

Courtyard view

Main entry with foyer/auditorium on Eilenburger Strasse

30 45 60 90 135

MUMMELSO

GITARRE

Berlin-Hellersdorf
Special Needs School

Location
Eilenburger Strasse 4,
12627 Berlin-Hellersdorf

Year
1st prize competition 1993
completion 2001/2002

Team
Florian Fels, Heinz Jirout, Olaf Menk,
Jacob van Ommen, Ricard Owers,
Matthias Schirrmacher

Client
Bezirksamt Hellersdorf und Marzahn
von Berlin, Hochbauamt

Technical planners
CBF Engineering GmbH, Berlin
(structural engineering)
HL-Technik Engineering Partner GmbH,
Munich (building services)
Krüger & Möhrle Freie Landschaftsar-
chitekten BDLA, Stuttgart (open space
planning)
BATTLE McCarthy Consulting
Engineers & Landscape Architects,
London (HVAC technology)

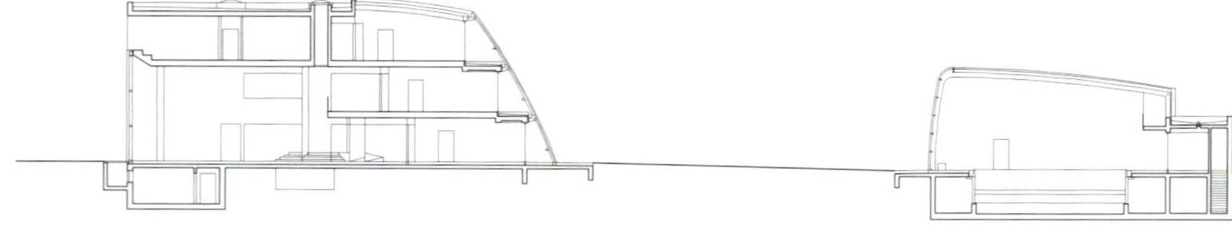

Cross section

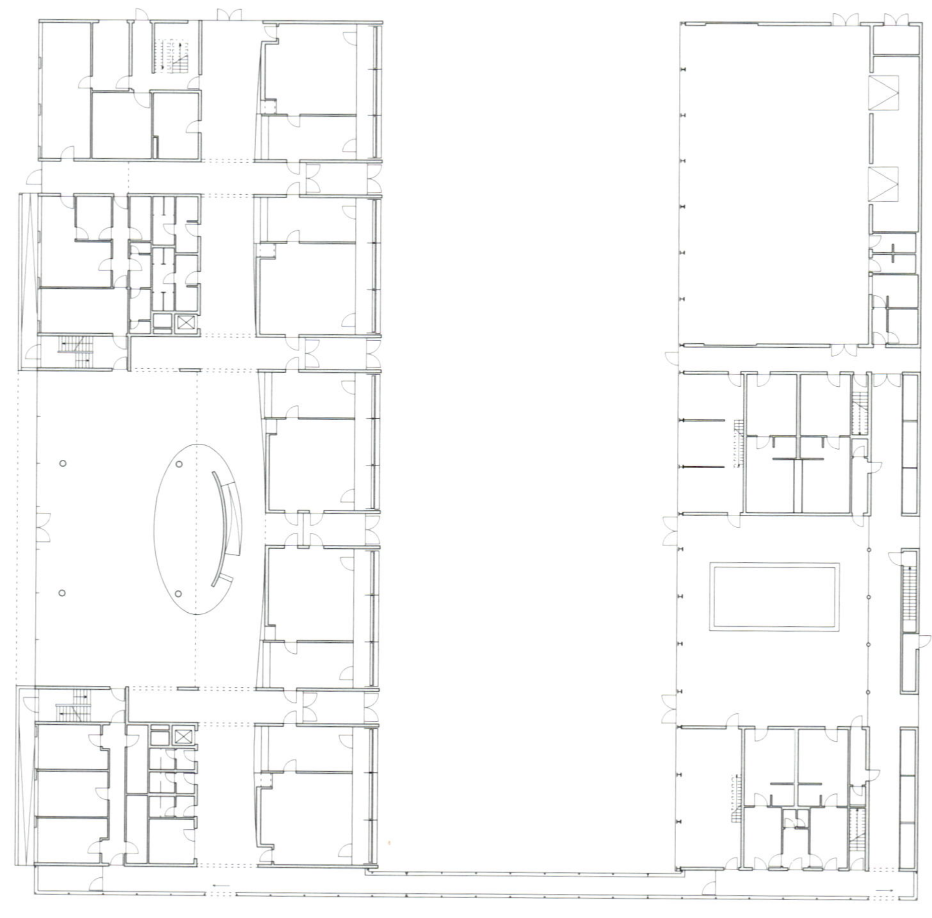

Ground floor

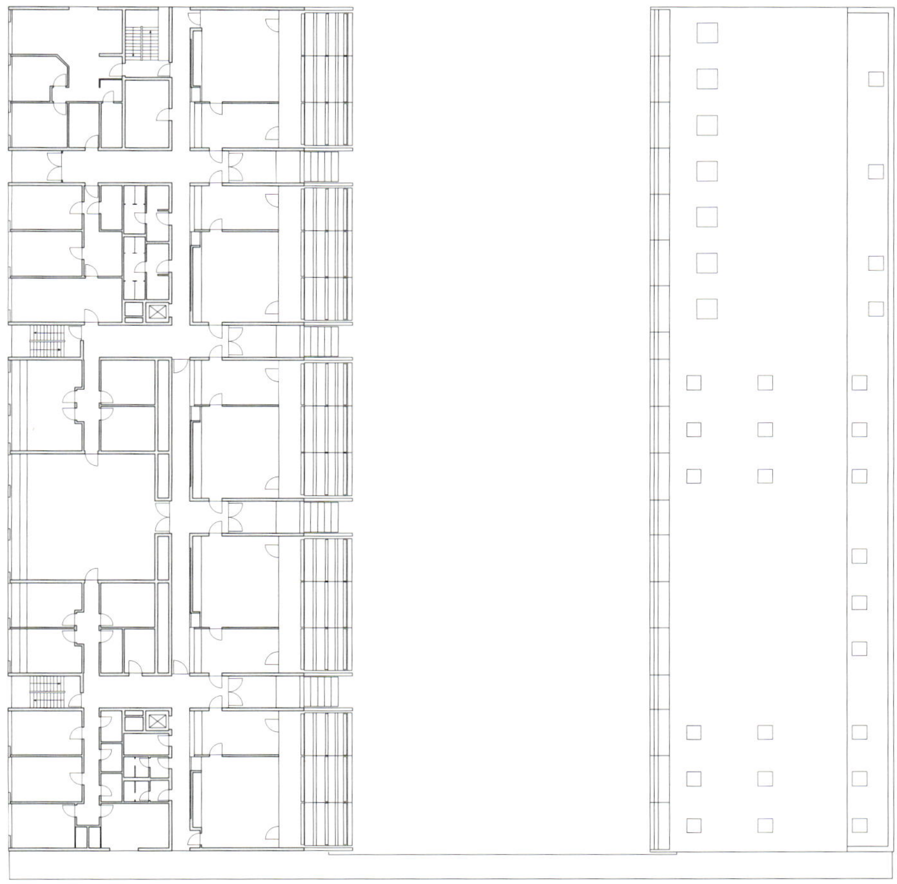

2nd floor

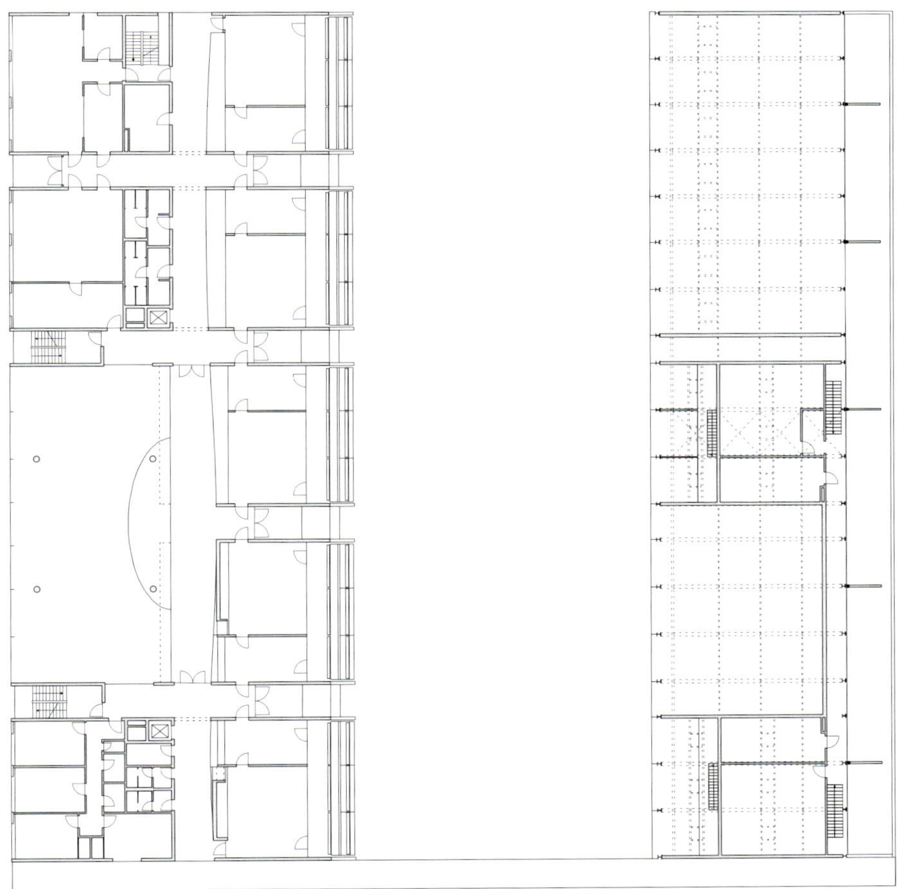

1st floor

The Bruno-H.-Bürgel-Grundschule, Berlin

This project was under enormous time constraints. The Berlin senate had to expand its existing buildings to meet the requirements of the federal government's new all-day school programme by August 2006. The initiative began with an investigation of which sites were most suitable for the architectural expansions that would support the midday meal and after-school activities. The idea was to determine whether a particular school site could be adapted to satisfy the new laws.

Our task was to produce a design study that investigated a school site in Berlin-Lichtenrade. If an expansion proved to be feasible, this was to be implemented in time for the new school year – which left us only a few months to complete the project.

The development adjacent to the site was heterogeneous and consisted mostly of small single-family homes, as well as two modular, exposed-aggregate concrete containers that had been placed at the edge of the schoolyard a number of years earlier as a temporary extension.

The exposed-aggregate containers had just been dropped into place, as they were, not really integrated with the existing buildings. The question we faced was: how could we complement the existing ensemble of structures and, at the same time, offer the students a new identity for their school?

As there was no unoccupied space available on the existing grounds, we replaced one of the exposed-aggregate concrete containers with a new, larger building – taking up as little of the schoolyard's open space as possible. The ground-floor cafeteria's façade is so open, it seems as though the students at their lunch table are sitting out in the schoolyard. Classrooms are laid out on the storey above. These new units practically float above the schoolyard next to the gymnasium, forming a generous canopy.

The 100-metre track, although it wouldn't fit on a map of the school grounds anymore, simply runs beneath these new structures. Because of the restrictions on space, we had to nest features in overlapping spaces, while still trying to keep them roomy. In summer, you can open the double doors, and the students can set up their tables between the building, the façade, and the hundred-metre track.

Courtyard elevation of the existing building

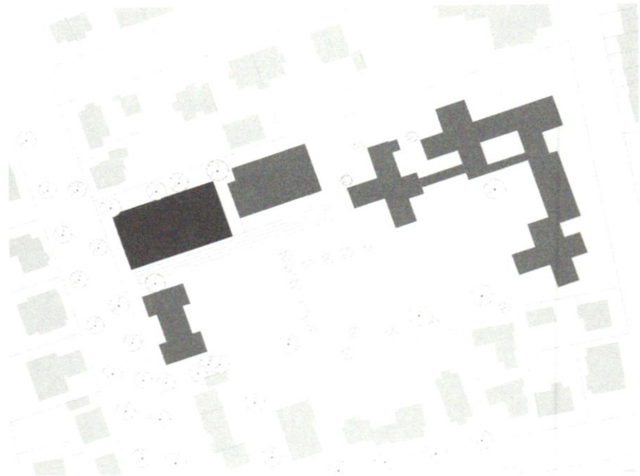

Integration of the new construction into the existing ensemble

The school is named after Bruno Bürgel, an astronomer who specialised in studying planetary rings – hence our use of circles as a motif. We wanted to create a connection with the world of Bruno Bürgel.

Yes, we expressed this theme quite directly with the façade. We designed a homogenous cladding of coloured aluminium sheets that wraps around the building completely, and is perforated with sections of circles in varying sizes.

Inside the building, the impression is very different. Appearing much lighter, almost like a veil, this perforated metal screen fosters a certain kind of intimacy. At the same time, it provides protection from the sun.

On the ground floor, children look up at the cladding from below. Here, we arranged the lighting in such a way that the illuminated rings set into the ceiling look as if they are floating above your head.

Incidentally, the Year 2 children dubbed the new building the "Käseburg", the "Cheese Castle" – but when they reach the higher classes they recognise the reference to the planets. We made a more specific reference to the theme in the cloakroom area. In collaboration with the artist Folke Hanfeld, we incorporated box lighting elements with representations of planetary rings.

This school building needed an update. Today, schools perform more functions than they once did: they are simultaneously learning and leisure zones, with the children playing at school and eating their midday meal at school. This changes any number of things – the school's structure has to be read in a different way. The existing building needs to be recoded as well as expanded.

Invitation to the school's opening

Julian

SPORTCO
3

Bruno-H.-Bürgel-Grundschule

Location
Rackebüller Weg 70, 12305 Berlin

Year
completion 2006

Team
Erik Behrends, Olaf Menk, Florian Fels, Jacob van Ommen and Catharina Gebel, Anja Fischer

Client
Bezirksamt Tempelhof-Schöneberg von Berlin, Hochbauamt Abt. Immo GHI

Technical planners
GTB-Berlin Gesellschaft für Technik am Bau mbH, Berlin (structural engineering)
RM Ingenieursgesellschaft Ridder und Meyn mbH, Berlin (building services)
Folke Hanfeld, Berlin (art)

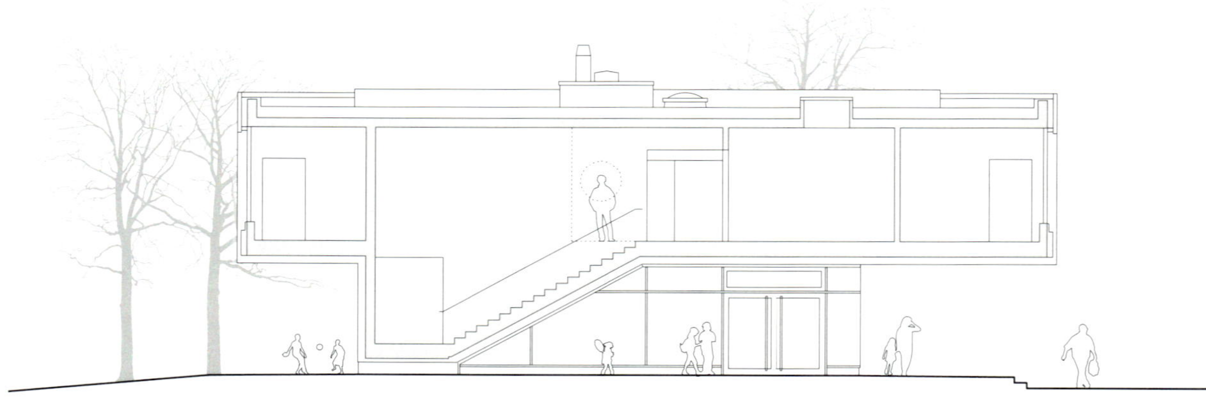

Cross section

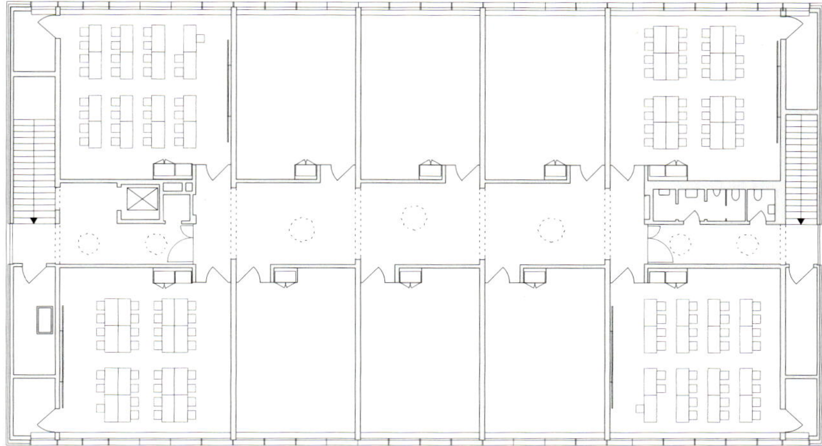

1st floor

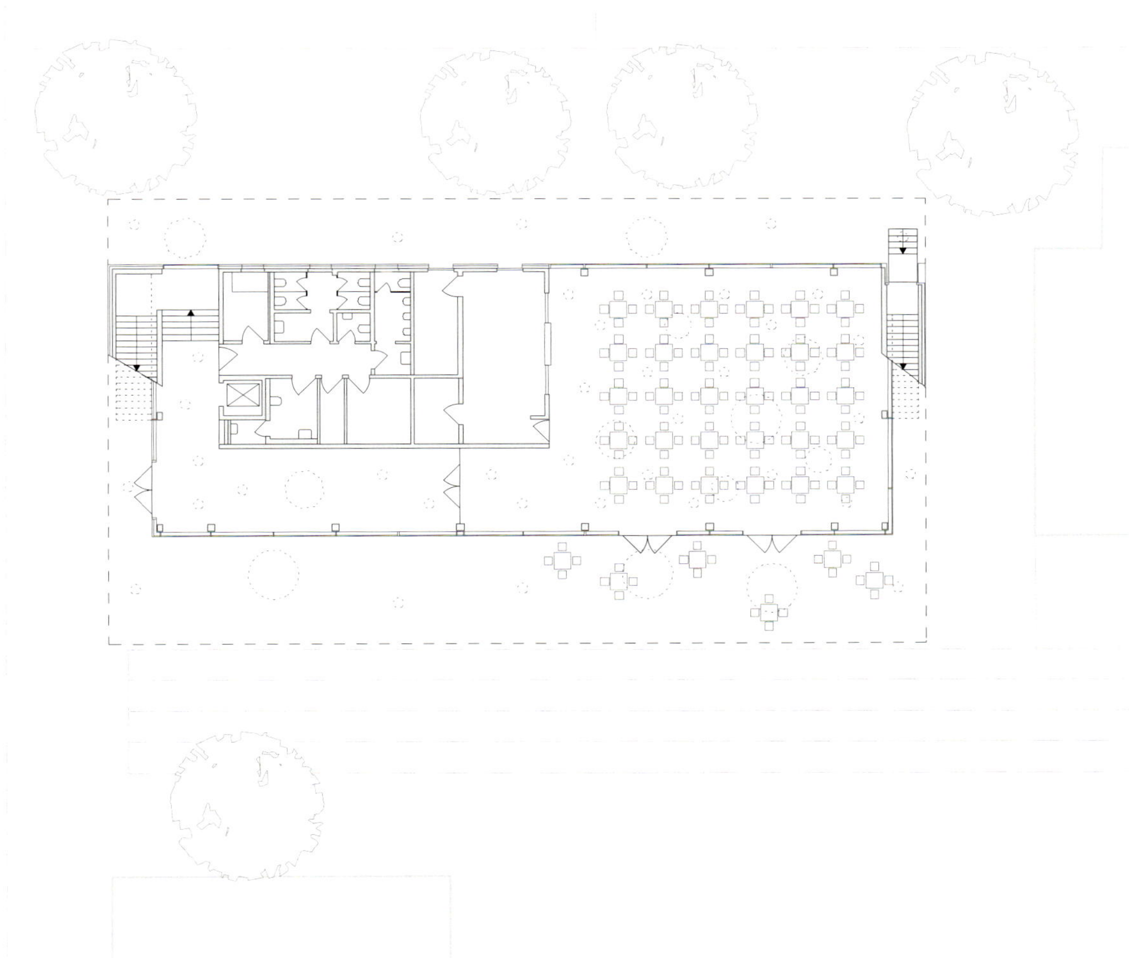

Ground floor

Marie Curie
Gymnasium

The Marie-Curie-Gymnasium, Dallgow-Döberitz

It was always important to us not to design a school with heavy wooden doors and high doorknobs, where you'd feel trapped as soon as the door closed.

In designing the Marie-Curie-Gymnasium, we wanted to create a bright building that would welcome students, not present them with emotional barriers. They needed a chance to talk amongst themselves before the start of the school day. For this reason, the school building's foremost features are not the teachers' and directors' rooms – instead, we put the students and their meeting spaces in the foreground.

This was one of the reasons why we won the competition. The jury was pleased with the sequence of foyer, multipurpose room, and cafeteria on the entrance level because it provides a flexible space for the students' social and informal lives.

The break area on the first storey is also a gathering place. In the morning, students can meet up there on the deck, where they can look down on the street and greet their teachers and classmates as they arrive at school.

Many students live locally, but some even come from Berlin, as the school's reputation for excellent science instruction is unusual enough to be of interest to Berliners. For this reason, the school was designated as an all-day school in the competition phase.

Actually, it's not really a long way from Berlin: Dallgow-Döberitz is in Havelland, and the Döberitz regional station is only a 17-minute train journey from Berlin's

View of the school from the housing estate

Zoo station. Currently, however, most of the students are children from the immediate neighbourhood. The school is also a significant driving force for regional growth – a whole carpet of single-family homes has since spread out around it.

We found the school's location in Berlin's so-called *Speckgürtel* ("fat belt", a term used to describe affluent suburbs) particularly challenging. As an architect, you have to treat the city's periphery very carefully. How do you impose a boundary on the city? It's a question to which we gave a great deal of thought – after all ninety more hectares of land are developed every day in Germany.

When the competition was held, almost fifteen years ago, the area was pretty much just meadows and countryside. The school grounds were explicitly intended to be a capstone or border for city growth: the city would expand to this point, but no further. In that respect, the building

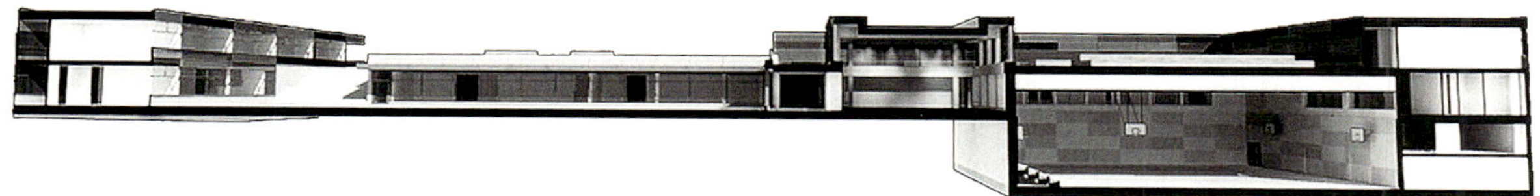

serves as a barrier to protect the natural space beyond. At the same time, we wanted to allow people to experience those surroundings as much as possible. The relationship with the natural landscape was a vital part of the school's design.

Every part of the school is embedded in a hillside – the gym is recessed in it and the auditorium passes clear through. The buildings containing the classrooms flank a raised schoolyard that expands into the landscape. In spite of being composed of many separate elements, the school presents clear lines that follow the road, with a centre and an enclosed courtyard. The school's central axis runs through the building and out into the landscape.

So, what's urban about a school on the periphery of the city? It was an important question for us: how can you build a model of urban space out in the countryside? It was very important to us that we should convey to the children growing up in this "green Nirvana" a certain sense of urban life. For that reason, we wanted to make Dallgow-Döberitz a dense and urban place without simply sticking a large structure in the midst of these little houses.

The conditions of the competition brief specified that none of the school's buildings should be longer than sixty metres. Still, we had to moderate the leap in scale from a community of small single-family homes to a large educational institution.

It was also important to make orientation easy; pass through the corridors and enter the auditorium, and you can look down into the gym, while at the same time you're also able to see the outside space. So you have lots of spatial and sensory impressions, plus many possibilities for communication – which we see as a defining urban quality.

On the one hand, then, the building creates a certain urban impression, while, on the other, it blends into the landscape, which comes right up to the roof. From the break area on the school roof, you can see far over the roofs of the family homes – a striking change in perspective!

But this raised deck does more than that: it also makes the building readable, helping people to find their way. It separates the two L-shaped upper-level blocks that house the classrooms from the special subject and laboratory rooms on the ground floor. The wooden superstructures of the break area provide seats, stages and a place to climb. At the same time, they house skylights for the gym.

Some of them have integrated periscopes, too, which draw the eye down into the building, visually connecting the wide landscape above with the darker hallway zones beneath the deck. Conversely, the students in the hallways can watch what's happening on the deck or look out into the landscape.

Sunken gyms are unusual in Berlin because, as you might expect, they're significantly more expensive to construct. Because they save energy, however, you can balance the construction costs against the operating costs. This buried gym gives the school site an impressive density, as well as a very good ratio of interior to exterior spaces. The school building owes its efficiency to its compact lower-level construction.

The gym, however, is by no means a dark bunker space – it's lit by skylights concealed in locations like the stepped seating of the rooftop break area, so it feels very open.

Periscopes visually connect interior and exterior spaces

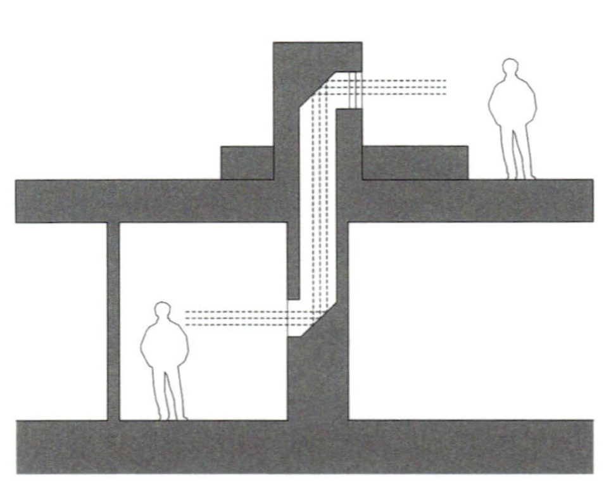

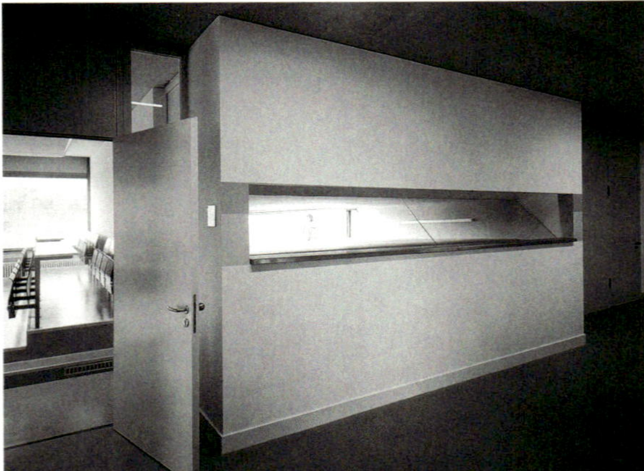

The school's everyday activities are visible to passers-by, thanks to a row of windows facing the road. This feature encourages locals to see the building as a public space they can use outside of school hours. We, for instance, organised a football match in the gym with some architect friends of ours as part of the project's opening celebrations.

The acoustic installation designed especially for the building by Johannes Sistermanns, which used copper wires to cause all the façade surfaces to resonate, was extremely impressive.

The gym should be used not just for physical education, but for parties and other large events too.

We worked to create diverse spaces throughout the school. The auditorium, for instance, can grow and shrink: folding doors and the main axis of the hallway space allow it to be extended as far as the inner courtyard in order to accommodate large events. When exams are being administered there, on the other hand, all the doors and the full-height panels on the side of the gym can be closed in order to create a self-contained working atmosphere.

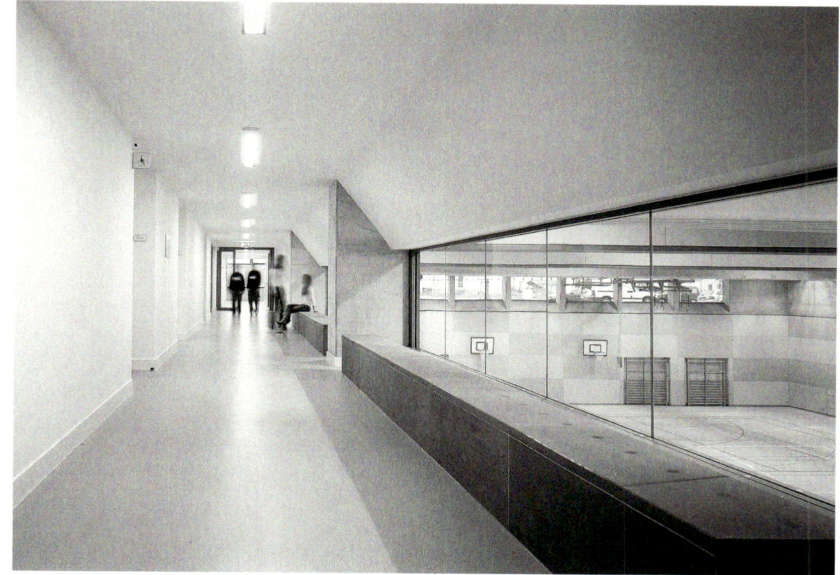

The sightlines are diverse: from the auditorium, you can look down and see the gym, and you can look up and see the break area. This space is a kind of visual junction point for the school.

Through these diverse visual connections, the students can perceive themselves as part of the school community. This increases group identity and the feeling that "this is my school". Incidentally, the film "Die Welle" ("The Wave") was filmed here – another testimony to the school's succinct design.

We wanted to convey the unique identity of the Marie-Curie-Gymnasium to the school's students on a number of different levels. For instance, we made the natural sciences the theme of the building's *Kunst-am-Bau* (integrated art work) project. The artist Folke Hanfeld created graphic representations of the work of a number of Nobel Prize winners, which we used as identifiers for the classrooms in place of numbers. This helps students – and teachers – to increase their familiarity with the research work of figures such as Niels Bohr and James Watson.

Another important question was what the façade – the face of the school – should look like. Here, again, we wanted to increase the visibility of the school's focus on the natural sciences and to highlight the achievements of the school's namesake. The outer walls are divided up into fields, which lie over and adjacent to each other in layers. There's a line of white text on the façade – from a speech by Marie Curie, who read it out during her acceptance of her Nobel Prize. The text is displayed on the floor, too, as a high contrast, magnified projection. There are

Gymnasium with views towards the surrounding corridor, auditorium and street

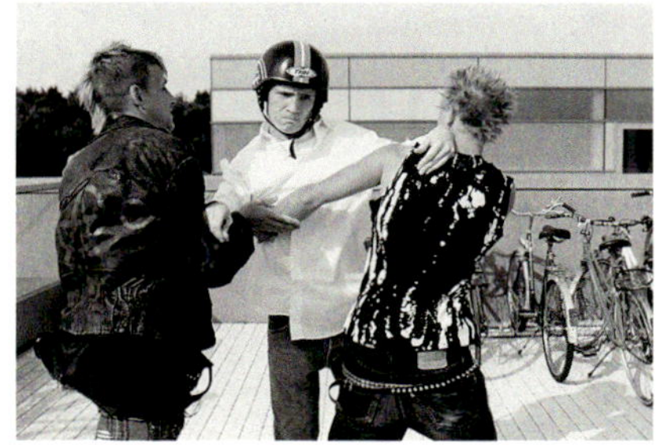

Still from the movie "The Wave", 2008

also glass elements of various different colours that form part of the school's guidance system; they're decorated by silkscreen printing on the panes and by perforated sheet metal elements applied to their inner surfaces.

As with many of our buildings, we thought it was important to specifically plan both the daytime and nighttime impact of the façade – after all, in the winter, it's still nighttime when school begins.

We came up with a kind of patchwork of fields with different degrees of transparency and translucency. The fields follow the movement of the sun, creating a dynamic impression of space and sensory stimulation that also extends to the classrooms.

We regarded the building as a teaching instrument on a number of levels: the stimulating colour fields in the façade reinforce perception, as do the periscopes. The building's technological performance can be taken in the same sense.

For instance, there's the night cooling system: the heat that builds up in inside the building is expelled at night with the aid of electronically controlled openings in the façade. Flaps above the doors are raised to permit transverse ventilation. At first, the custodian found this disconcerting – and for systems like this, acceptance by users is an important factor. After some training, however, man and machine became accustomed to one another.

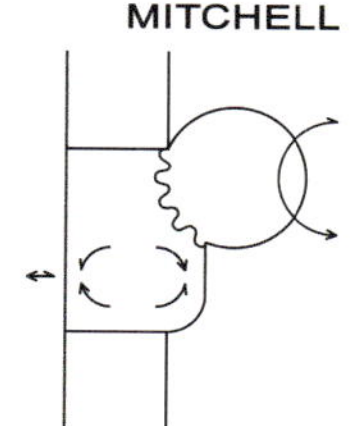

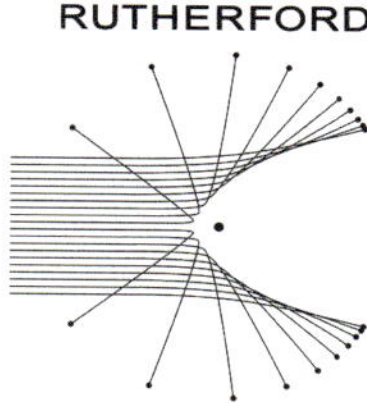

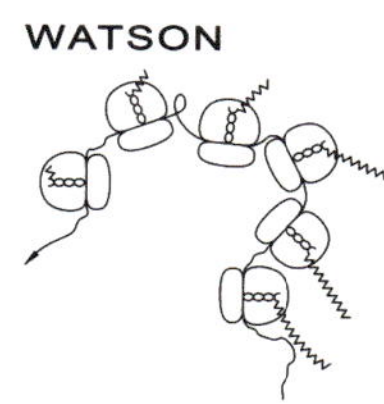

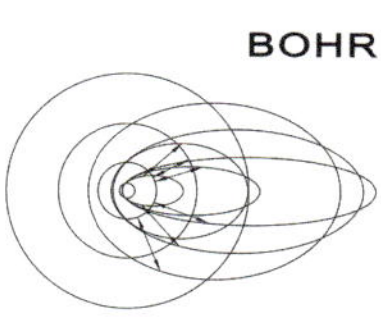

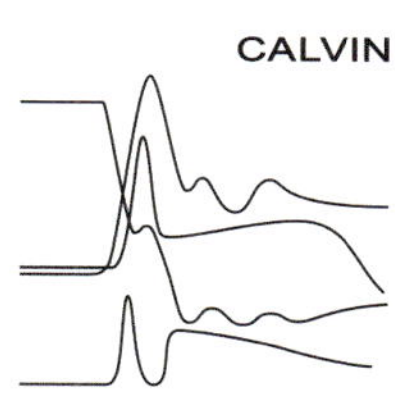

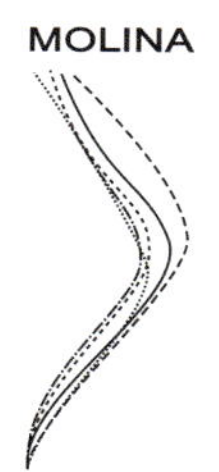

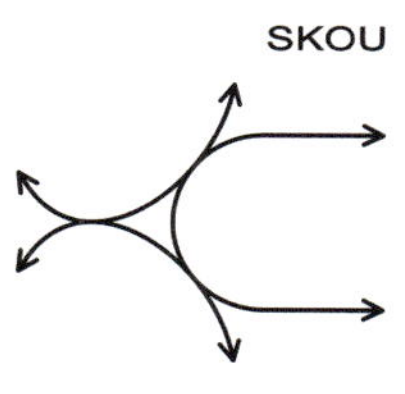

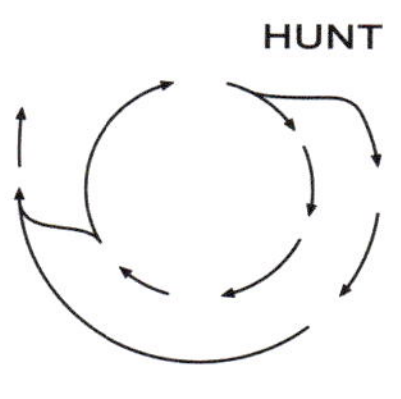

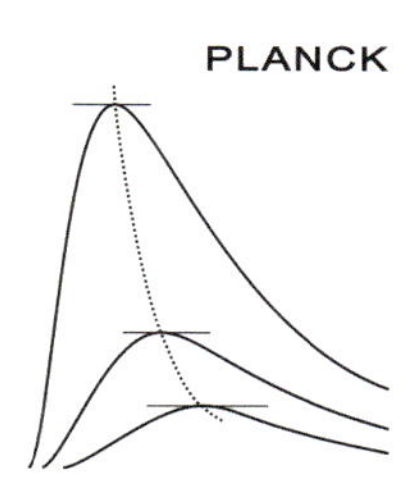

Artist Folke Hanfeld's graphic representations of Nobel Prize winners and their work

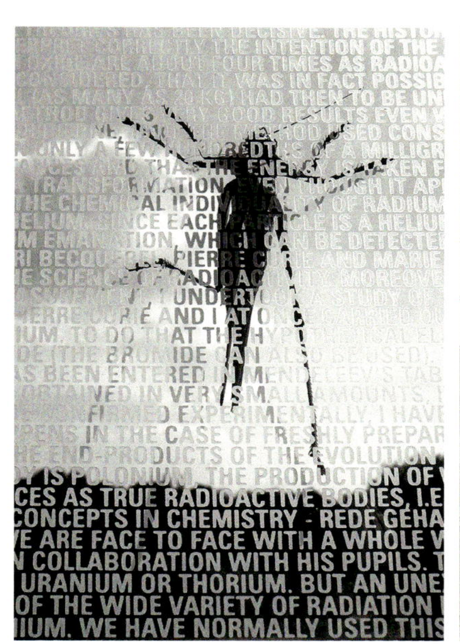

Marie-Curie-Gymnasium

Location
Marie-Curie-Strasse 1, 14624,
Dallgow-Döberitz near Berlin

Year
1st prize competition 2001
completion 2005
(2nd construction phase: 2009)

Team
Erik Behrends, Florian Fels, Olaf Menk, Jens Schoppe, Jacob van Ommen and Christian Jähnig, Dominika Plümpe, Kristin Hulzer, Mareike Münstermann, Volker Raatz

Client
Landkreis Havelland, Der Landrat, Dezernat IV/Hoch- und Strassenbau

Technical planners
GTB-Berlin Gesellschaft für Technik am Bau mbH, Berlin (structural engineering)
Brendel Ingenieure, Berlin, and Ingenieurbüro-Knoop GmbH, Mönchengladbach (building services)
Topotek 1 Gesellschaft von Landschaftsarchitekten mbH, Berlin (open space planning)
Lichtvision Design & Engineering GmbH, Berlin (lightning design)
Folke Hanfeld, Berlin (art)

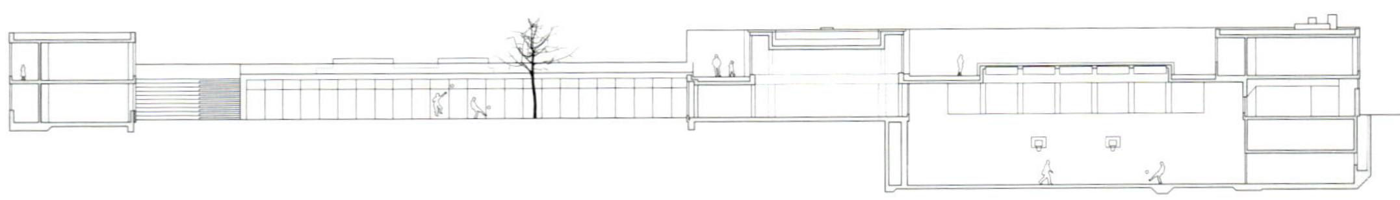

Longitudinal section

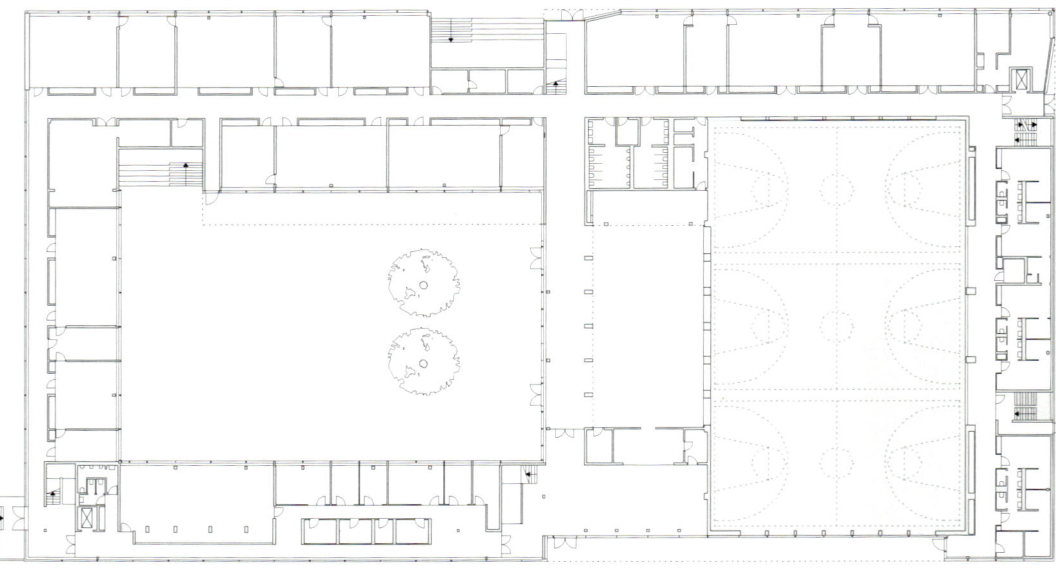

Ground floor

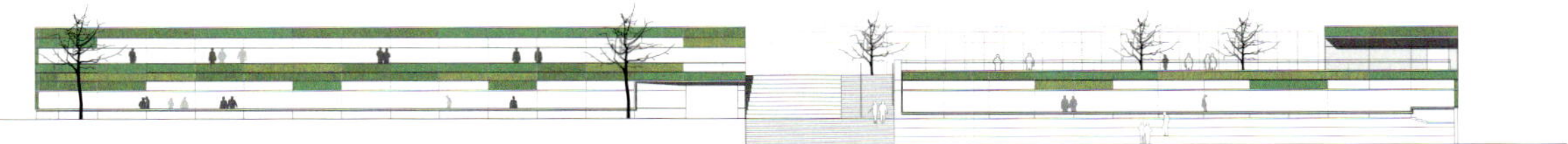

Elevation

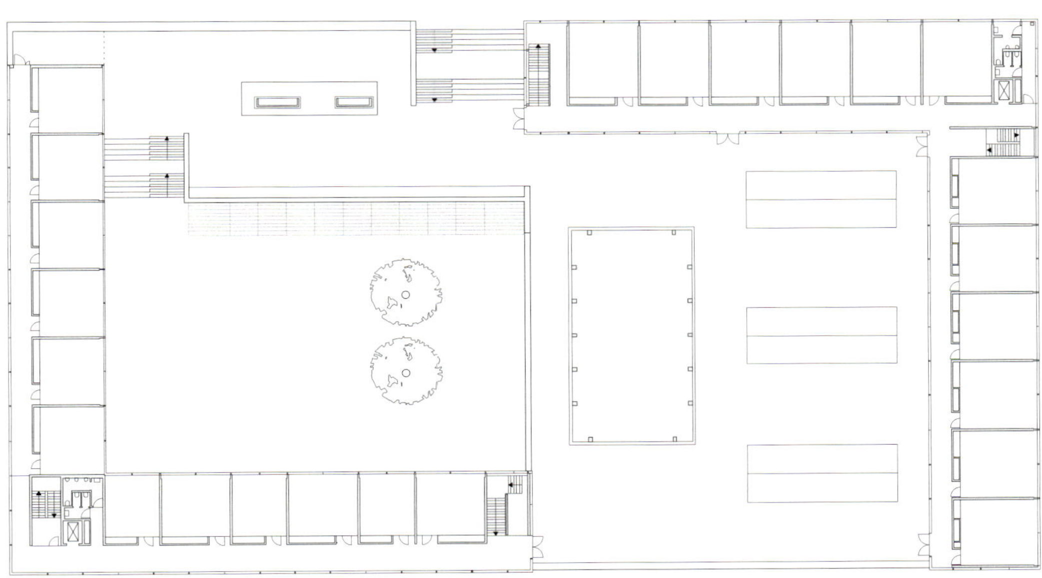

1st floor

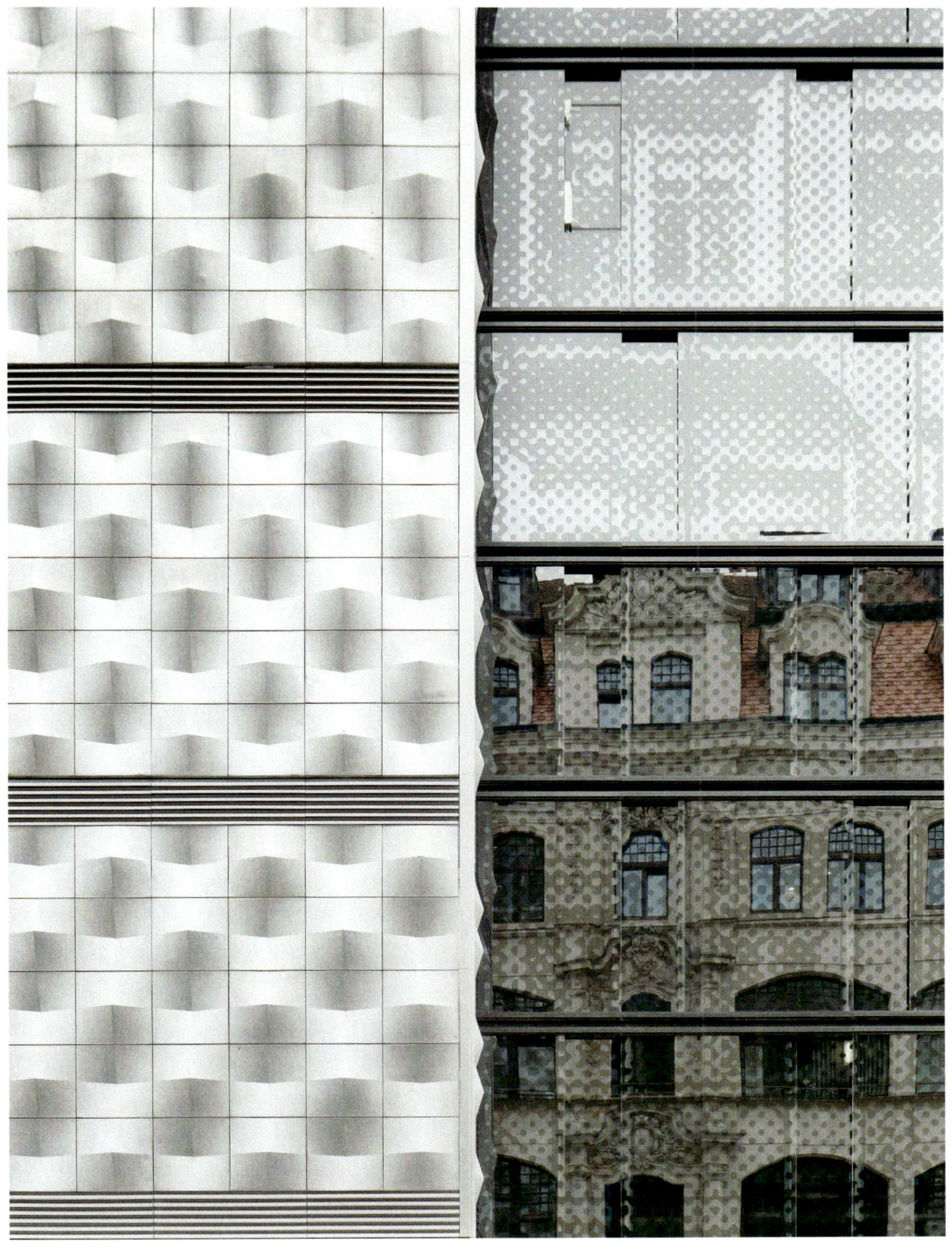

ADAC
ADAC
WTM PM 888

LUKAS
ald's

Site in 2010 (top) and the department store with residential towers in 1969 (bottom)

The Höfe am Brühl department store, Leipzig

The Brühl is one of the oldest streets in Leipzig. It was largely destroyed during the Second World War and rebuilt during the GDR period in the 1960s. Like Prager Strasse in Dresden, the new Brühl was a large modernist structure, consisting of a department store at one end of the plot and three residential towers just behind it. Located in direct proximity to the historic city centre, the development had become an icon of socialist urban design.

When we began to work on the design, the buildings were still there physically, but the feasibility of leaving them in place was under investigation. Ultimately a study by the firm Steidle persuaded the city to demolish most of it. A competition was held for a new building on the property; unfortunately, restoration and expansion simply weren't options. Only the department store – known to the people of Leipzig as "die Blechbüchse" ("the Can") – was to be preserved.

Well, that's the short version. This building has a very long history, all of which influenced our design. The house where Richard Wagner was born once stood on this site, although it was demolished in the late 19th century – and was replaced by what might be described as a *Gründerzeit* shopping mall (the "founders' time" was the period of industrialisation and economic growth in the second half of the 19th century). However, the building was gutted by fire during the Second World War. In the sixties, it was given a metal façade by the artist Harry Müller – hence its nickname. The *Gründerzeit* façade, parts of which had been preserved, is a protected structure –the sheet metal façade is too, actually. The project goals stated that it was to be left in place.

Thankfully! It's among the most beautiful GDR façades that we have. Unfortunately, only fragments of the *Gründerzeit* façade survived the war.

The sheet metal façade has a real magic about it. This simple principle – the aluminium elements curve in opposite directions – is great duplicated across the whole surface. The dynamism of the façade, combined with the hyperbolic paraboloid elements, is truly remarkable.

Behind and beyond the sheet metal façade, a huge new building was to be constructed, extending across the boundaries of the demolished buildings. One major challenge in dealing with this design assignment was coping with the scale. An implanted monofunctional

Partially disassembled metal façade, with late 19th-century *Gründerzeit* façade behind it, 2010

Space between the façades

structure of this size would have entirely broken with the proportions of Leipzig's inner city. To mitigate this, we structured the new volume so that it would fit into the scale of the historical urban layout and tried to incorporate its access points into the city's grid. For instance, we incorporated the route of the old Plauensche Strasse – now it crosses the main axis again as a public road.

We took on the proportions of the urban environment by dividing the large structure into distinct house-like units, giving them different façades and offset volumes. The staggering gives the roof silhouette a certain sense of movement, giving this 400-metre behemoth a far less oppressive appearance.

We developed six different types of façade for the new building in order to create complexity.

And we consciously played with alternating glass and stone façades. The stone façades were given a lamellar structure. We applied a musical score – the overture of "Parsifal" – to the slat façade as a motif; you might be able to read the melody across the pattern of stone slats.

Some of the glass façades are printed with motifs representing the façades of old houses that once stood on the Brühl.

The façades were something we constantly had to fight for. We wanted to do a good job on them, in spite of the cost pressures on the developers. Of course, they wanted to cut out any features of the design that were not absolutely necessary.

The outer façades continue into the interior, framing the shopping mall space like a city street. In a departure from the standard shopping centre model, we created courts and alleyways along the main axis in order to create contrasting spaces.

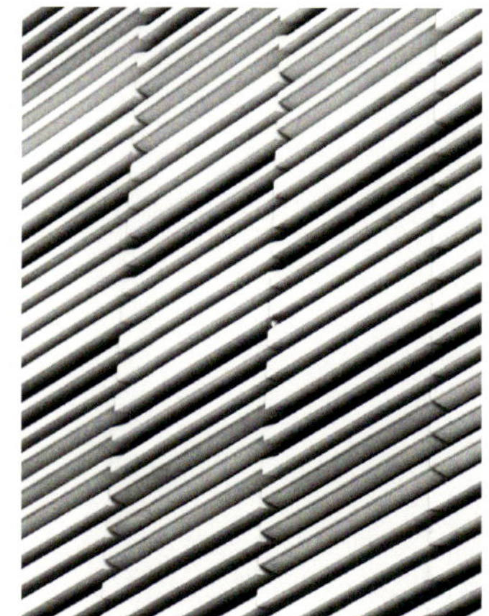

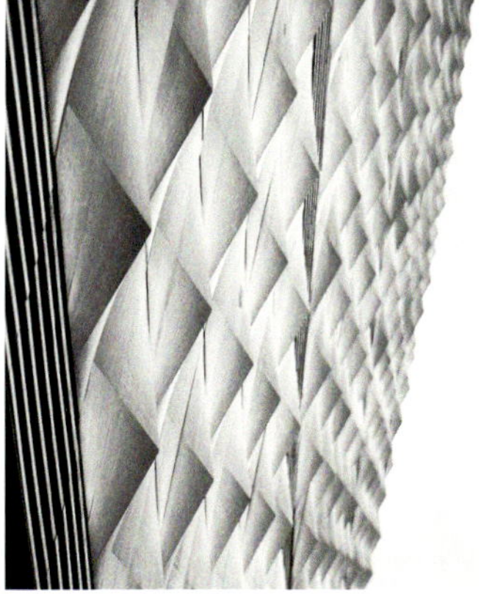

Our aim was to reproduce the matrix we'd seen in the historic infrastructure. For instance, we have historical photographs of large fur warehouses on the Brühl, with alleyways, galleries and bridges. There are also photographs of fur trade fairs on the Brühl, where traders would lay pelts over the parapet. The pelts united the storeys of the building, looking almost like a kind of building envelope.

The mix of functions was important to us too. We zoned the building vertically. The shopping areas are located in the lower storeys, with the parking areas immediately above and apartments at the top.

Cars cross the pedestrian spaces in the mall via bridges. This creates a stimulating effect: it makes me think of films like "Metropolis" or "Blade Runner". Alternatively, we could have built a standard underground garage, with complex utilities, smoke extraction and ventilation.

However, if you think in the long term, these underground areas would be impractical for subsequent use. Car use may change drastically in the near future, in which case there will be advantageous ways of repurposing the aboveground spaces. Besides, spaces that are aboveground and naturally lit are less likely to feel oppressive. The parking was very important to the investors – it was supposed to be the hub for the whole of the old city!

Our participation in the whole project was premised on the question: can we afford to turn down a "bad", commercial job, or might we be in a position to turn it into something positive? We'd never designed a shopping centre before. We were surrounded by firms with plenty of experience in shopping mall design, who all knew how to handle this kind of project – in Germany, in Holland or anywhere else in the world.

Archival material on historic courtyards and bridges along the Brühl

And, incidentally, one question that's always important to politicians: how is this project different from a project in Düsseldorf or Frankfurt?

In fact, it presented us with a moral conflict: did we want to be involved in such a huge project, on this site, in the middle of the city? But we also saw a chance to take advantage of the small amount of room for manoeuvre offered by such a competition.

The city was heavily involved in planning and demanded high quality – perhaps because putting a shopping centre in the inner city was so controversial, and local citizens took a considerable interest.

In recent decades, a noticeable tendency has developed to see the city as a playground and a stage for art, culture, and shopping, as well as for temporary uses. The historical city centres are being reprogrammed – they've become sites of self-expression for a wide range of societal groups.

If there's no day-to-day life going on there, the city centre eventually becomes simply a backdrop. For instance, there are very few children living in the inner city of Leipzig – and because of that, the inner city offers only few amenities for children. This project poses fundamental questions about the future of our inner cities, and so the vital mix of functions was very important to us. This includes the housing on the building's upper storey – these are patio houses accessed via a shared outer area. The effect is almost suburban and could be of interest to families.

Patio apartments with semi-public terraces on the roof

HÖFE AM BRÜHL

Höfe am Brühl department store

Location
Richard-Wagner-Platz 1, 04109 Leipzig

Year
1st prize competition 2007
completion 2012

Team
Erik Behrends, Arno Löbbecke, Olaf Menk, Jens Schoppe, Alessio Fossati, Jost von Fritschen, Kristina Herresthal, Stefan John, Götz Hinrichsen, Kai Arne Löper, Dirk Nachtsheim, Karsten Schuch
and Carolin Döpfer, Andrea Höpfner, Remy Jalade, Tobias Klein, Lisa Knoll, Jakob Kortemeier, Martin Sulzbach

Client
mfi Höfe am Brühl Leipzig GmbH & Co. KG, Essen

Technical planners
Schüßler-Plan Ingenieurgesellschaft mbH, Düsseldorf (structural engineering)
HTW, Hetzel, Tor-Westen + Partner Ingenieurgesellschaft mbH & Co. KG, Düsseldorf (building services)
Licht Kunst Licht AG, Bonn (lightning design)
FAMED, Leipzig (art)

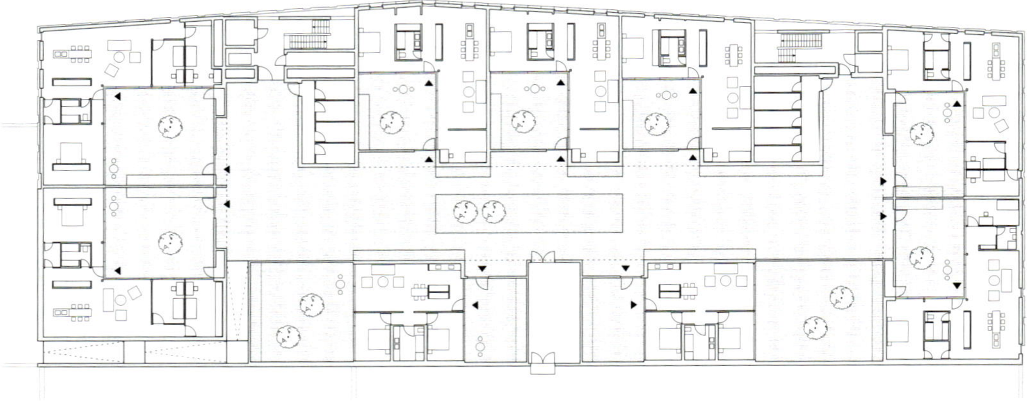

Detail of patio apartment floor plan

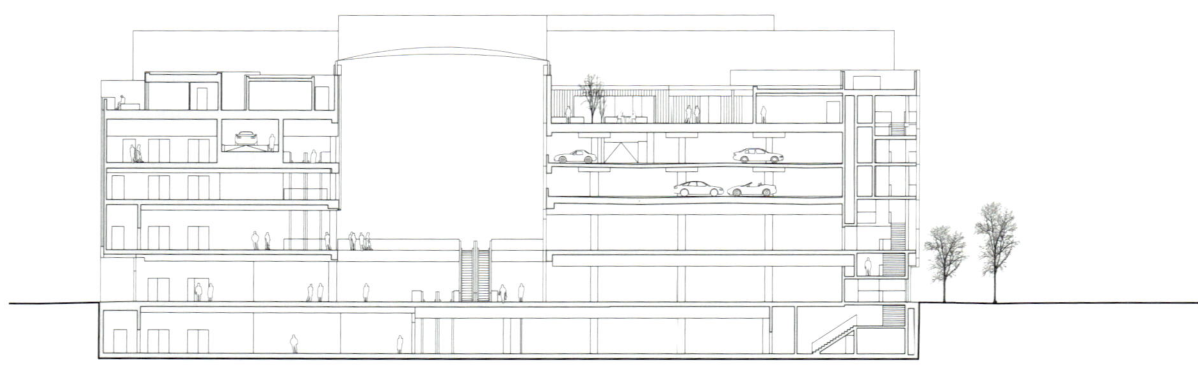

Cross section

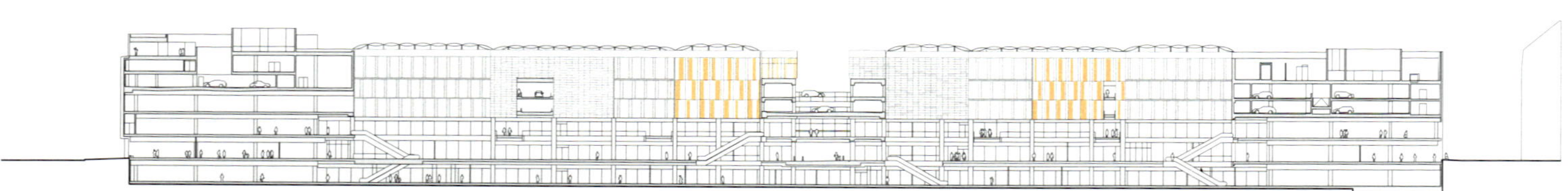

Longitudinal section

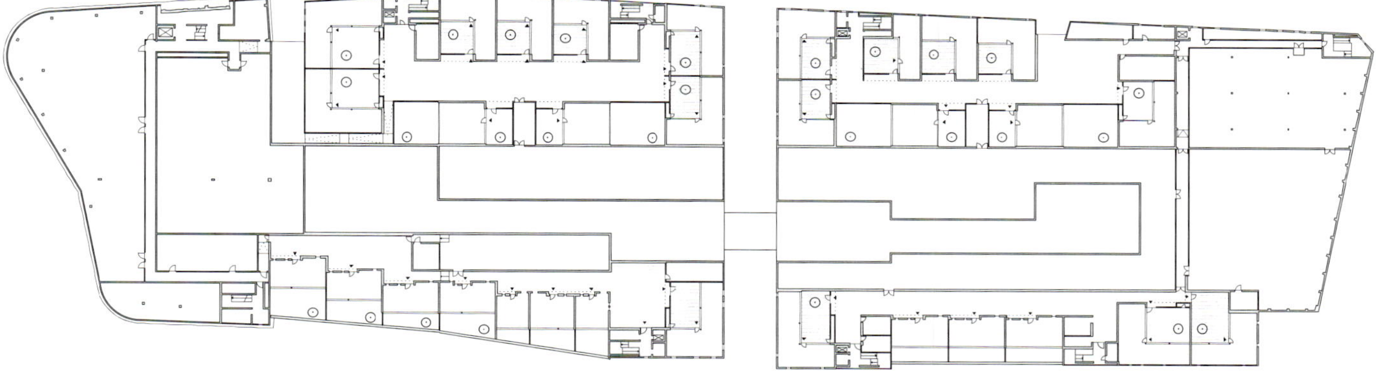

4th floor

2nd floor

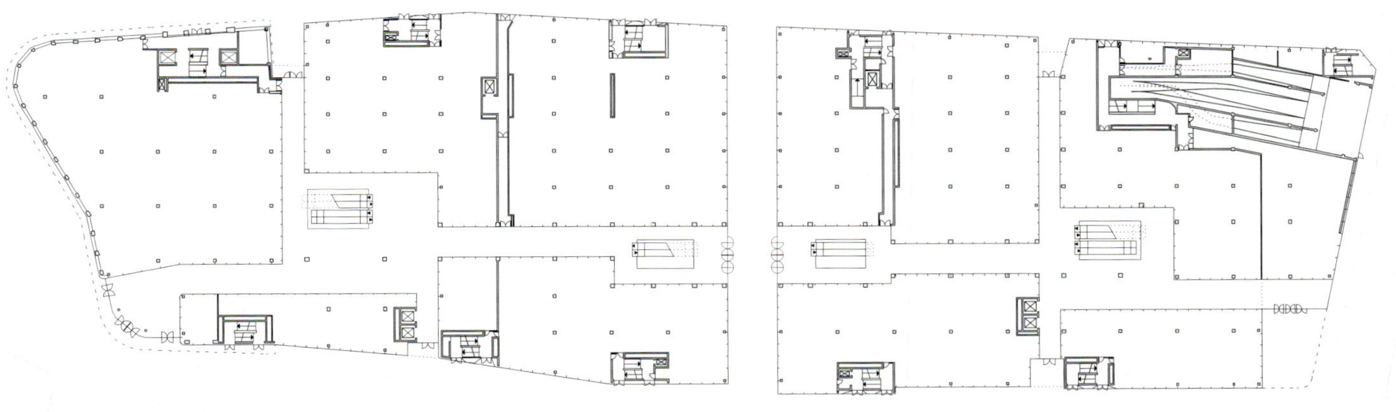

Ground floor

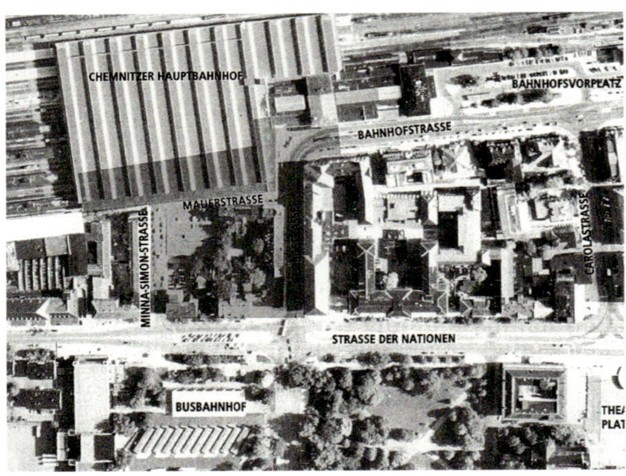

Station prior to conversion (top) and rendering of the design with opened-up ground floor and new illuminated façade (bottom)

Conversion Chemnitz Train Station

The project was to expand the existing train station in Chemnitz, which consists of a historical building and a station hall from the seventies.

The actual heart of the project was the plan to combine mass transit and long-distance traffic under one roof: some of the fast trains no longer stop at Chemnitz, and this allows the local tram to use the former Deutsche Bahn rails. About 150 million euros are going into the conversion of the rail system, but nobody will to be able to "see" the money at the end. We were therefore tasked with designing a face for this transformation.

This represented a design challenge: the tram now runs all the way into the station on the standard train tracks, making it necessary to create a new opening in the façade.

However, there was another important factor: previously, when you arrived by train at Chemnitz, you had no sense of connection to the city. You disembarked into a kind of sealed can, with no visual connection to the surrounding environment. We wanted to counteract this and create a spatial gesture of welcome.

For this reason, much of our project revolved around removing parts of the building and opening the station invitingly to the city. We called this the "Stadtbaldachin" or "city canopy". We wanted to strip the introverted station hall down to its load-bearing structure without wasting resources. We removed the façade and only replaced the upper part of it. The load-bearing structure was left unchanged, apart from a few small changes to the supports.

Stripped supporting structure during construction

Test installation of the illuminated façade in the office

The city wants to develop academic facilities along the rearmost tracks. We therefore hope to activate the station as a proper transit space, so that you can reach these buildings directly from the station platforms, without having to cross the road. A bus station is also to be built here. The new station will therefore be a very intensive transit space, bringing together many forms of transport – railway, tram and bus – and optimising both functional and visual connections with the city.

Green space also plays a vital role in connecting the station with its environment. There's always an informal green space along train tracks, and we extended this theme into the city. The idea was focused by an intervention that we developed in association with the artist Carsten Nicolai: a mirror affixed to the underside of the station roof projects the green outdoors into the heart of the station.

During the competition stage, we conveyed the idea of connecting the station with its surroundings by marking the surfaces of the station, as well as the flat surfaces of the city directly adjacent to it, in vivid orange, showing that the paving would extend beyond the station into its immediate urban environment. The plaza extends further than the station roof, and the space receives you before you enter the actual building – making the station the gateway to the city!

The station's new envelope also facilitates communication: we created an interactive installation for it together with the light artists rAndom International. It takes the movements of passers-by – and also of vehicles and the trains on the rails – and transmits them to the façade as energy impulses. This creates a subtle interplay of light that also represents a dialogue with the surrounding environment. We developed this idea based on model studies.

We opened up the façade in the lower area. You quickly realize that the area around the station has quite a pronounced topography. Earlier, this hadn't been so apparent, because you could only reach the platforms via the old station building. Together with the landscape architects Topotek, we responded to this spatial situation by creating a dynamic environment of steps and levels, turning the station into a geometrised landscape.

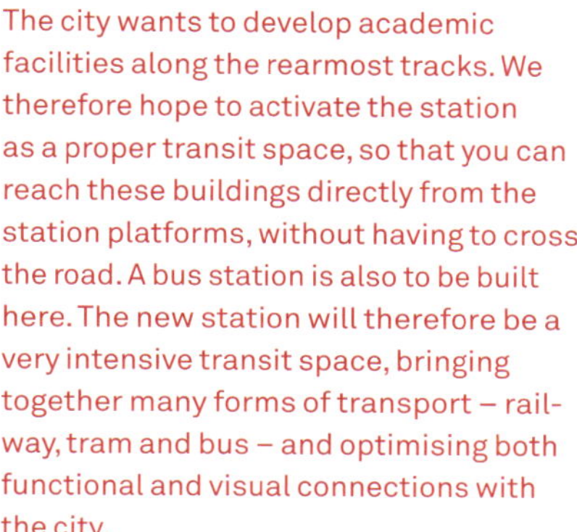

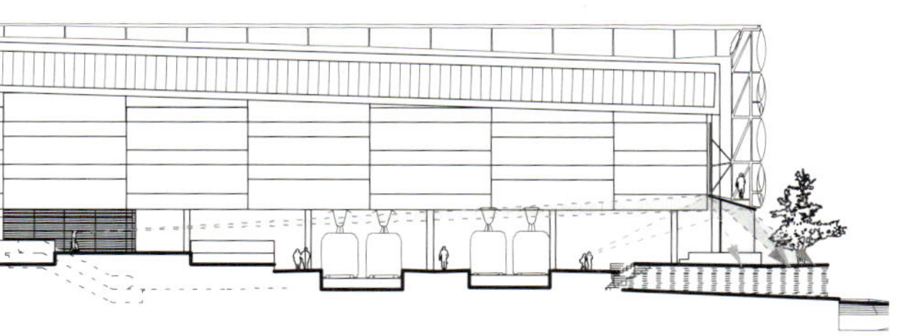
Section showing the mirror projecting the green outdoors into the station

AOK PLUS – Gesundheit in besten Händen.
Kasse einsteigen: AOK PLUS
AOK PLUS

Conversion Chemnitz Train Station

Location
Bahnhofstrasse 1, 09111 Chemnitz

Year
1st prize competition 2004
completion 2014

Team
Jost von Fritschen, Florian Fels, Arno Löbbecke, Olaf Menk, Jens Schoppe, Erik Behrends, Jacob van Ommen, Matthias Schirrmacher, Robert Tesch and Jon C. Ferrer, Peter Menken

Client
Verkehrsverbund Mittelsachsen GmbH

Technical planners
Buro Happold Ingenieurbüro GmbH, Berlin (structural engineering/building services)
Dr.-Ing. Wolfgang Stucke / Dr.-Ing. Thomas Klähne, Berlin (inspection engineers)
Ingenieurgesellschaft Lachmann-Dominok mbH, Oelsnitz (building services)
Topotek 1 Gesellschaft von Landschafts-architekten mbH, Berlin (open space planning)
rAndom International, London (art)
Carsten Nicolai, Berlin (art)

Competition sketches

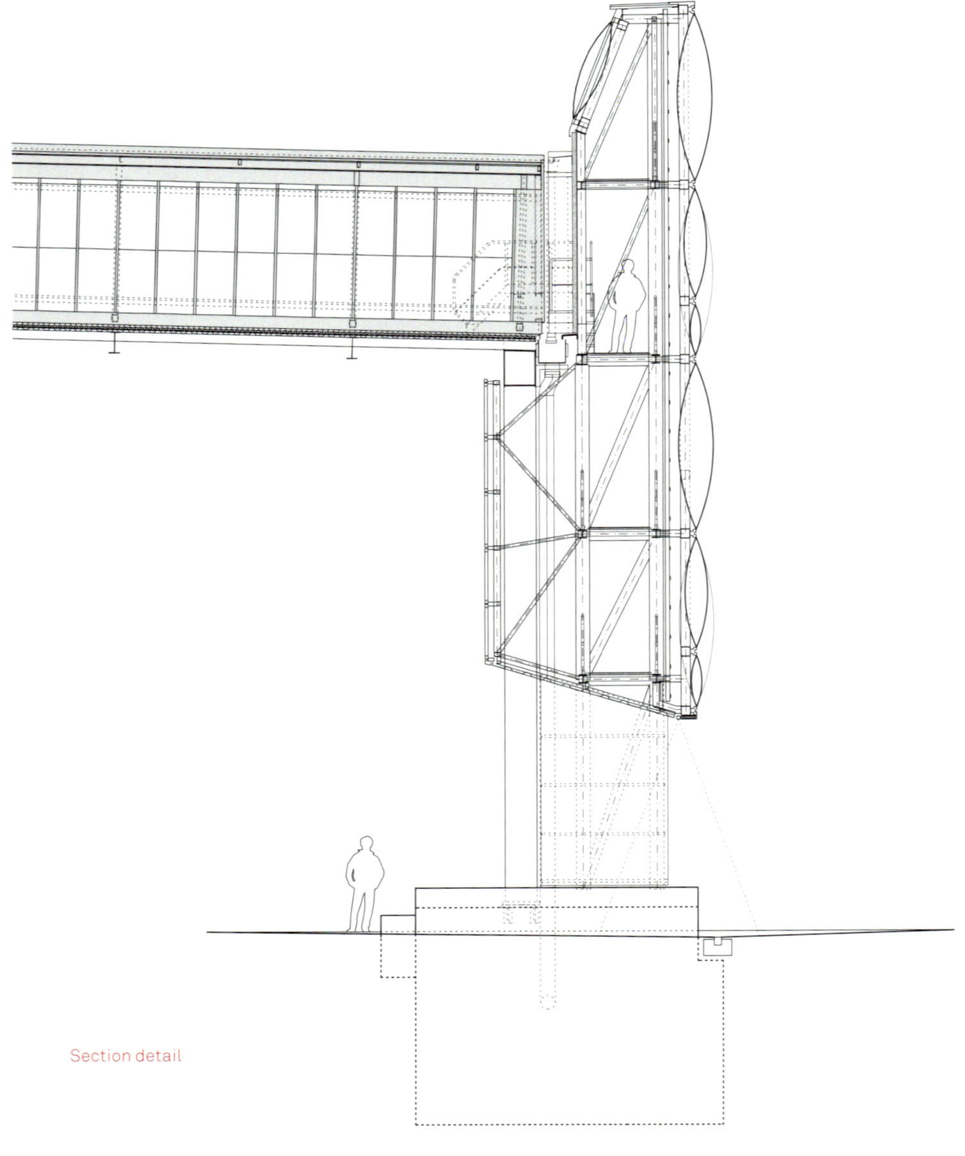
Section detail

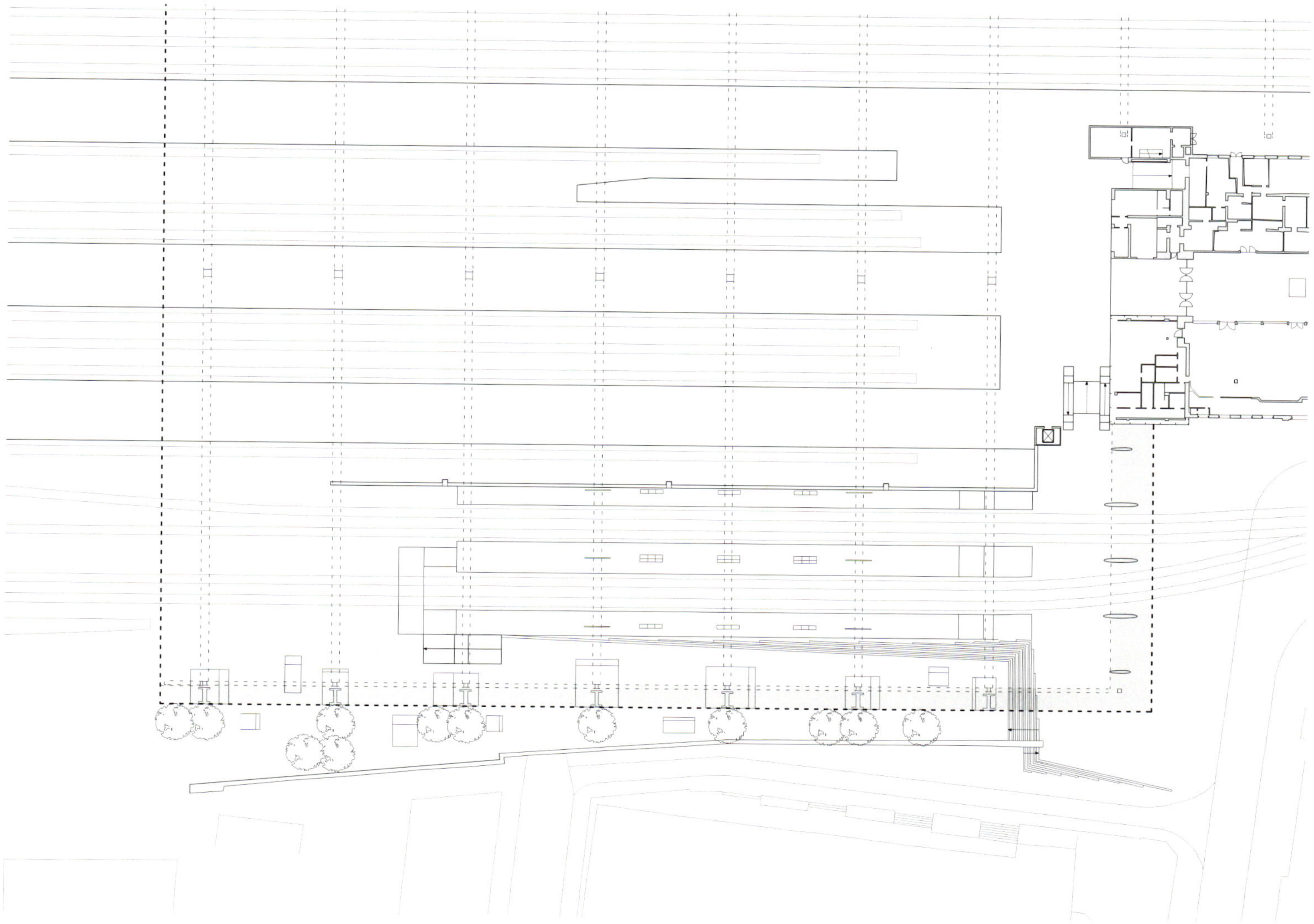

Ground floor

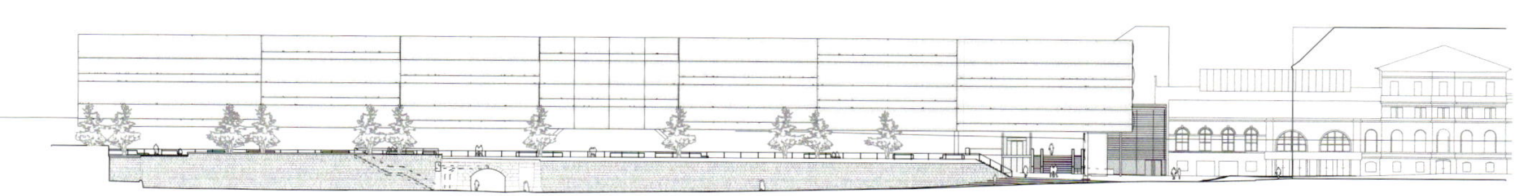

Elevation

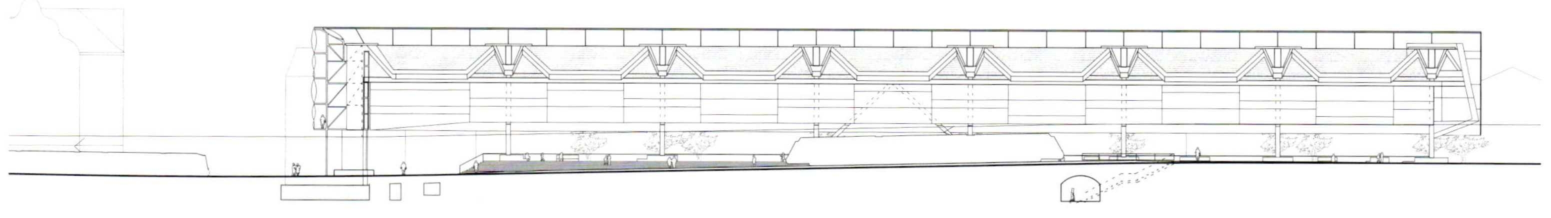

Longitudinal section

HANS

Four new buildings on shared polder

The Hamburg-Neumühlen office building

As far as I know, the Hamburg-Neumühlen am Elbufer office building was the first in Germany to incorporate building component activation. We developed this radical concept in association with Hansjürg Leibundgut, a specialist in low-energy concepts. Because there were no buildings in Germany that could be used as a reference, we flew to Switzerland. For us, and perhaps for him as well, this project marked a historic milestone.

The essence of the concept was that all the building services – all the heating, cooling and air supply lines – should be embedded in the concrete ceilings. In addition, we needed relatively wide support spans of 11.5 metres. This led to a ceiling thickness of approximately 40 centimetres, to provide enough space to install the necessary cables and conduits.

This produces what you might call invisible building services. No heating units or ventilation units can be seen anywhere in the building – formally, the structure is extremely minimal. Essentially, all you see is the floor, the ceiling, and the double façade that encloses them.

The whole of the building's floor and the whole of its ceiling are currently harnessed for heating. The activation of these expansive surfaces permits us to work with very low flow temperatures. In the summer, cool water passes through this same system of conduits, and there's a ventilation system with a single to double air exchange that's also used to control the temperature.

In spite of this, the windows can also be opened manually. However, a system like this can only operate in a space bounded by a very efficient façade. At Neumühlen, we constructed a classical double-skin façade with a relatively large space between the panes – approximately 0.8 metres (in some areas, this increases to 1.5 metres). This arrangement improves the aerodynamic conditions between the two layers. Depending on the direction in which you open the windows, you can control the ventilation. In the winter, opening the window lets only pre-warmed air inside.

Where the double façade is especially deep, people even place chairs in the intervening space. The area inside the double façade becomes a sort of common room, almost like a conservatory!

We've since implemented a number of buildings with building component cooling systems, though perhaps nothing as radical as this design. In Neumühlen, we also employed geothermal probes for heating and cooling – more than a hundred copper rods, extending 100 meters into the ground. The use of heat pumps and heat exchangers allowed us to significantly reduce the building's energy needs.

As architects, we were interested in the architectonic and spatial implications of applying intelligent building technology. We were able to construct a building that was glass-clad on all sides. In this specific site, on the waterfront, this was a very attractive idea. Our building joins a new "string of pearls," the Hamburg harbour development. Resting on a shared polder structure, our building projects beyond the waterfront promenade. We wanted to maximise the visual connection with that outdoor space.

On each floor, you feel like you're floating above the Elbe. On the one side is water; on the other the green heights of the park. You feel immediately present in this natural space, remarkably unconfined.

The conference rooms, on the other hand, were placed in the centre, as their purpose requires them to be more enclosed. Here, the walls are panelled with wood on three sides, and the windows can be closed so that daylight enters the room only from above, creating a space that feels almost like the cargo bay of a freighter. On the other hand, you can extend the conference area into the outdoors, both visually and physically: in front of this space is a large wooden deck facing the water.

We also found it interesting to design a building that could be adapted to modern, ever-changing working conditions in an uncomplicated way. We didn't use any kind of load-bearing wall or building services that would hinder adjustments to the floor plan.

Because the office space was to be leased, we couldn't discuss ideas for cubicle, combination or open-plan offices with the tenants. And with such rapid technological developments in the working world, it's impossible to definitely predict the workspace of the future.

We therefore wanted to create a working environment in which the architecture imposed as few requirements as possible, in order to ensure maximum flexibility. Within this setting, any project team could set up their own individualised workspace.

It could also be permanently adapted and reversibly deconstructed. The tenants could install individual offices, set up group workspaces and so forth wherever they wished.

We were working for two clients, a pair of shipowners who were to divide the office space between them and also wished to rent out part of the building. In 1996, when we personally presented our competition entry in Hamburg, we opted for an idiosyncratic interpretation of the master plan's C-shape. There are two functionally symmetrical office blocks and, in the middle, the access, conference and lobby areas – those key functions that make an office building a meaningful address.

With its three sculptural, freestanding access towers, the entrance hall is perhaps one of the building's most striking architectonic elements. Concentrating the access systems in these tower-like structures makes the hall very permeable, and permits a view down the banks of the Elbe to the harbour. Concealed light strips allow the textile-clad towers to be illuminated, creating various moods and lighting schemes.

The different lighting possibilities create a variety of architectonic states of matter – sometimes the towers are massive sculptural elements; sometimes their fabric coverings dissolve and you can see the staircases inside.

The towers penetrate the roof's surface, creating "islands" in the expanse of water on the roof.

The design of the roof was especially important to our clients. They had a particular interest in this because they so often see the building from the water. From the high deck of an eleven-storey cargo ship, they now look down on the roof of their five-storey building, as do their neighbours further up the banks of the Elbe.

Hamburg-Neumühlen office building

Location
Neumühlen 13–15, 22763 Hamburg

Year
1st prize competition 1996
completion 2002

Team
Kai Hansen, Florian Fels, Volker Raatz,
Jacob van Ommen

Client
Herrmann Ebel and Frank Leonhardt,
Schifffahrtskontor Elbe, Hamburg

Technical planners
Ingenieurbüro Dr. Binnewies, Hamburg
(structural engineering)
Büro freier Ingenieure Ansorg + Horn,
Berlin-Weißensee (building services)
Ludwig & Meyer, Berlin GbR (façade consulting)
Prof. Dr. Hansjörg Leibundgut, Zürich

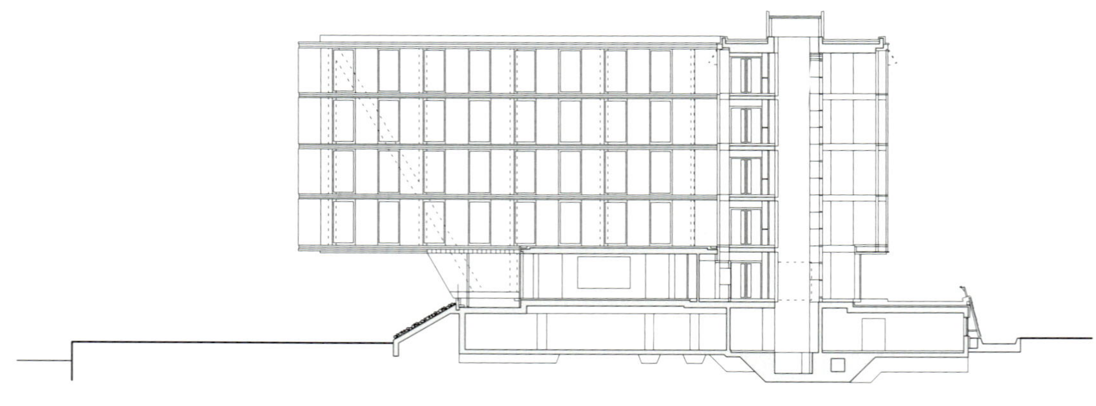

Section

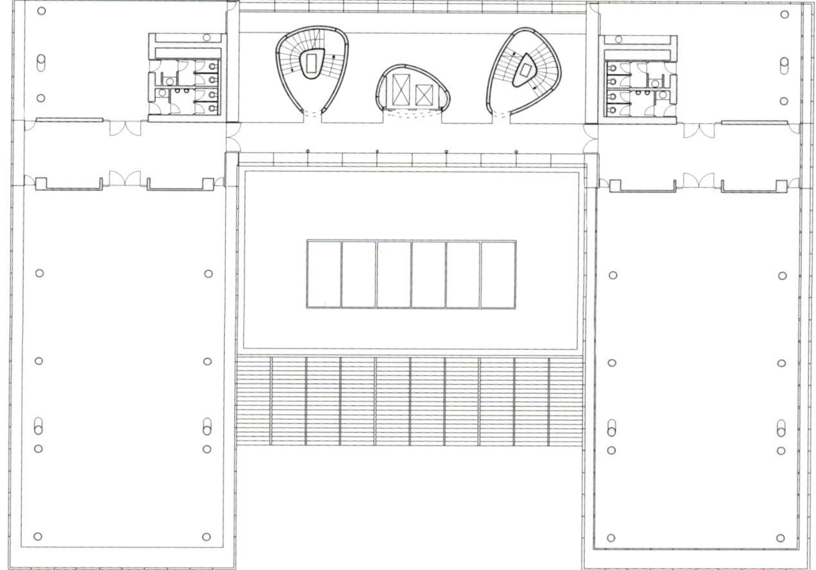

1st floor

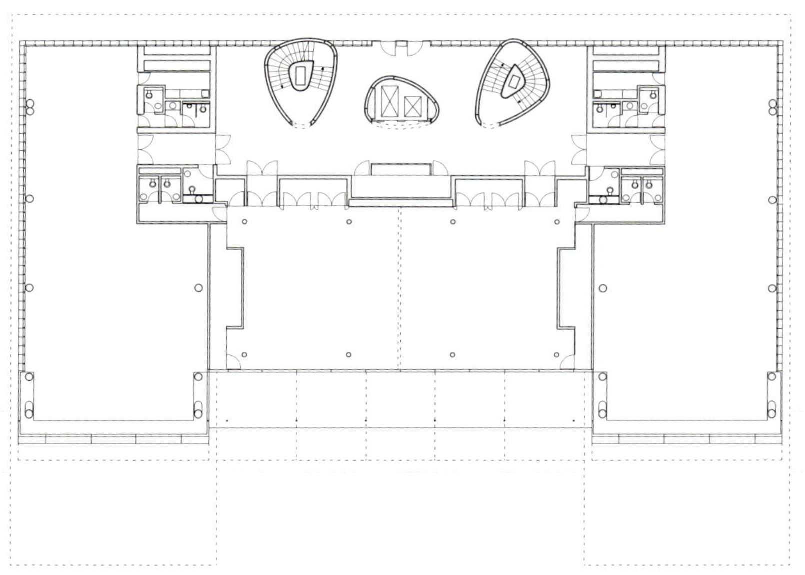

Ground floor

The ThyssenKrupp representative office, Berlin

The ThyssenKrupp building competition concerned a plot at Berlin's Schlossplatz, between the former Staatsratsgebäude (the state council building) and the site of the new Stadtschloss (the royal palace). The first thing we should say about this project is that, after the competition had been judged, it prompted a public discussion. This ultimately led to the plot being returned to the city and to the company distancing itself from the initiative.

Like other firms, ThyssenKrupp wanted to have a presence in Berlin. However, they didn't merely want an office in the German capital – they wanted a public building. The company wanted to give something back to the city, presenting itself as a kind of philanthropist or patron. After all, ThyssenKrupp has an interest in its image.

Its Berlin site was to be an inviting gesture, prominent within the urban space, not a kind of sealed capsule.

The site required a special approach to history. By rebuilding the Stadtschloss, Berlin is looking back to its past, but ThyssenKrupp wants an image that looks forward to the future.

What we found most interesting about the project was that it involved a private entity taking possession of a public site. The question was how to synthesise these different interests to create a balanced socio-political and architectural excursus.

The programme consisted of offices, discussion rooms and event spaces. You might compare this type of corporate office in a capital city to an embassy. The function of an embassy building is to provide a place for formal and informal discussions, a place to conduct business and host public events: this kind of space acts as a calling card for a nation – or for a company – which means that it requires showcases and exhibition spaces. Our design was conducive to all of this – particularly with regard to events. The public and the private merged to create a hybrid space that positively cried out for a programme of events.

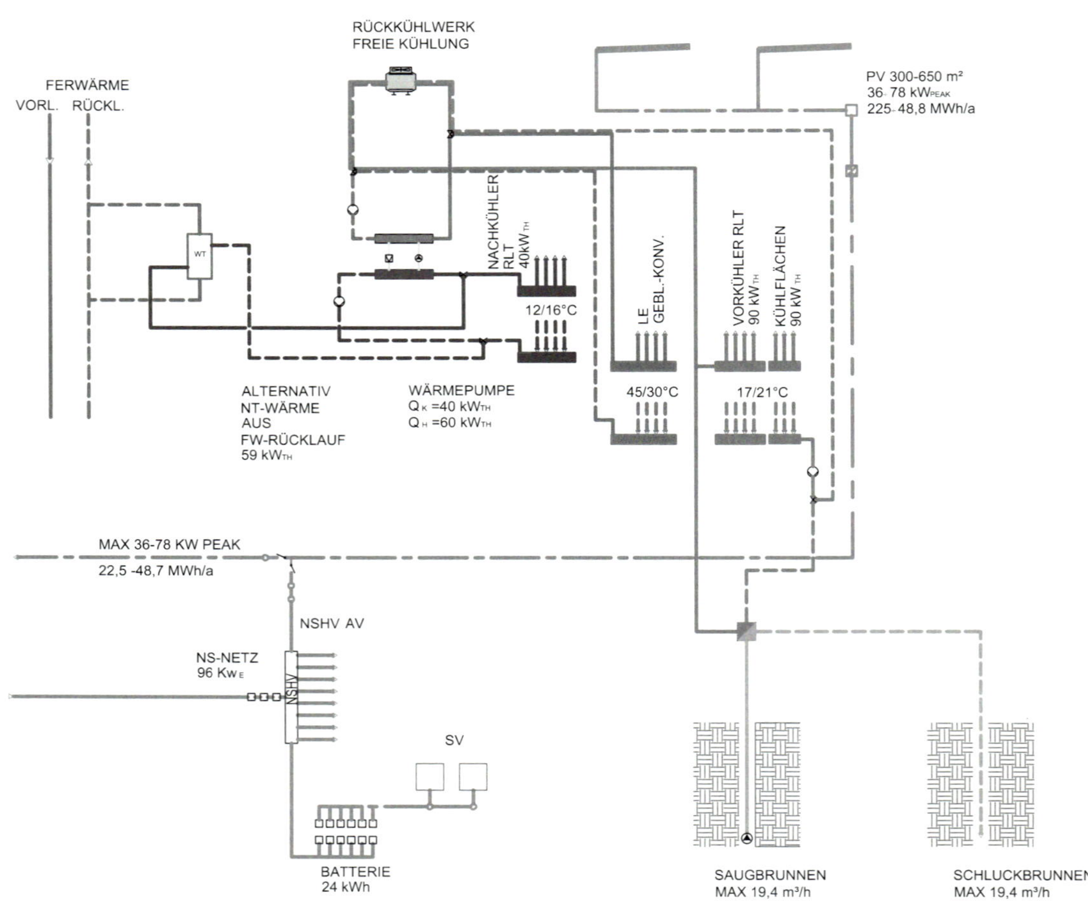

Scheme of the energy supply

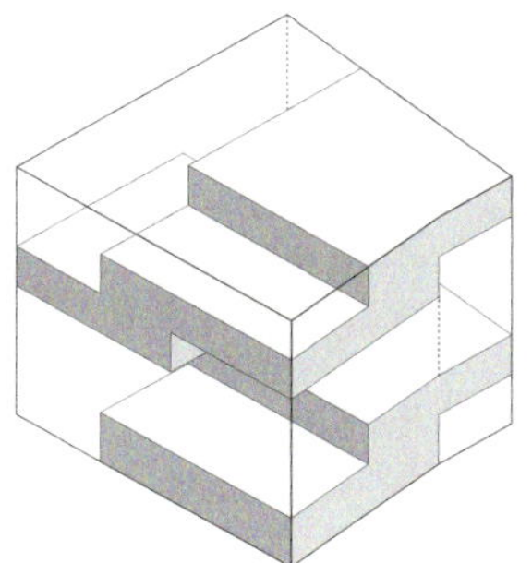

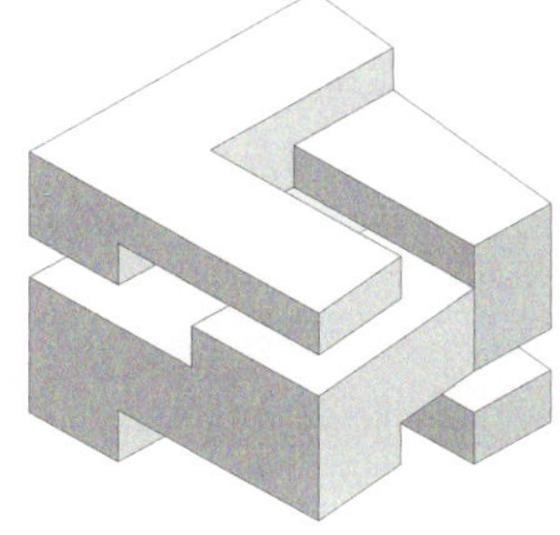

Public Areas

Private Areas

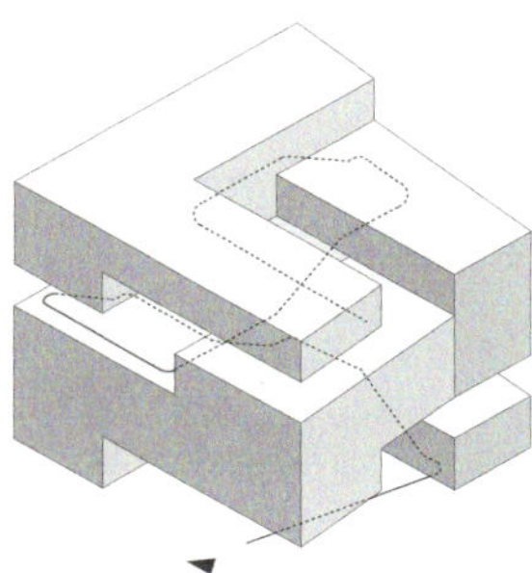

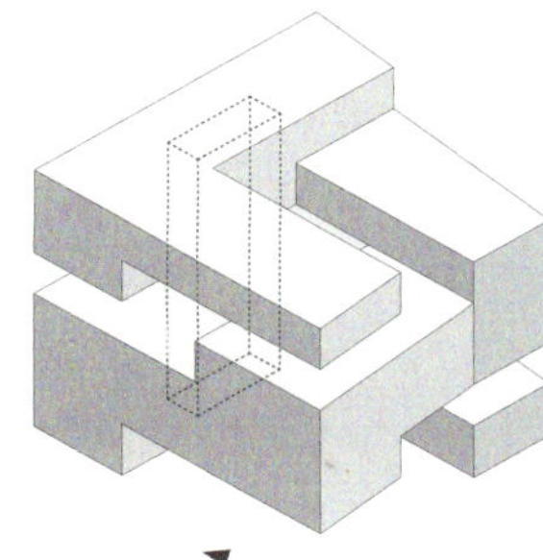

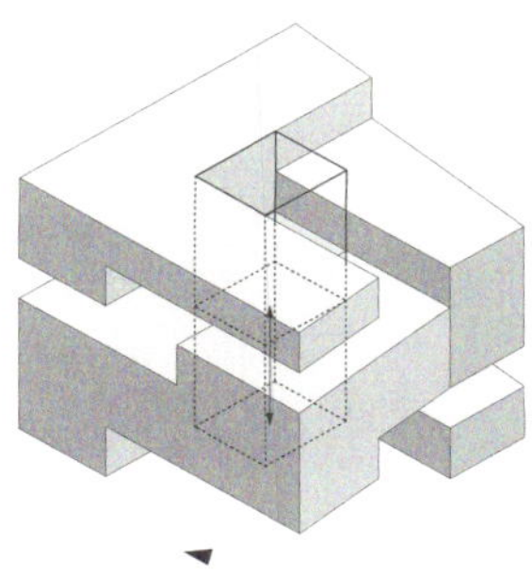

Representative Circulation

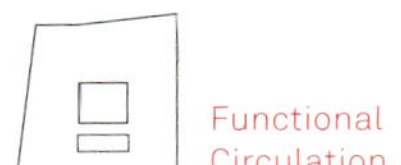

Functional Circulation

Plateau

At first glance, our design looks like a public building. You don't feel like you're looking at a corporate office. We felt that it would be fundamentally wrong to make a space like this, in a site like this, explicitly private – we felt that the challenge lay in creating a building that, though capable of being private, was primarily public in character.

The German Embassy in Oman, for which we won a prize, was built under very different circumstances. It's located in an area with no urban context and has a large private buffer in the form of a wall and a garden. At the Berliner Schlossplatz, however, the public space extends right up to the building, which is exposed on all sides. A building like this needs a façade that spans the full spectrum of mantled, sealed and opened spaces.

We therefore constructed two spatial spirals: one private and one public. They interlock to create a complex, three-dimensional space that jumps across boundaries. This is intended to reinforce the building's public character. Of course, visitors' access had to be regulated in some way.

The concept might be reminiscent of Rem Koolhaas' design for the Dutch embassy in Berlin: he also wished to make his building as public as possible. The realities of using a building like this, however, are rather different – an embassy must also be a confidential and secure place. The Dutch embassy isn't located in the centre of a plaza, and the public space is confined to the route leading to the roof – a grand gesture within a small spatial volume.

By contrast, the empty spaces that we designed are huge and need to be filled – they have the proportions of a museum, where spaces are twenty metres high and fifteen deep. The spatial geometry is complex, which isn't something you're used to seeing in normal, functional buildings, and therefore not something you associate with them.

For a corporate headquarters, this simply looks outlandish, but that's part of the attraction. You have to fill a building like this with life – a café on the ground storey isn't enough. That's why we designed a space that would call for a lively programme.

We envisioned our building in a number of different states. It'd look different – and be used in a different way – for each different kind of event. Alongside the clearly delineated administrative spaces, there'd be halls where activities could spread out. The surrounding plaza would provide an additional extension. Such a design requires that the building really be engaged with its location. A building in a location like this would have a constant visual connection to its immediate environment – without being able to control it.

As always when developing an architectonic design strategy, we interpreted both the role of the client and the assignment itself somewhat according to our own wishes.

That's true. But the location brings with it a duty – for the client and for the architect. If you just want a private building to occupy this space, you don't belong here. You can't isolate yourself in a place like this!

And yet there are some precedents for it: the Bertelsmann Foundation's reconstruction of the Kommandantenhaus at the beginning of Unter den Linden is a completely introverted space.

However, we wanted to define our project differently. And, after all, we were among the three runners-up, which means that our theme of public engagement must have been discussed.

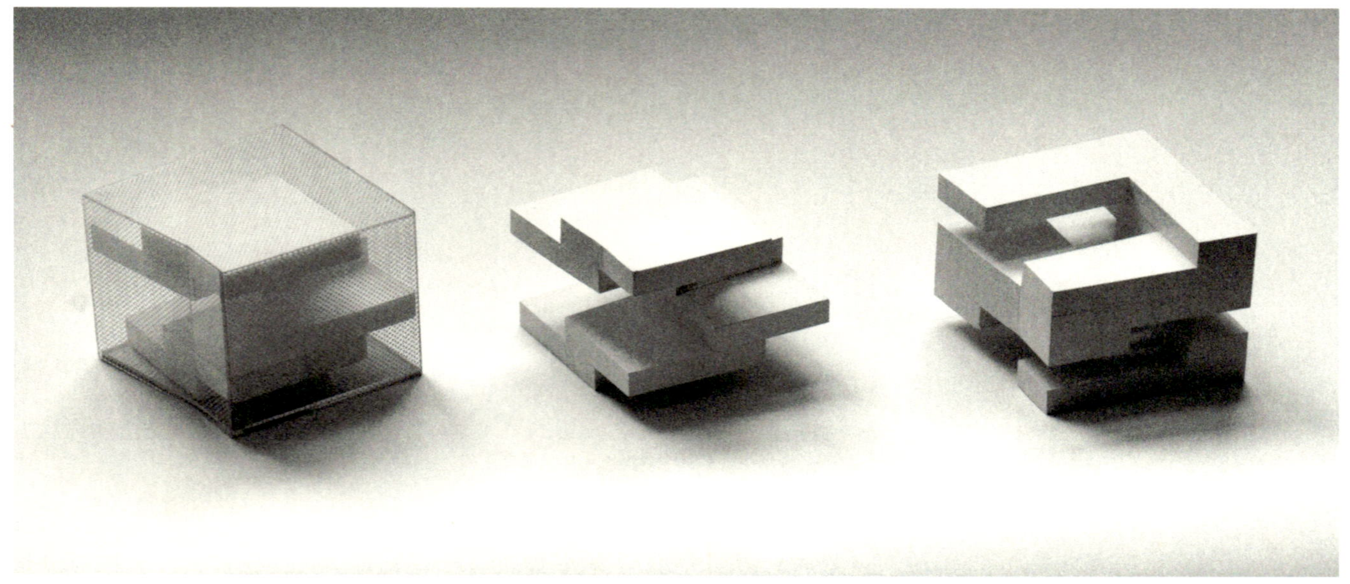

The winning design solved the dilemma in a different way. Its zoning is not spatially interwoven, but rather two-dimensionally stacked. There's a basement structure and a public terrace, with a private building above. At first, it seems like a good idea, an arrangement that would have been easier to use.

When you take a closer look, you realise that the concept doesn't work so well. Not only a café but also meeting rooms and the core of the corporate offices were to be housed on the ground floor. If you wanted to get to the supposedly public terrace on the upper storey, you'd have to cross this area, causing a disruption.

In the "Planwerk Innenstadt" (planning department's plan for the city centre), this site was to define the rear of the Schlossplatz – at the moment, it extends as far as the Foreign Office. The former Senatsbaudirektor (senate building director) Hans Stimmann wanted to recreate the historical urban plan. This, however, created a conflict: the historical plan had to be reconstructed while leaving a respectful distance around the Staatsratsgebäude.

ThyssenKrupp has since given the site back to the city. The main reason for this was that nobody was able to meet the demands of the site, the need to intelligently respond to both private and public interests. This resulted in fundamental questions about the property's development potential ...

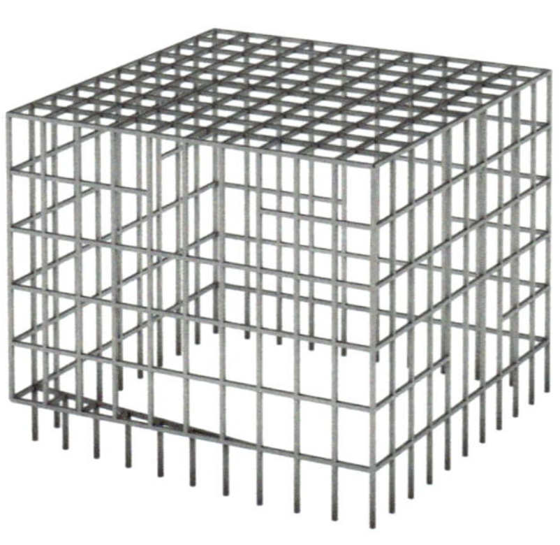

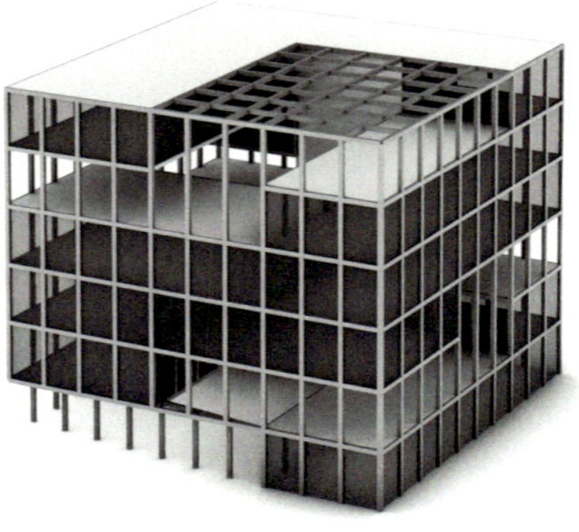

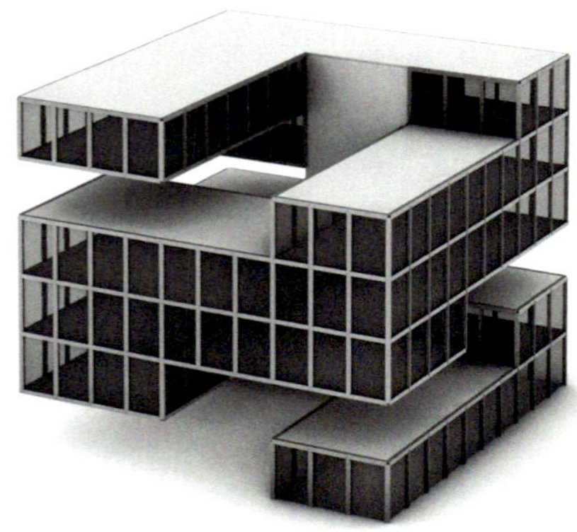

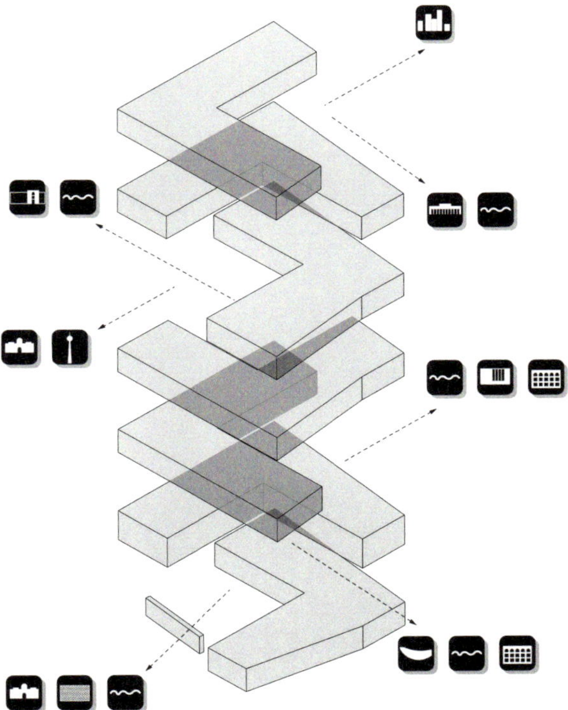

Visual links to the environment

This happens frequently – somehow, various interests manage to reach a consensus during the tendering stage, and it looks like it'll actually be possible to realise the design. Once the design has found a form and has been published, however, it becomes a target for all the criticisms that weren't sufficiently explored beforehand.

We made provisions for a certain spectrum of possibilities. Up to a certain point, we had the idea that we were going to completely open up the building's outer envelope. In an extreme case, we could have envisaged leaving the building's public space entirely without temperature controls. There would have been only a formal separation between interior and exterior, like a conservatory with single-glazed windows. In those areas where people are working at desks and therefore sedentary, of course, they'd get cold quickly, but in the circulation spaces, where they're in motion and where, in any case, they don't stay for long, it wouldn't have had to be so warm. As for events, the people in attendance are effectively heating elements in themselves. This approach would have allowed the space to be repeatedly redefined for rest or action.

Ever since we opened our own office, we've been concerned with liminal spaces and climates. We're talking about "buildings that can grow and shrink". In such buildings, there aren't uniform climatic conditions for everything. Instead – as in our first project, the special needs school in Berlin-Hellersdorf – there are various functional zones. That project included, for instance, multi-storey conservatories between the classrooms.

This liminal climate has a specific function – it promotes air exchange and serves as natural ventilation and exhaust. Our strategy accepts different climatic spaces for different functions. Better to put on a sweater than to wrap a whole building in insulation.

To come back to ThyssenKrupp: our work was partly concerned with transforming things that were associated with the company. The firm is known for its elevators, i.e. for vertical transport in enclosed spaces. Our design celebrates the open staircase – an entirely different form of circulation, which is almost considered old-fashioned nowadays. Steel is also associated with ThyssenKrupp. When you think of steel, you usually think of solid surfaces, but we dissolved the material into delicate and mobile netting.

This design possesses a number of theatrical factors: the stage-like space, the open staircases and, above all, the way movement within it is choreographed. Here, you perceive a room completely differently from each of its corners and in combination with what you can see outside. The building would have been a strong and confident neighbour for the reconstructed Schloss.

ThyssenKrupp representative office

Location
Schlossplatz 2, 10178 Berlin

Year
2nd prize competition 2011

Team
Stefan Schenk, Dominik Queck, Hugo Neto, Thiele Nickau and Carolin Döpfer, Finn Wilkie

Client
ThyssenKrupp AG

Technical planners
schlaich bergermann und partner, Stuttgart/Berlin (structural engineering)
HL-Technik Engineering Partner GmbH, Munich (building services)
Prof. Dipl. Ing. Klaus Daniels, Munich (energy technology)

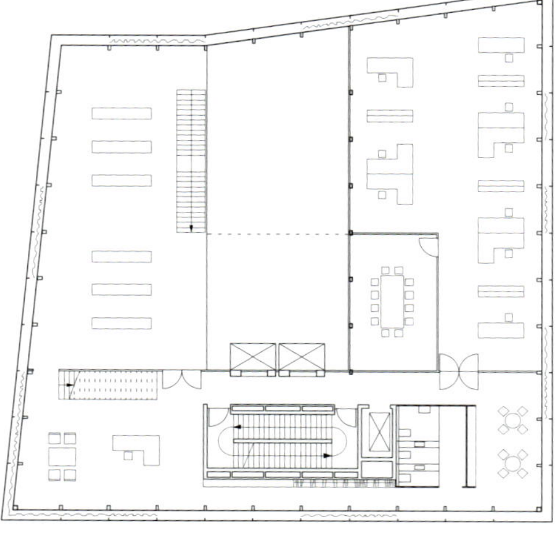

1st floor

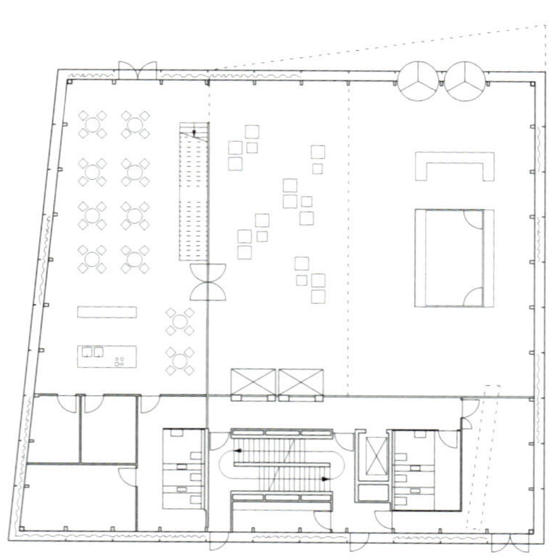

Ground floor

Elevation

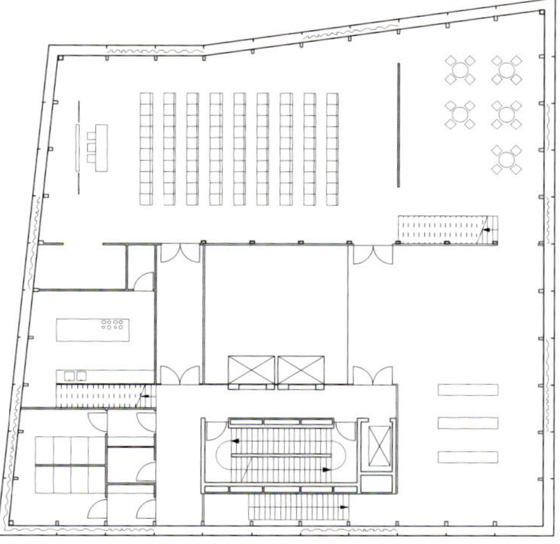

3rd floor

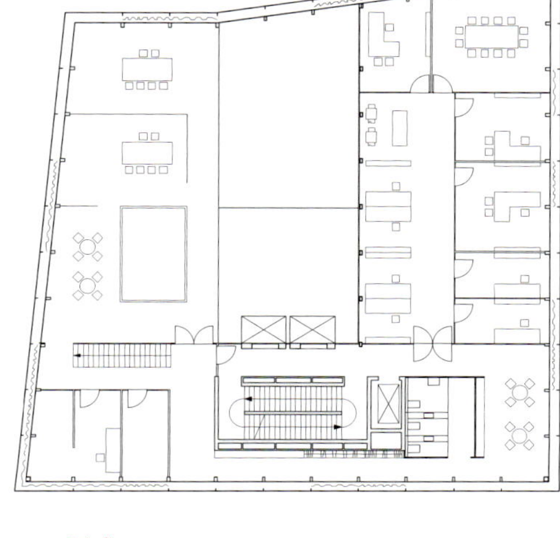

5th floor

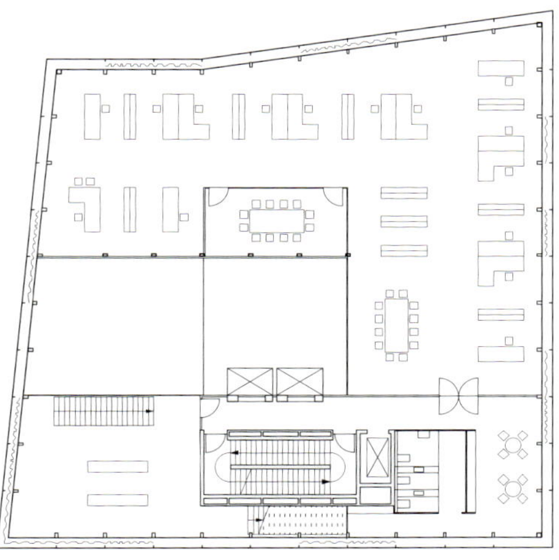

2nd floor

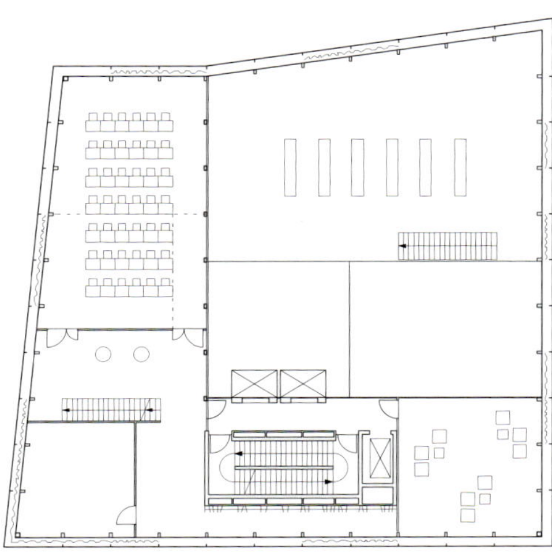

4th floor

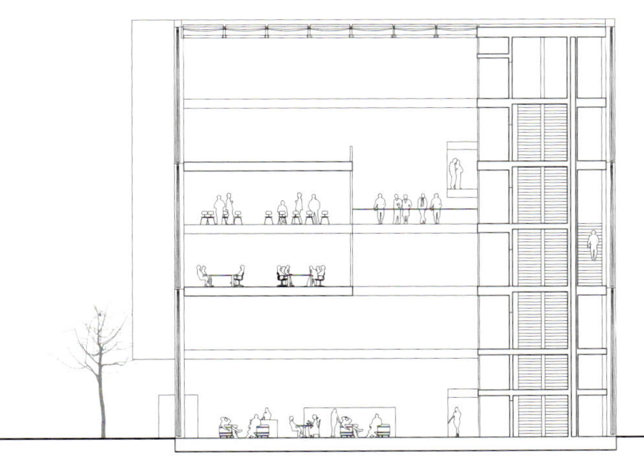

Sections

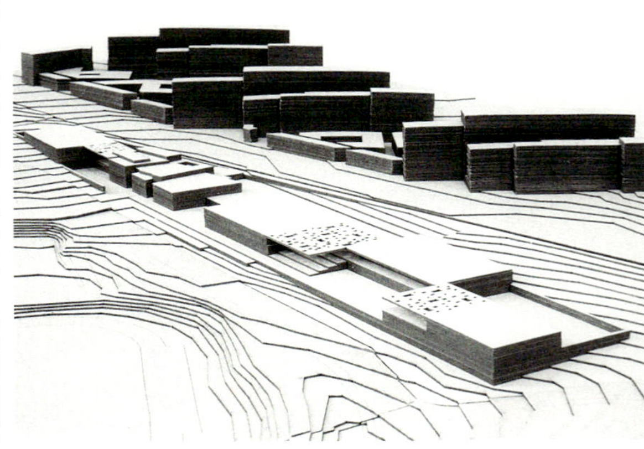

Jerusalem Museum of Nature & Science

As a matter of fact, we almost never take part in open competitions, but in this case, both the location and the assignment tempted us. A few months before the competition, we'd travelled to Israel, and we were delighted by, for instance, the atmosphere at the architecture faculty in Bezalel, where we gave a lecture.

Although it's hard to be pleased about barely missing out on first prize, it was great that, at the presentation of our competition entry, we were able to resume the contacts we made on our first trip.

Incidentally, it wasn't the first time that I'd visited the country: as a child, I lived in Jerusalem. My parents emigrated there from Riga, where I was born. After a year in Israel, however, we moved to Germany, back to my father's homeland.

Of course, your biographical connection made the location special for us. The assignment itself, however, was also great: the plan was to construct new buildings for the natural history and technology museums, plus an extension to the science museum, on a plot where a building belonging to the science museum already stands.

Jerusalem truly is a special place; partly, of course, because of the city's cultural and historical heritage, but also because of the way the city fits into the landscape. In many places, it really merges with the topography.

For this reason, we tried to work out a design that would integrate the large new building volume – it was around 25,000 square metres – into the hillside in as natural a way as possible. It was to be part of the urban landscape. We responded to this need by, for instance, positioning the ensemble of buildings so that they'd be perceived from the surrounding city as being only one- or two-storey structures.

The whole thing, however, is actually three staggered floors: on the upper level, we gave each functional area an individually readable volume. In terms of scale, we broke the ensemble down into individual pavilions. These, however, are linked by a common roof surfaces, allowing the ensemble to present a clear figure in urban planning terms.

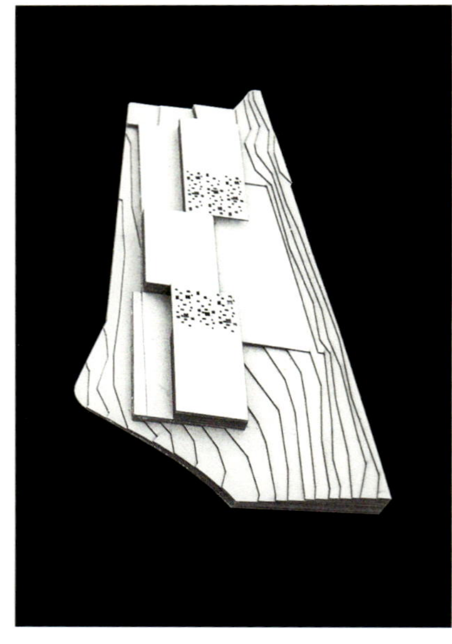

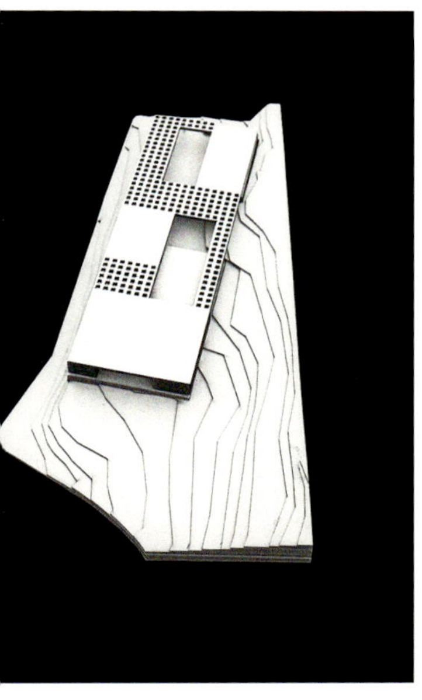

The path into the individual museums leads from the foyer of the entrance building down into the middle level, where an "inner street" connects the buildings: the natural history museum in the centre and the technology museum to the south, plus the old buildings of the science museum and its new extension to the north. From the passageway, there are visual connections to the exhibition areas and the museum gardens. In the basement, the lowest level, are functional spaces such as the underground garage and the conference rooms.

We wanted to achieve a further incorporation of the museums into the city by integrating the plot into the city's public road network, so that the new ensemble would become part of the everyday routes through Jerusalem –

– as with the Stuttgart library, the routes cross the terrain naturally. In this sense, an official route from the Knesset to the national library would have passed over our new open-air steps.

The open-air steps have a shade canopy over them. Their inviting width, and the plants and stepped seating, make them a place to spend time as well as a transit space.

This exterior space was of fundamental importance – partly as a public thoroughfare, but also as a visual connection to the city.

The terraces and garden spaces that we designed are also thematically differentiated – each of them has its own identity, depending upon which museum it belongs to. The technology museum, for instance, has a garden that functions as a sort of classroom, and the natural history museum's garden has a "sun" theme, with cacti and expanses of sand.

Incidentally, the fact that we were working with a very different climate than that of Germany opened up new creative opportunities. The site's hillside position means that most of the building adjoins soil and the façade is open on only two sides. The large glass surfaces are provided with solar protection by projecting roof overhangs. The sides that face the sun are fairly compact and enclosed, with natural stone walls made from typical Jerusalem stone. Across these, as on the shade canopies, we distributed small openings.

In terms of sustainability, we relied upon architectural climate protection: the virtually unbroken wall surfaces on the sunny sides keep the summer heat out. The roof surfaces are shaded by photovoltaic elements. They're mounted so that air can circulate beneath them; the wind cools the roof's concrete surfaces, which transport that coolness into the rooms.

Interestingly, while we were doing the research for this competition, we discovered that architects used similar construction elements back in the twenties. Richard Kaufmann, for instance, used shade canopies with airflow below them in a number of his projects.

Jerusalem Museum of Nature & Science

Location
Sderot HaMuze'onim
Givat-Ram, Jerusalem 91904

Year
finalist, competition 2012

Team
Daniel Strassburger, Stefan Schenk, Dirk Nachtsheim, Dominik Queck and Nora Brinkmann

Client
municipality of Jerusalem

Technical planners
TRANSSOLAR Energietechnik GmbH, Stuttgart (energy technology)
Topotek 1 Gesellschaft von Landschafts-architekten mbH, Berlin (open space planning)

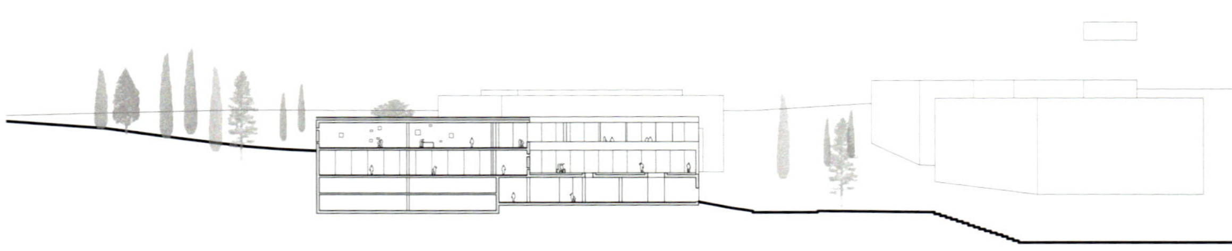

Sections

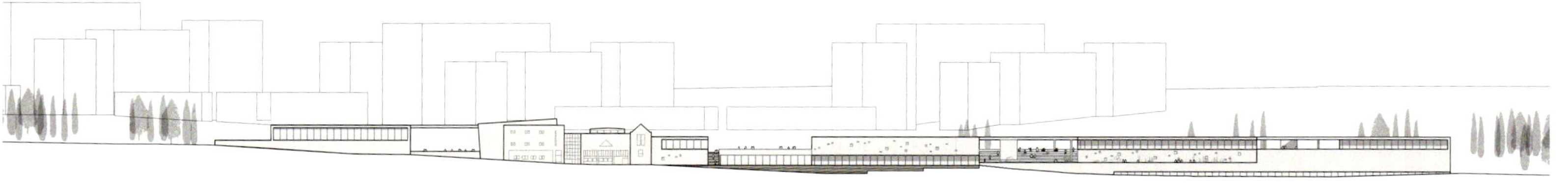

Elevation

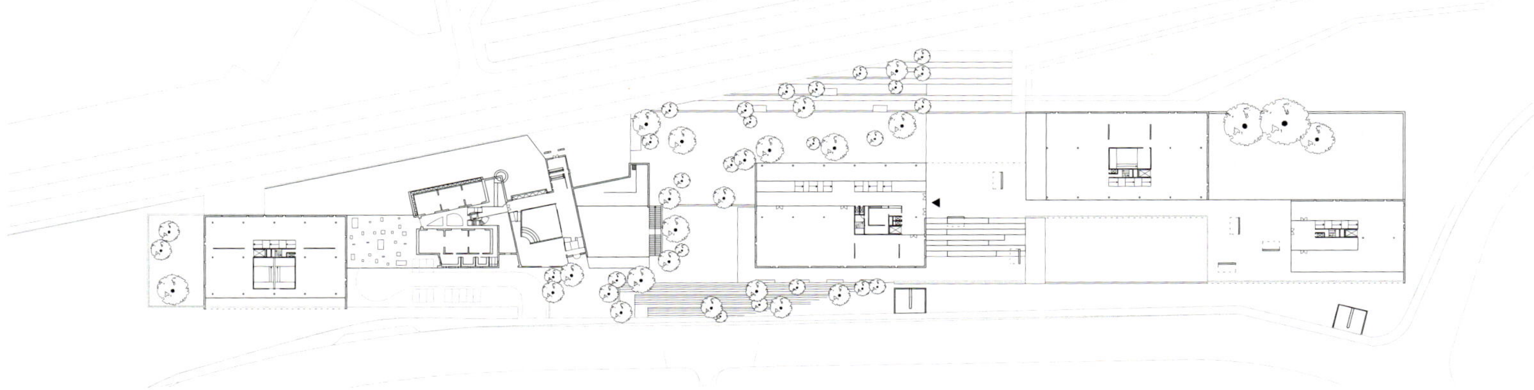

Ground floor

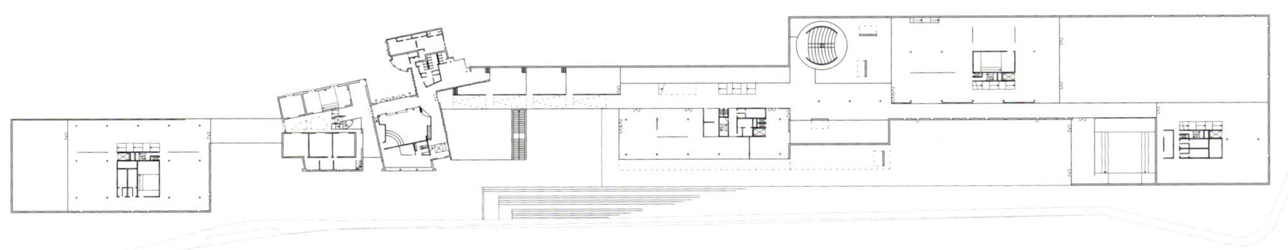

1st basement floor plan

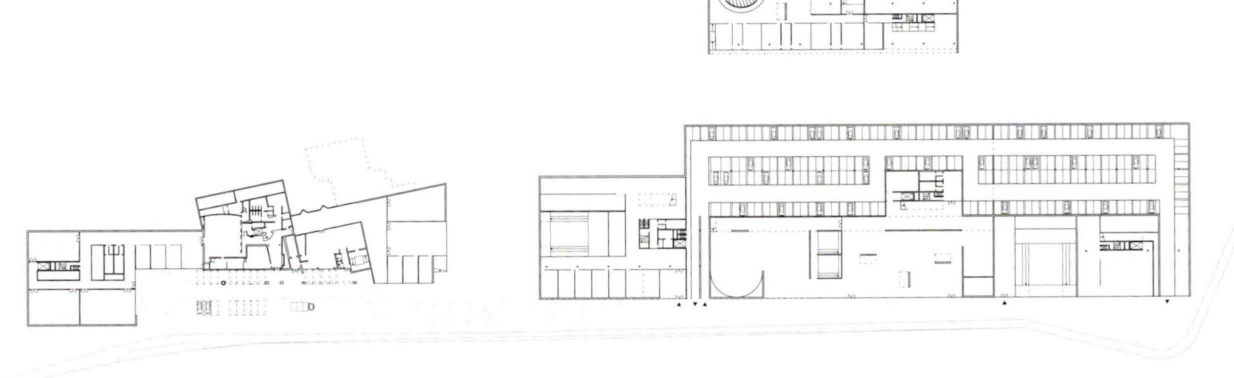

2nd basement floor plan

CONVERTIBLE
GERMANIA

USCITA

Convertible City – the German contribution to the Venice Architecture Biennale, 2006

The German Pavilion at the Venice Architecture Biennale was an exceptional project for us as architects – after all, we're not curators in the usual sense of the word. Although, really, all architects are curators!

In any case, the project left a very lasting impression. It gave us a chance to sum up certain themes from our day-to-day work and place them in a wider context.

The aspect that I found most interesting was that creating the catalogue involved interviewing people from completely different disciplines – scientists and artists, for instance. Conversations like these were a way of contemplating architectural issues in a wider context. For instance, we discussed the dividing line between public and private space – and the artistic interpretation of this theme – with the choreographer Sasha Waltz. Then there was Wim Wenders, whose impressions of Brasilia we found very interesting. He was disappointed by this textbook example of modern urban planning; in his contribution he describes a flea market under a motorway bridge as the only living place in the city.

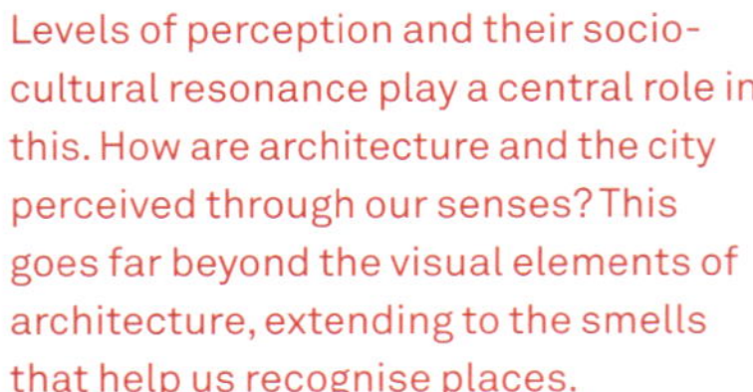

Levels of perception and their socio-cultural resonance play a central role in this. How are architecture and the city perceived through our senses? This goes far beyond the visual elements of architecture, extending to the smells that help us recognise places.

It's a question of our emotional response to the city. East Berlin smells different to West Berlin, that sort of thing. We remember smells better than we do buildings.

The theme of our pavilion, entitled "Convertible City", is the city and how to work with existing buildings and, by the same token, how to handle existing identities. This is obviously more challenging than erecting a solitary building out on a greenfield site.

Pavilion in 1909 (top) and in 1938 (bottom)

It puts architecture in perspective. Of course, there's the question of architecture's future. Is it a formal solution? Or a socio-political model? The Biennale has always been a showcase for the newest, hippest formalism: postmodernism was born there, as were deconstructivism, the Liquid Surfaces, and so on. The interesting thing about the 2006 Biennale, which was curated by Ricky Burdett and entitled "Cities, Architecture and Society", was that, paradoxically, architecture had shifted toward art – in terms of socio-political relevance rather than in terms of formal representation! This suggested a question to us: what role can architects play in this debate if they no longer use the traditional tools of architecture?

Good architects are always alchemists who can make gold out of dirt, who can produce unexpected potential from a seeming disadvantage – from a substandard existing building, for instance. Of course, this is part of what "convertible" means – like driving a soft-top car and being able to create a whole new feeling, a different way of life, simply by pulling a handle.

Today, people are turning away from the tabula rasa mentality of modernism. More and more architects are realising that you can't always start from scratch. Transforming existing structures is one way of getting past the hostility so many people have toward contemporary architecture. Architecture can reach people on an emotional level – which doesn't happen purely through the utility of a building, something that may not be significantly changed by renovation. Instead, it's a question of creating a sense of emotional attachment – something that many people feel has been lost in post-war architecture. There are also highly significant applications in terms of sustainability.

I once spent a year studying in Venice, and I knew the pavilion very well. I've always wondered how we could get rid of the "Germania" feeling, this burden, this weight. How could we create a comfortable, optimistic atmosphere in a building like this – an atmosphere with the kind of lightness that people don't expect from the Germans?

Of course, we also enjoyed doing something about this hulk of a pavilion and the way that it makes you feel small and separates you from the lagoon, even though you're so close to the water you can smell it. Our strategy was to use the roof as a belvedere – to overwrite the obsolete form of national representation inherent in the pavilion by helping people experience this magnificent location while still allowing the original intention to remain legible.
A long staircase takes the visitor from the pavilion's main inner space through a portal and toward the group of trees crowning the roof – at first, you wouldn't know where the path was taking you. This new element – the terrace atop the pavilion – makes the pavilion at once a showcase for exhibits and an exhibit in its own right.

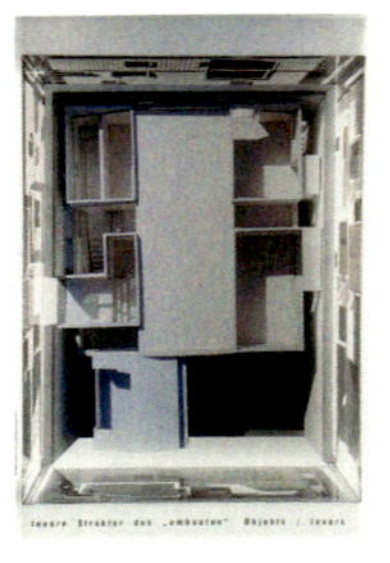

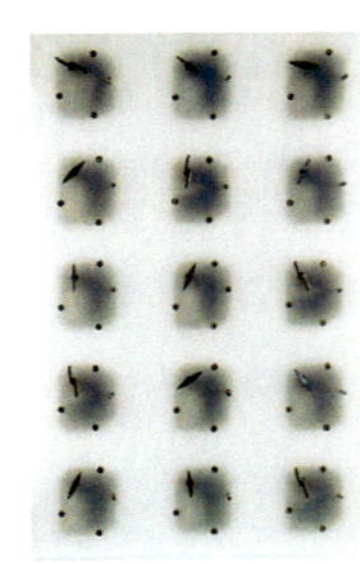

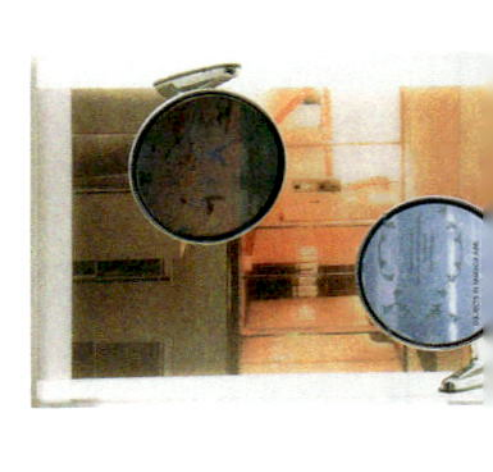

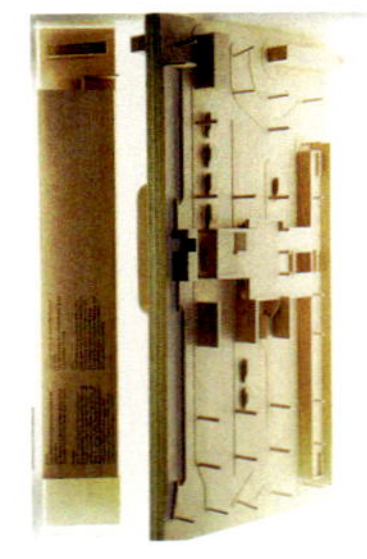

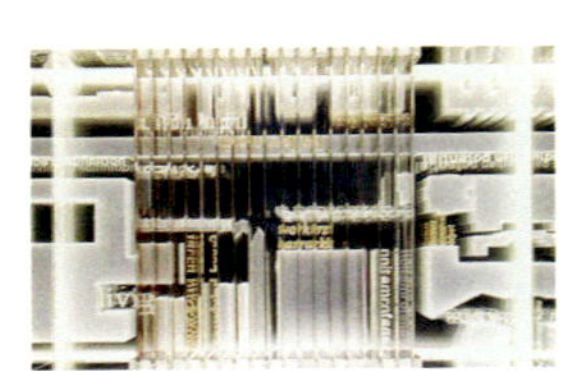

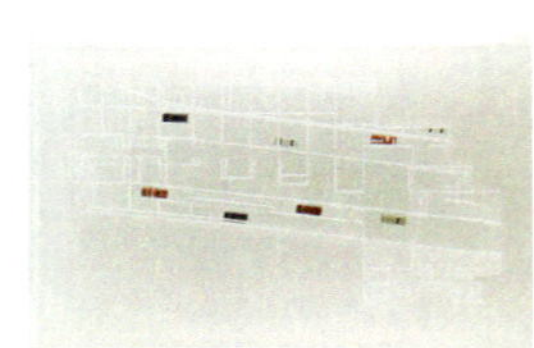
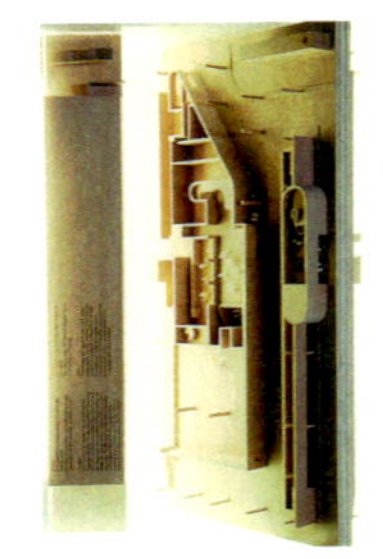

westhafen-pier
schneider+schumacher

BELOW
YOU CAN SEE A
VIP
WHO TRANSFORMS CITY
IT´S UP TO
YOU!

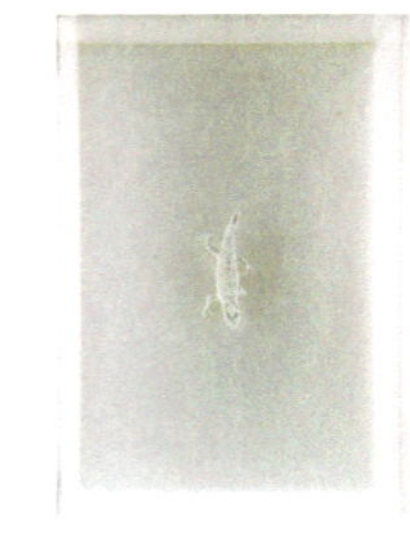

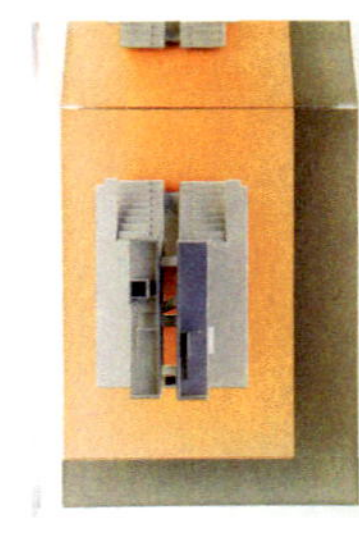

We also held a number of events on the roof – for instance, there were podium discussions on urban renewal and on the future of cities. The idea of utilising the roof in this way, however, did create a number of problems for us. The Bundesbauministerium (the federal construction ministry) was so shocked by the collapse of the ice-skating hall in Bad Reichenhall in 2006 that we had to subject the roof to a magnetic resonance test to prove that it would take the strain. The pavilion certainly looks solid, but it was built with limited uses in mind, so it was perfectly reasonable to demand a test of the roof's load capacity.

The other problem was the path through the sixty-centimetre-wide skylight passage. The ministry thought that you couldn't expect people to use it – but the passage in a Deutsche Bahn train is no wider. In any case, during the anxious period of preparation, after the image of the route up to the roof had already been published, there were constant questions as to whether it was even practicable. It wasn't always plain sailing – we had no Plan B. We had to make various efforts of the most absurd kind in order to remove all doubt.

The implemented pavilion didn't look like our rendering, because the densely planted trees never permitted it to be viewed in the round. The first image – which won over the jury – was never realised. However, it got us through the project.

Inside, we set up ten-metre-high banners, which hung freely in the main space. Visitors moved through this spatial installation, which featured examples of modern urban renewal projects. The stepped spatial arrangement of the individual project images gave viewers the illusion of standing in an urban space.

For the presentation of selected projects in the side wings, we developed an object that was a hybrid of a table and a book; the visitors could open the boxes (which had been designed by different architects) to discover images, objects and models.

We asked each participating architect or artist to create an item for the exhibition and put it in a Plexiglas box, with no rules as to the contents, material or form. This was in itself a daring curatorial decision – we had no guarantee that the overall effect would be successful. Our gesture of trust in our colleagues, however, produced a collection of idiosyncratic items to stimulate the visitors.

The element of surprise created by opening the boxes provided a further activating element, and the individual exhibits took advantage of this adroitly. There was, for instance, a box by the MESS group that contained a mirror. The lettering around its edge read: "here you see a major player in urban transformation."

IBLE
CITY
MANIA

CONVERTIBLE CITY

Convertible City – German contribution to the Venice Architecture Biennale, 2006

Location
German Pavilion, Giardini della Biennale, Castello, 30100 Venice

Host
Bundesministerium für Verkehr, Bau und Stadtentwicklung

Commissioners
Armand Grüntuch and Almut Grüntuch-Ernst

Team
Arno Löbbecke, Lukas Feireiss, Julia Wolter, Sybille Fanelsa, Beate Engelhorn and Eleonora Fassina, Alessio Fossati, Caroline Steinchen, Anja Fischer

Technical planners
KRONE Ingenieurbüro GmbH, Berlin (structural engineering)
cfk Architetti, Venedig (local partner)
Licht Kunst Licht AG, Bonn (lightning design)
Dorén + Köster, Berlin (graphic design)
Stilkonzil, Berlin (website)

Catalogue: ARCH+ 180
Armand Grüntuch, Almut Grüntuch-Ernst (editors-in-chief)
Lukas Feireiss, Sophie Lovell, Anh Linh Ngo, Stephan Becker, Martin Luce (editorial staff)
Walter Schönauer (graphic design)

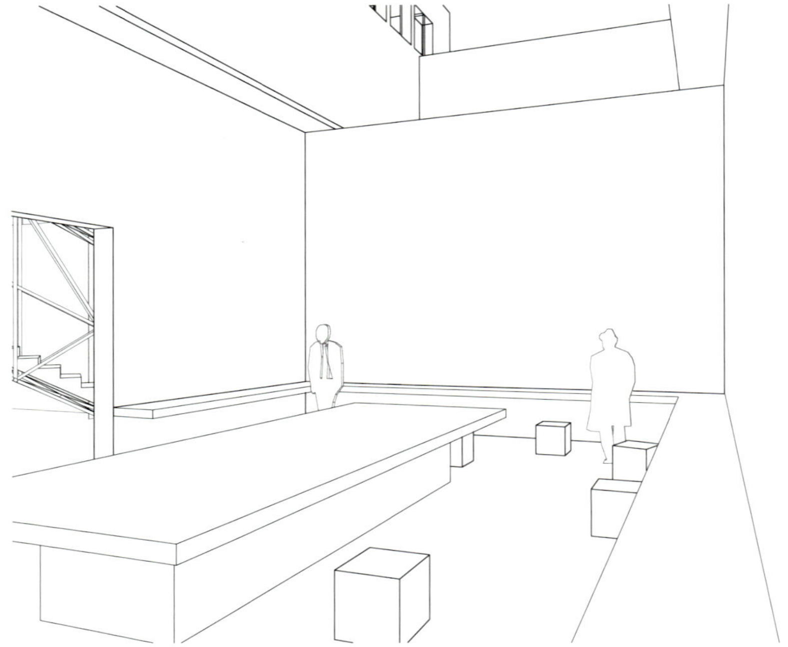

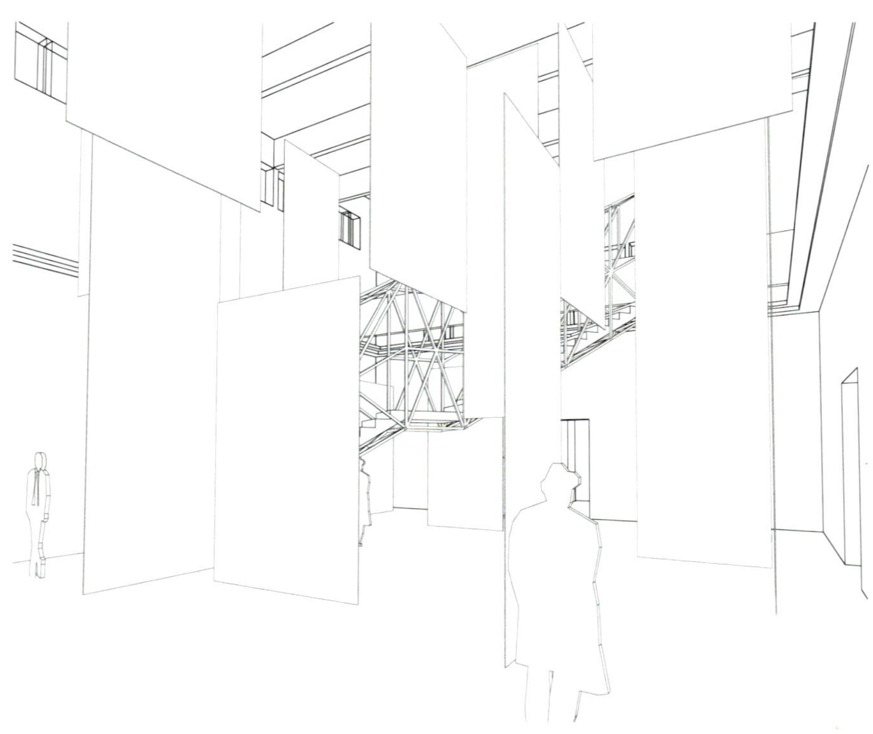

Competition sketches

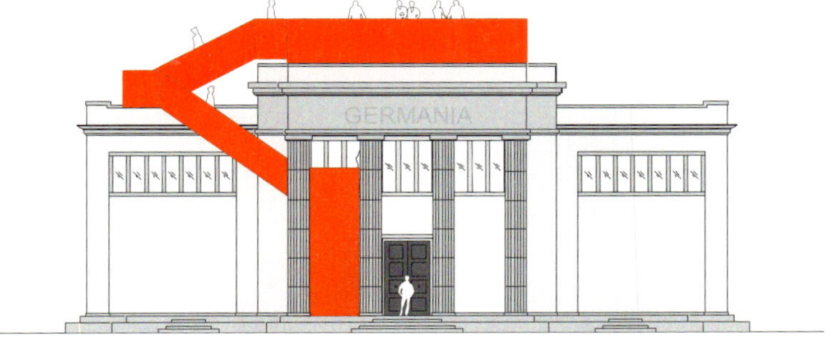

Elevation

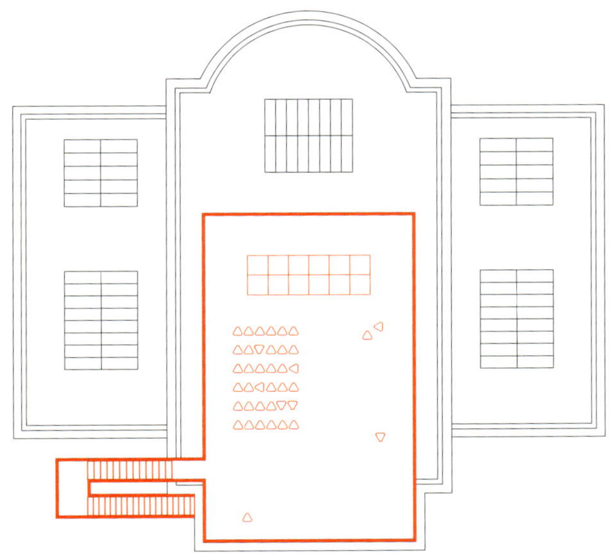
Roof

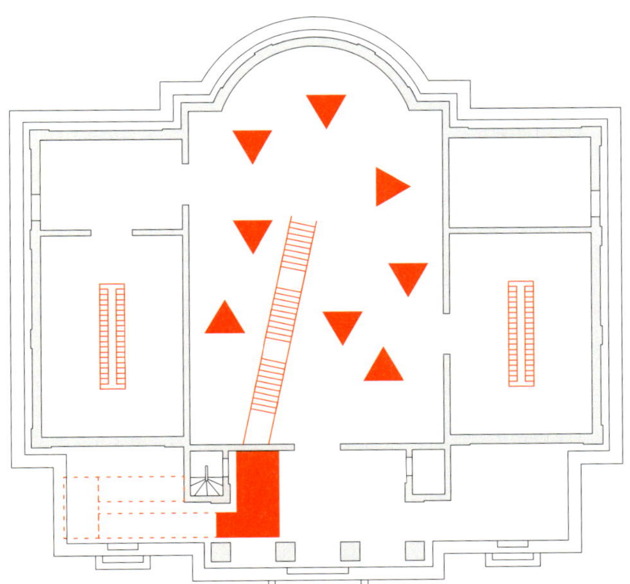
Ground floor

The Deutsche Schule Madrid

The Deutsche Schule in Madrid is one of the oldest German schools abroad, founded in 1896. This meant that it had a fabulous inner-city location. The expansion project is taking it to an entirely different location, on the city periphery.

The new plot somehow feels like no-man's-land. The location looks so peaceful and idyllic, and there's a cemetery nearby – but the ring road runs directly below it.

Since 2003, a whole new suburb began to spring up here. When the competition was being held, the ground-floor properties were still impossible to sell. For this reason, the ground floors were empty and mostly boarded up, and the areas between the buildings were wasteland ... it was a total non-place, really.

The view, however, is wonderful! You can see snow-covered mountains. That's one advantage of a location on the edge of the city.

Of course, for us this evoked memories of the school in Dallgow-Döberitz. Again, the suburban site encouraged us to bring urban qualities to the periphery.

And here in Madrid, landscape was again the theme of the design. Rather than creating a natural landscape, however, we wanted to create a geometric one that would be capable of forming a network structure for the whole campus, thereby securing a high degree of flexibility for the design.

At the same time, we wanted to create a location with a sense of identity, one that united openness with introspection and security. We based our design on a monastery typology.

Adjacent residential area

Integration into the landscape in model and aerial view (top and bottom)

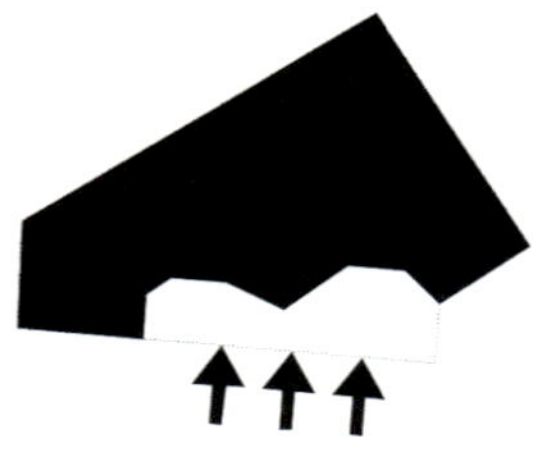

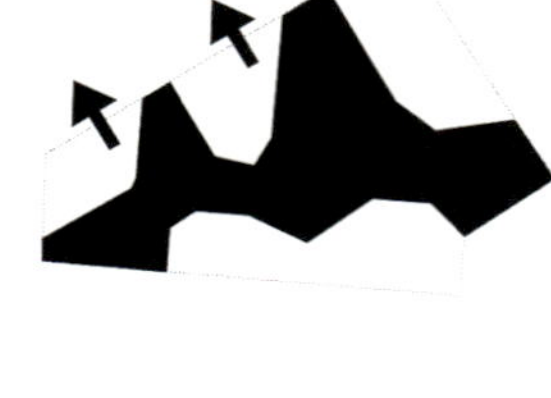

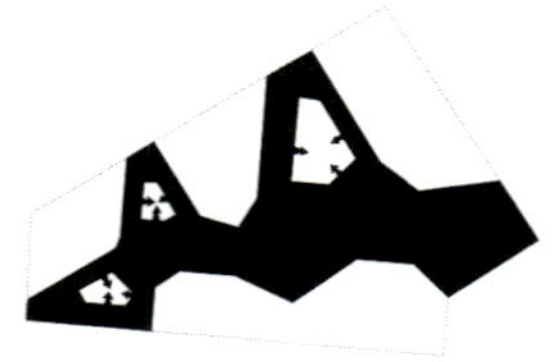

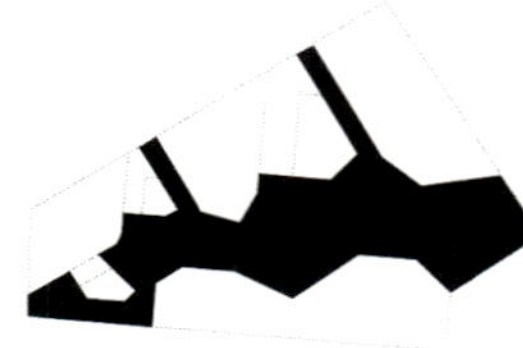

Monastery buildings made an impression on me from the very first time I read about the Carthusians, about whom Le Corbusier also wrote a great deal. The residential cells in a monastery are grouped along the inner transverse cloister and have a small garden. It's like an urban structure.

We began this project by investigating the themes of the cloister passage, the courtyard arrangement and the transverse cloister. The biggest question that we faced, however, was how to fit all the required functions onto the site. The programme was to be divided among three central sites: the kindergarten, the *Grundschule* (primary school) and the *Gymnasium* (academic secondary school). Additionally, however, the school should have a shared central area.

On top of that came the other large communal spaces, like the cafeteria, gym, and auditorium.

Façade models in the design phase

Mock-up of the façade on site in 2013

Don't forget: the school will have 2,000 students! That's a lot of people. We thought it was important to break up the large expanses of the courtyard spaces so that the children could find their own way around, but still feel like a part of the group.

We divided the individual schools into distinct blocks, then fit them together again to form an ensemble. The sports fields had to be laid out in the remaining spaces – it was a real puzzle! In designing a school, architects always have the same problem with the 100-metre track: if you don't think of it at the beginning, you'll never be able to fit it in!

Providing access to the individual schools was also a challenge: because the kindergarten, for instance, doesn't have the same operating hours as the others, it has to be kept separate, with its own entrance.

Everything, however, was to be brought together at a central location. We created a courtyard – we call it the foyer courtyard – to provide a special zone between outside and inside. This is the reception area, where all the students first arrive.

The courtyard has shaded areas – the Spanish climate demands that you plan for spaces where people can take refuge from the sun and heat. However, we also provided bright areas open to the sky.

These polygonal openings create interesting interplays of light and shadow – they also serve as "wind catchers", channelling cool northerly wind into the courtyard.

All our previous school projects had been around Berlin. Spain has an entirely different climate, and that obviously had an impact on the design.

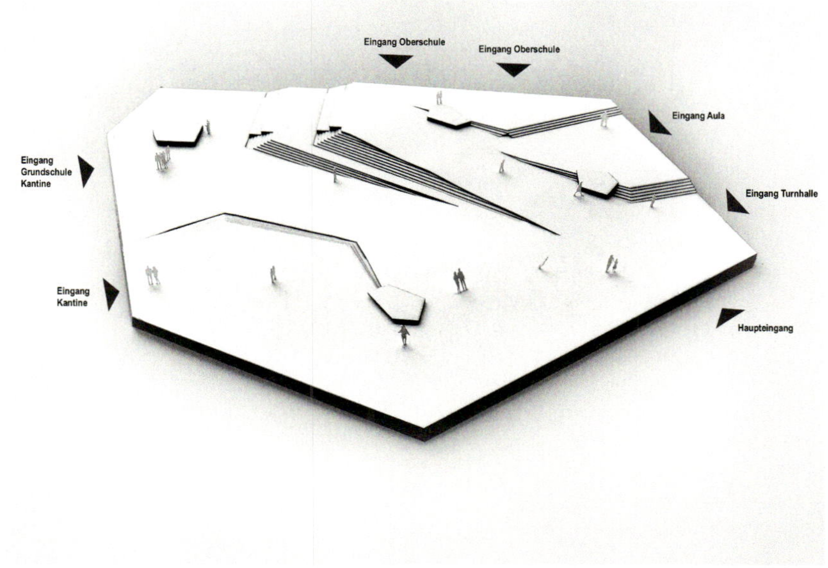

Model of the base of the foyer courtyard: a landscape of ramps and stairs

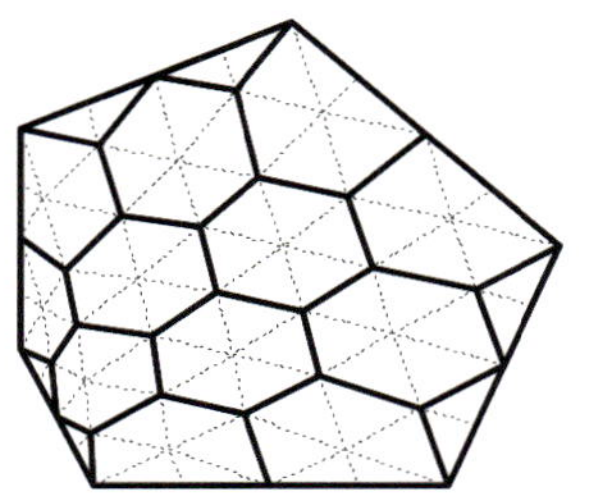

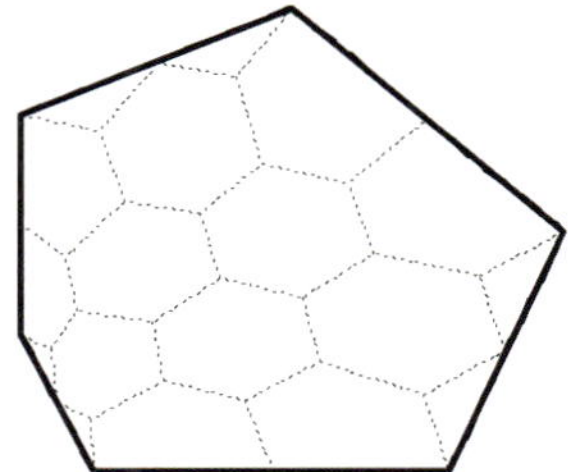

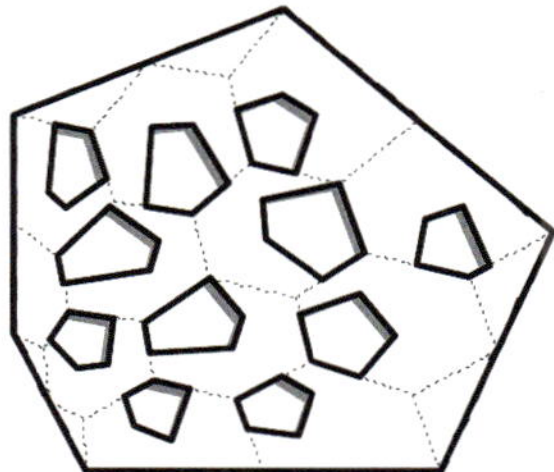

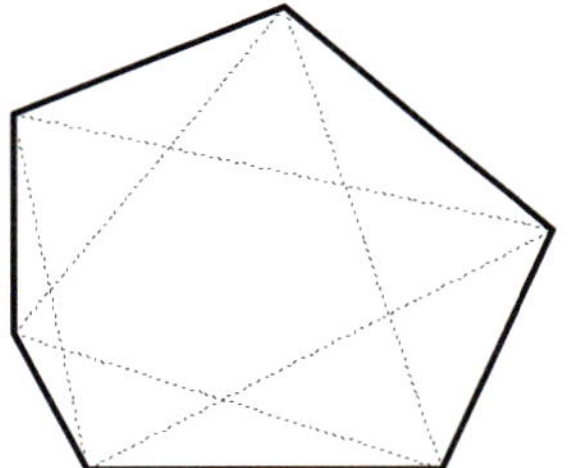

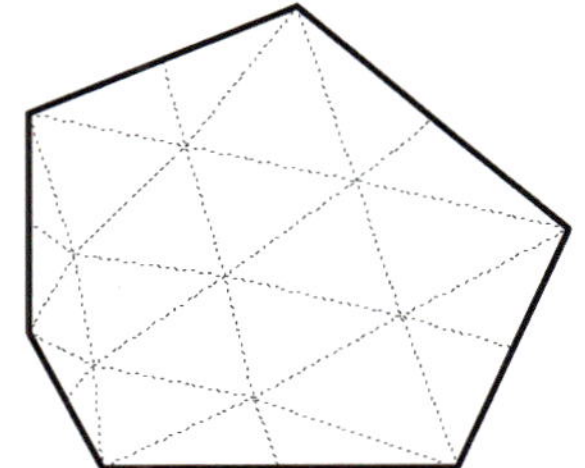

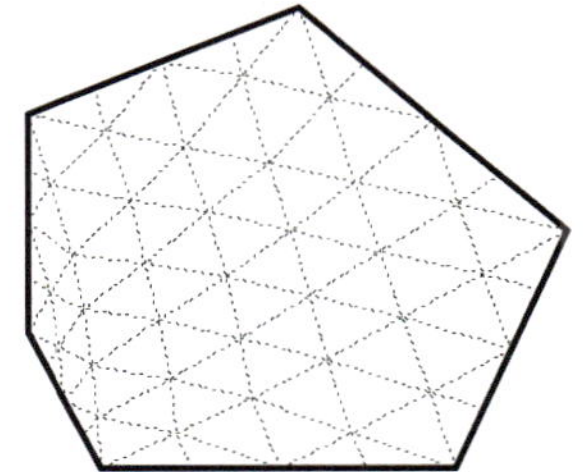

Design studies of the roof of the foyer courtyard

Generally, temperatures are high, but they also vary significantly over the course of the day and over the course of the year. To help us understand how to cope with the weather conditions, we looked at traditional building techniques used in this climate and adopted the basic principles – for example, the Roman hypocaust, or hot air heating system.

We combined these traditional techniques with the architectural innovations of our own age. For instance, we built a "thermal labyrinth" under the school. This system uses geothermal energy to cool or warm the air, saving energy.

Above all, school buildings should look to the future: they play a key role in sustainability, because they shape the day-to-day life of future generations.

As the competition brief put it, international schools are also "a foreign policy instrument". They're a site for intercultural encounters.

We tried to unite all these different requirements in a project that would also have a strong sculptural presence. We wanted to combine clearly readable individual sections to form an ensemble that would constitute one organic, comprehensible structure. Eventually, we felt that everything was just right – the way structures of varying heights related to each other and the way they were staggered.

This also helped us develop the right relationship between intimacy and openness. The special features of our design are, on the one hand, the introverted, enclosed patios, which radiate a certain intimacy, and, on the other hand, the view out to the mountains from the point where the schoolyards come together to form one large yard.

During the design process, we spent a lot of time on the plot and the basic geometry. Triangular forms are difficult to perfect – they always leave a system of leftover spaces and we have to work with a lot of rectangular forms, the sports fields for instance. The triangle itself is a very difficult architectonic form, which offers no reference points: you never know where you are.

Model study of the cafeteria

Model study of the foyer courtyard

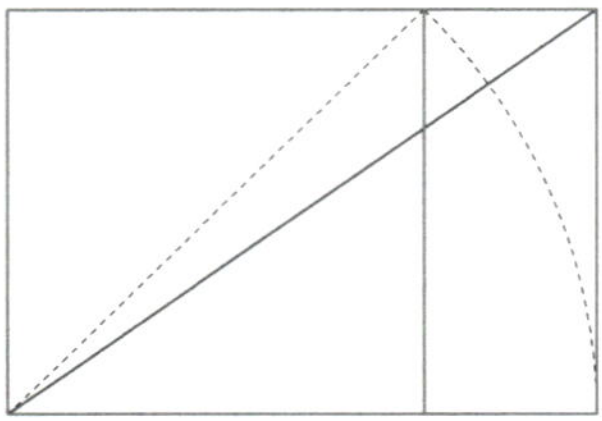

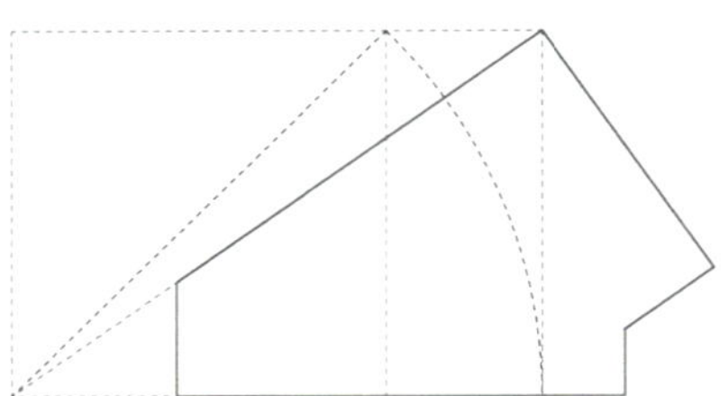

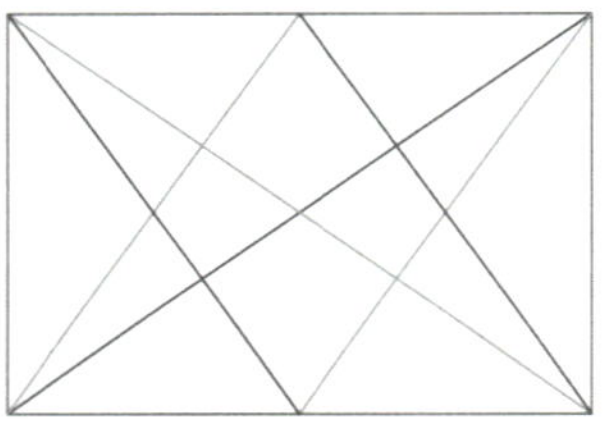

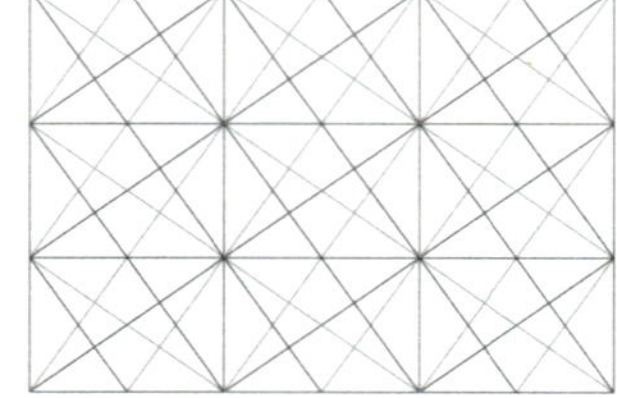

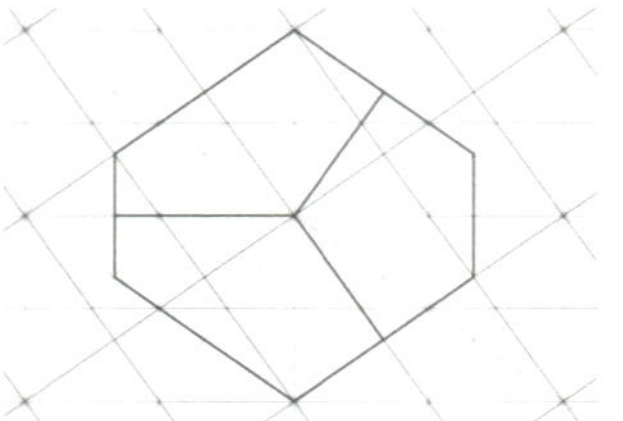

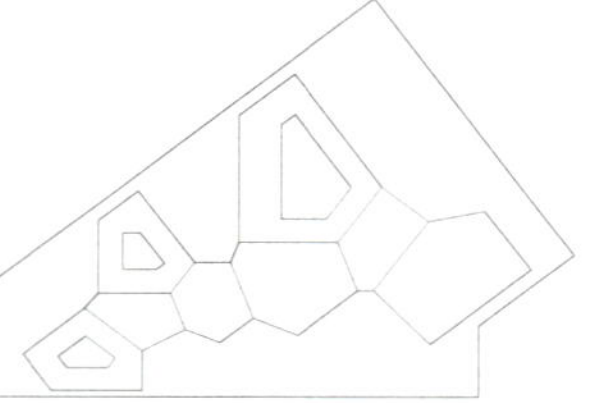

Design studies of the building's geometry

It poses questions like: how can you create regularity, what can you derive from a situation like this? As an architect, you always hope that all the problems will disappear once you find the source code.

It can sometimes be very helpful to start with the right module size and think outwards. Suddenly, fractals come into play and help to generate very different sizes – down to the tile pattern. If you're lucky, these observations can also be applied to the floor plan. In our design for the school, we discovered a ratio of lengths, which, as it turned out, gave us a system that defined everything. It was like a game of patience – suddenly everything just clicked.

We always design in two directions: on the one hand, we approach the building's form in an impulsive and intuitive way, and, on the other hand, we subdue it into a geometrical form. You can spend a great deal of time on the process of finding the form – it's fun. However, you should be careful that the end result is a building, not gift-wrap.

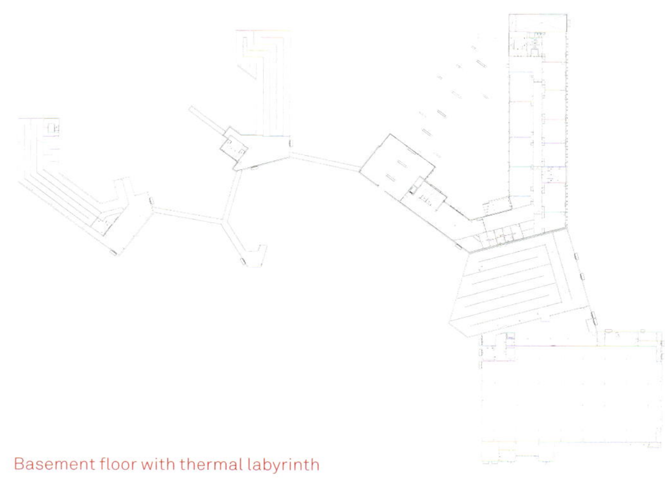

Basement floor with thermal labyrinth

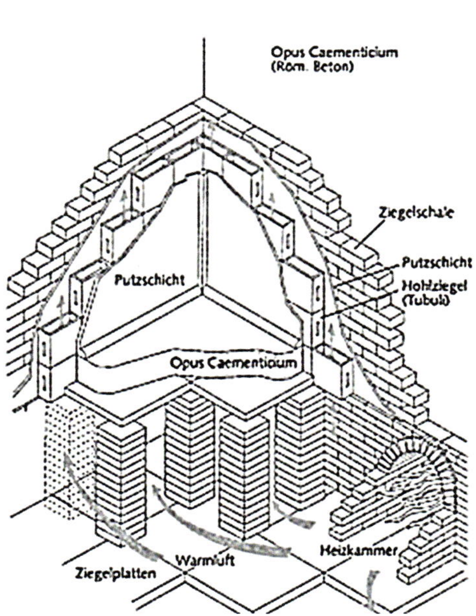

Roman hypocaust (hot-air heating system)

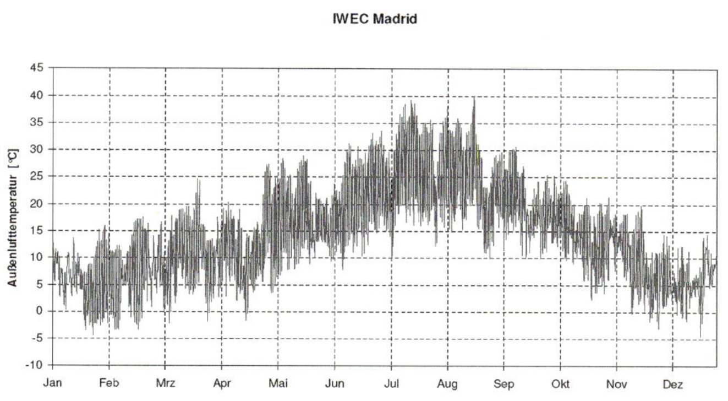

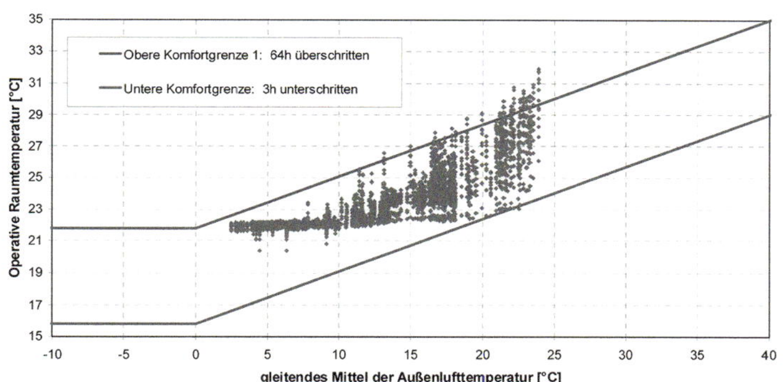

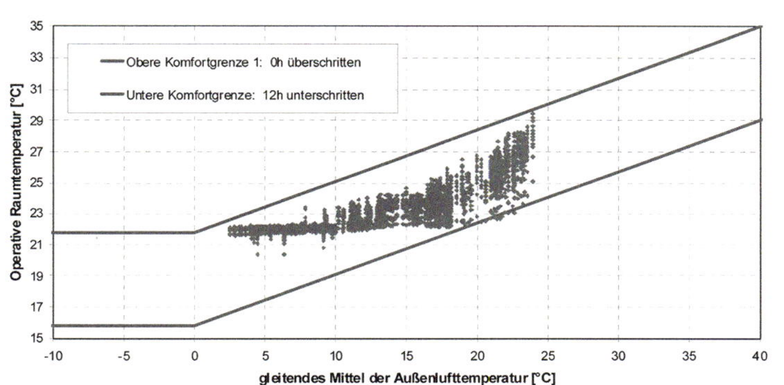

Temperature gradation through the year (top) and temperature with and without thermal labyrinth (middle and bottom)

Location
Calle del Monasterio de Guadelupe 7, 28049 Madrid-Montecarmelo, Spain

Year
1st prize competition 2009
completion 2015

Team
Erik Behrends, Florian Fels, Olaf Menk, Arno Löbbecke, Markus Lassan, Jens Schoppe, Benjamin Bühs, Victor Casado, Matthias Cremer, Jost von Fritschen, Isabell Gruchot, Kristina Herresthal, Rebeca Juárez, Elena Martínez del Pozo, Dirk Nachtsheim, Vera Martinez, Jaime Promewongse, Karsten Schuch, Kerstin Thomsen, Anna Wolska, Mar Ballesteros, Cristina Baixauli Garcia, Julia Naomi Henning, Johannes Blechschmidt, Andreas Nemetz, Dominik Queck, Henning Wiethaus

Client
Federal Republic of Germany, represented by the Bundesministerium für Verkehr, Bau und Stadtentwicklung (BMVBS), represented by the Bundesamt für Bauwesen und Raumordnung (BBR)

Technical planers
GTB-Berlin Gesellschaft für Technik am Bau mbH, Berlin (structural engineering)
Prof. Dr. sc. Mike Schlaich / schlaich bergermann und partner, Stuttgart/Berlin (inspection engineers)
Ingenieurbüro für Haustechnik KEM GmbH, Berlin (building services)
TRANSSOLAR Energietechnik GmbH, Stuttgart (energy technology)
Müller-BBM GmbH, Berlin (building services)
Lützow 7 Garten- und Landschaftsarchitekten, Berlin (open space planning)
Lichtvision Design & Engeneering, Berlin (lightning design)
Carsten Nicolai, Berlin / Folke Hanfeld Berlin (art)

Section detail

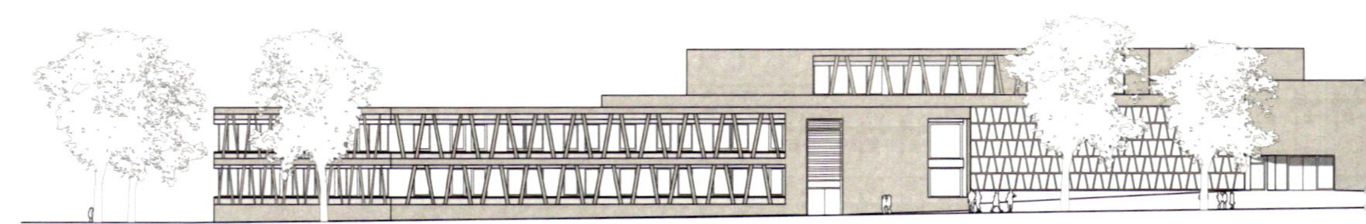

Elevation

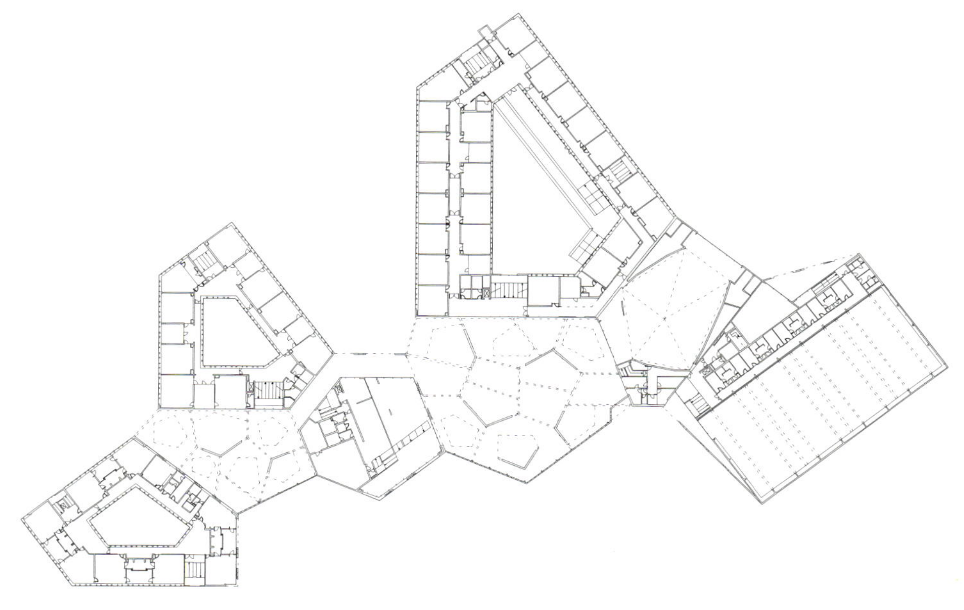

1st floor

Ground floor

Armand Grüntuch
Architect BDA, born 1963 in Riga (Latvia)

Diploma in Architecture with special award at RWTH Aachen; DAAD-scholarship in Venice Istituto Universitario di Architettura.
1987–89 in the office of Norman Foster, London; since 1991 office in Berlin with Almut Grüntuch-Ernst. Academic teachings and lectures in Architecture, Design and Construction at renowned universities in Germany and abroad, including Universität der Künste, Berlin; Kunstakademie Düsseldorf, Bezalel Academy of Arts and Design in Jerusalem, Israel; Penn University in Philadelphia, USA, as well as participation in conferences and symposia including Palma de Mallorca (Architectural Association NRW), Santiago de Chile (Expo Allemania), London (Goethe-Institut) and New York (Center for Architecture). Regular participation as chair or member in national and international juries. Commissioner of the German Contribution for the 10th International Architecture Exhibition, Venice Biennale, 2006.

Almut Grüntuch-Ernst
Architect BDA, RIBA, born 1966 in Stuttgart

Diploma in Architecture and Urban Development at Universität Stuttgart; DAAD-Scholarship in London at the Architectural Association.
1988–89 in the office of Alsop & Lyall, London; since 1991 office in Berlin with Armand Grüntuch. Academic teachings and lectures in Architecture, Design and Construction at renowned universities in Germany and abroad, including Universität der Künste, Berlin, Kunstakademie Düsseldorf, Bezalel Academy of Arts and Design in Jerusalem, Israel, Penn University in Philadelphia, USA, as well as participation in conferences and symposia including Palma de Mallorca (Architectural Association NRW), Kuala Lumpur (Asia Design Forum), London (Goethe-Institut), Berlin (Bundesministerium für Wirtschaft und Technologie) and Israel (Women Festival Holon). Regular participation as chair or member in national and international juries. Commissioner of the German Contribution for the 10th International Architecture Exhibition, Venice Biennale, 2006. Since 2010 member of the consultant committee for town planning in Munich. Since 2011 chair of the Institute of Design & Architectural Strategies at TU Braunschweig.

Ilka Ruby
Architect, born 1969 in Gießen
Andreas Ruby
Architecture historian, born 1966 in Dresden

Foundation of *textbild,* an agency for architecture communication in 2001 and of the publishing house RUBY PRESS in 2008.
Publications include *Re-inventing Construction,* Berlin, 2010; *Riegler Riewe. The depth of the surface,* Berlin 2009; EM2N. Both And, Zurich, 2009.
Curatorial work includes the exhibitions Druot, Lacaton & Vassal at DAM (Deutsches Architekturmuseum) in Frankfurt and DAZ (Deutsches Architektur Zentrum) in Berlin, 2012/2013 or *Machen!* An exhibition about the prizewinning German projects of the Holcim Award 2011/2012 at Aedes architectural forum, Berlin.
Academic teachings and lectures in Theory of Architecture and Design at many renowned universities including Cornell University, École Polytechnique Fédérale de Lausanne; École Nationale Supérieure d'Architecture de Paris; Universitat Politècnica de Catalunya in Barcelona; Technische Universität Graz; Universität der Künste, Berlin and Peter Behrens School of Architecture Düsseldorf.

Current

Erik Behrends
Florian Fels
Arno Löbbecke
Olaf Menk
Dirk Nachtsheim
Dominik Queck
Jens Schoppe
Jost von Fritschen
Mar Ballesteros
Tina Balzereit
Benjamin Bühs
Ulrike Gardeler
Kristina Herresthal
Götz Hinrichsen
Andreas Hoppe
Markus Lassan
Jaime Promewongse
Stefan Schenk
Karsten Schuch
Christoph Schubert
Daniel Strassburger
Robert Tesch
Anna Rose Wolska
Victor Casado
Matthias Cremer
Max Kaske
Dorith Landwehr
Elena Martínez del Pozo
Victoria Monari
Freia Stieger
Clémence Touzet

Conny Pergande
Elke Stamm
Brigitte Haas
Sabine Trappe-Roesler
Ekkehard Endruweit

1992–2013

Tobias Ahlers
Andreas Ammon
Alexis Angelis
Gregor Arlt
Elke Atanassow
Miriam Baehrens
Cristina Baixauli Garcia
Robert Banovic
Katja Barthmuss
Nicola Baumann
Karl Baumgart
Ingo Beckmann
Andrea Berghoff
Johannes Bernhardt
Katrin Bertsch
Florian Beyer
Thomas Birk
Johannes Blechschmidt
Silke Blechschmidt
Florian Böhm
Hagen Brandt
Nora Brinkmann
Ulli Bucher
Janine Burdack
Pascale Busch
Miguel Carrilho Branco
Esther-Maria Charles
Andreas Cormann
Janina Cornelius
André Debus
Holger Deppe
Carolin Döpfer
Hana Draskovic
Marc Drewes
Andrea Ehlert
Thomas Ellinghaus
Richard Emge
Beate Engelhorn
Tristan Ernst
Benjamin Falch
Sybille Fanelsa
Eleonora Fassina
Lukas Feireiss
Jon Celestino Ferrer
Björn Fiedler
Sebastian Finke
Anja Fischer
Alessio Fossati
Birgit Franz
Peter Friedrich
Martin Fuchs
Stefanie Gaasch
Philipp Gantenbrink
Sigrid Gaubert
Catharina Gebel
Christian Daniel Geyer
Ulrich P. Goertz
Claudia Große-Hartlage
Markus Gröteke
Isabell Gruchot
Christoph Haag
Bernd Haller
Kai Hansen
Helen Hart
Mark Hartz
Hermann Sebastian Hauser
Arnd Hawlina
Dennis Hawner
Bianca Hejl
Julia Naomi Henning
Claudia Herrmann
Anne Christine Heucke
Hannes Heyer
Sandra Hirseland
Andrea Höpfner
Ralf Huber
Kristin Hulzer
Alexander Huston
Rémi Jalade
Heinz Jirout
Stefan John
Rebeca Juárez
Alexander Kader
Tobias Klein
Sonja Killat
Annegret Kirchner
Lisa Knoll
Olaf Koeppen
Sergej Kolessov
Sebastian Kordowich
Jakob Kortemeier
Martin Helge Koschlig
Miriam-Sylvelin Kotte
F. J. Johan Krol
Julian Krüger
Bernd Lampe
Stefan Laub
Tom Lazar
Meike Lenfers
Sandy Lindner
Kai Arne Löper
René Lotz
Felix Lupatsch
Andri Gunnar Lyngberg
Arnd Manzewski
Arun Markus
Vera Martinez
Maren Mengert
Peter-René Menken
Nicolas Morales
Steven Morgan
Annika Müller
Mareike Münstermann
Birthe Nagel
Eva Nagl
Andreas Nemetz
Hugo Neto
Thomas Neumüller
Thiele Nickau
Michel Obladen
Richard Owers
Ulrike Pabel
Jana Patzer
Bettina Paucke
Anni Peller
Sophie Peters
Dominika Plümpe
Maike Pohl
Dorothea Pollok
Volker Raatz
Axel Rahmstorf
Johannes Raible
Jemima Retallack
Amir Rothkegel
Johannes Rueb
Jan Rützel
Tina Schelz
Alexander Schierbaum
Matthias Schirrmacher
Mareike Schlatow
Guido Schmidt
Sebastian Schmidt
Fabian Schmitz
Saskia Schneider
Roland Schreiber
Hans-Christoph Schultz
Beate Schwabe
Barbara Senepart
Jan Skuratowski
Jea-Woan Son
Maren Sostmann
Ines Spitzner
Gernot Stangl
Caroline Steinchen
Martin Sulzbach
Sabine Tastel
Stefan Tebroke
Kerstin Thomsen
Sven Abe Tjalma
Jakob Ulbrych
Caro van de Venne
Jacob van Ommen
Julius von Holst
Barbara von Raffay
Ina Vössing
Mark Wachendorfer
Oliver Walkiewicz
Ivonne Weichold
Tanja Werner
Florian Wiedey
Henning Wiethaus
Finn Wilkie
Julia Wolter
Sebastian José Zell
Rose-Marie Zimmermann
Dirk Zimmermann

Consultants

Amstein + Walthert, Zürich

Arup GmbH, Planer und Ingenieure, London/Berlin

Battle McCarthy Consulting Engineers, London

Brendel Ingenieure AG, Berlin

EGS-plan Ingenieurgesellschaft für Energie-, Gebäude- und Solartechnik mbH, Stuttgart

Freie Planungsgruppe Berlin GmbH, Berlin

GTB-Berlin, Gesellschaft für Technik am Bau mbH, Berlin

GuD Consult GmbH, Berlin

Folke Hanfeld, Berlin

Happold Consulting Engineers Ltd., Bath/Berlin

HHP Berlin, Ingenieure für Brandschutz GmbH, Berlin

HL-Technik Engineering Partner GmbH, München/Berlin

ifb Ingenieurbüro für Bauwesen, Berlin

IBT Ingenieurbüro für Tragwerksplanung GmbH & Co. KG, Mannheim

Horsch Planungsgesellschaft bR, Berlin

HTW, Hetzel, Tor-Westen + Partner Ingenieurgesellschaft mbH & Co. KG

Hussak Ingenieurgesellschaft mbH, Lauingen

Ingenieurbüro Dr.-Ing. Binnewies, Hamburg

Ingenieurgesellschaft Ridder und Meyn mbH, Berlin

Ingenieurbüro Krone, Berlin

Kardoff Ingenieure Lichtplanung GmbH, Berlin

KBP Kühn Bauer Partner, Hallbergmoos

Ingenieurbüro für Haustechnik KEM GmbH, Berlin

Ingenieurgesellschaft Lachmann-Dominok mbH, Oelsnitz

Prof. Dr. Hansjürg Leibundgut, Zürich

Leonhardt, Andrä und Partner, GmbH, Berlin

Levin Monsigny Gesellschaft von Landschaftsarchitekten mbH, Berlin

Licht Kunst Licht AG, Bonn
Lichtvision Design & Engineering GmbH, Berlin

Lützow 7 Garten- und Landschaftsarchitekten, Berlin

Müller BBM GmbH, Berlin

Schlaich Bergermann & Partner, Stuttgart, Berlin

Schüßler-Plan Ingenieurgesellschaft mbH, Düsseldorf

Topotek 1 Gesellschaft von Landschaftsarchitekten mbH, Berlin

Transsolar Energietechnik GmbH, Stuttgart

Service Engineer Ingenieurbüro Weltzer, Berlin

Publications (selection)

architektur aktuell
"'Höfe am Brühl', Leipzig, Deutschland – Ein Stück Singapur mitten in Leipzig", Ulf Meyer, 01/13

vdaw-online.org
"Westerwelle legt Grundstein für Deutsche Schule Madrid", 04.02.13

EL PAIS
"El Colegio Alemán invertirá 56 millones", 24.01.13

EL PAIS
"El Colegio Alemán se va a Montecarmelo", 24.01.13

DBZ Deutsche BauZeitschrift
"Kochen und Kunst statt Sport und Unterricht – Ehemalige Jüdische Mädchenschule, Berlin", 18.01.13

Self Made City Berlin – Stadtgestaltung und Wohnprojekte in Eigeninitiative
"August 51", Kristien Ring (ed.), Jovis Verlag, Berlin 01/13

DBZ Deutsche BauZeitschrift
"Bestand als Ressource für die Zukunft", 01/13

ELLE
"Townhouse in Berlin", Alexander Bartl, 01/13

Südwest Presse
"Ringen am Sedelhof", Hans-Uli Thierer, 23.11.12

baunetz.de
"Höfe am Brühl – Einkaufszentrum in Leipzig von Grüntuch Ernst Architekten", 10.10.12

Leipziger Volkszeitung
"Höfe am Brühl: Leipzigs modernstes Einkaufscenter öffnet heute", Kerstin Decker/ Jens Rometsch, 25.09.12

Freie Presse Chemnitz
"Eine Fassade wie an der Allianz-Arena", Grit Baldauf, 11.09.12

Augsburger Allgemeine
"Auftakt für die Sedelhöfe – Im September beginnen die Abbrucharbeiten in der Keltergasse", Michael Ruddigkeit, 31.08.12

Bauwelt
"Kaminzimmer mit Schlossblick – Schinkelplatz Berlin", Nikolaus Bernau, 08/12

Baumeister
"Befruchtung!", Stimmungsbild zur Frage: 'Brauchen wir noch Biennalen?', Armand Grüntuch, 08/12

AIT
"EAT + ART – Umbau der Jüdischen Mädchenschule zu einem Haus für Kunst und Esskultur", Uwe Bresan, 06/12

wettbewerbe aktuell
"Deutsche Schule Madrid", 06/12

marereise HAMBURG
"Im Hafen (nichts) Neues", Till Briegleb, 06/12

Bauwelt
"Vorhang auf! – Kunst am Bau für die Deutsche Schule", Dorothea Külbel, 06/12

Augsburger Allgemeine
"Sedelhöfe: Ulms neues Stadtviertel", Oliver Helmstädter, 21.05.12

Frankfurter Allgemeine Zeitung
"Es geht ja doch ein Leuchten in die Zukunft", Frank Peter Jäger, 03.05.12

sz-online.de
"Die Rückkehr der Blechbüchse", Sven Heitkamp, 02.05.12

Baumeister
"Vorher/Nachher – Ehemalige Jüdische Mädchenschule, Berlin-Mitte", Frank Peter Jäger, 05/12

DBZ Deutsche BauZeitschrift
"Kunsthandel statt Kunstunterricht – Umbau der ehemaligen Jüdischen Mädchenschule in Berlin", Frank Peter Jäger, 05/12

db deutsche bauzeitung
"Klassenfest", Jürgen Tietz, 05/12

Südwest Presse
"Einstimmig für Sedelhöfe", Jakob Resch/ Hans-Uli Thierer, 26.04.12

wettbewerbe aktuell
"Museums- und Kulturforum Südwestfalen in Arnsberg", 04/12

Berliner Zeitung
"Aufeinander bauen", Stephan J. Bultmann, 20.03.12

stylepark.com
"Das Stadthaus als Heilmittel", Heinrich Wefing, 15.03.12

The New York Times
"New Chapter for Berlin School", Rachel B. Doyle, 09.03.12

dbz.de
"Schweger & Partner bauen für ThyssenKrupp", 03/12

Sauerland Kurier
"Das wird Arnsberg aufwerten – Architekturwettbewerb zur Museums-Erweiterung in vollem Gang", Gaby Decker, 26.02.12

kunstmarkt.de
"Ein neues Herz für Mitte", 10.02.12

zibb
"Eröffnung Mädchenschule", rbb Rundfunk Berlin-Brandenburg, 09.02.12

art-in-berlin
"Neueröffnung der ehemaligen Jüdischen Mädchenschule", 07.02.12

SPIEGEL online
"Haus für ‚Kunst und Esskultur' – Warhol und Pastrami to go", Ingeborg Wiensowski, 07.02.12

baunetz.de
"In der Zeitmaschine – Jüdische Mädchenschule in Berlin umgebaut", 07.02.12

Stilbruch – Das Kulturmagazin
"Jüdische Mädchenschule soll zur Galerie werden", Julia Riedhammer, rbb Rundfunk Berlin-Brandenburg, 02.02.12

wettbewerbe aktuell
"Neubau Wissenquartier 'Intelligent Quarters' (IQ), Hafencity Hamburg", 02/12

wettbewerbe aktuell
"ThyssenKrupp-Haus Berlin", 02/12

Der Tagesspiegel
"Am Schlossplatz ist der Würfel gefallen", Ralf Schönball, 27.01.12

Bauwelt
"Der Konzern am Schlossplatz – ThyssenKrupp-Haus in Berlin", Dieter Hoffmann-Axthelm/Heiko Haberle, 01/12

baunetz.de
"ThyssenKrupp-Haus – Schweger gewinnt am Berliner Schlossplatz", 27.01.12

Berliner Morgenpost
"In der Jüdischen Mädchenschule eröffnet das Kunsthaus", GW, 12.01.12

Berliner Woche
"Immobilienpreis für Marthashof", 04.01.12

Handbuch und Planungshilfe Stadthäuser
"Stadthäuser als Ensembles; Mehrfamilienhäuser in Baulücken; Bauteilkatalog", Hans Stimmann, DOM publishers, Berlin 11/11

Baumeister
"Architekten. Vorkommen. Haltung. Vermehrung", Dr. Wolfgang Bachmann, 11/11

Berliner Morgenpost
"Neuling in Mitte", Isabell Jürgens, 16.10.11

ARCH+
"Fassaden – von Kaufhausschlössern und Schlosskaufhäusern", Cornelia Escher, 10/11

Chemnitzer Morgenpost
"Die tollste Schaustelle der ganzen Stadt", 10.09.11

baunetz.de
"Königshof an der Wilhelmstraße – Wettbewerbsentscheidung in Berlin", 05.08.11

VMS mobil
"Das Chemnitzer Modell entwickelt sich", 06/11

stylepark.com
"Wohnhaussiedlung Marthashof", 05.04.11

Baumeister
"T-Shirt und Zweireiher? Drei Lückenschließungen in Berlin", Falk Jaeger, 04/11

ARCH+
"Urban Villages – Ein Reisebericht über die Suche nach dem Berliner Townhouse", Tim Rieniets, 03/11

wettbewerbe aktuell
"Quartier am Mailänder Platz in Stuttgart", 03/11

wettbewerbe aktuell
"Science Park Center Kassel", 02/11

Welt am Sonntag
"Die hohe Schule der Kunst", Julia Siepmann, 30.01.11

Stuttgarter Nachrichten
"Hinter dem Bahnhof entsteht ein Luxushochhaus", Konstantin Schwarz, 20.01.11

artnet.de
"Ein Kunsthaus für die Auguststraße", Marcus Woeller, 10.01.11

Berliner Zeitung
"Zwischennutzung für 30 Jahre", Ingeborg Ruthe, 08.01.11

baunetz.de
"Alte Ziegelei. Wettbewerb in Speyer entschieden", 03.01.11

kassel.de
"Wettbewerb für Science Park Center Kassel entschieden", Stadtverwaltung Kassel, 23.11.10

wettbewerbe aktuell
"Europa-Viertel in Freiburg", 10/10

wettbewerbe aktuell
"Deutsche Botschaft in Maskat, Oman", 09/10

wettbewerbe aktuell
"Fachbereich Gestaltung der Folkwang Universität in Essen", 09/10

Leipziger Volkszeitung
"Baustart für 'Höfe am Brühl'", Klaus Staeubert, 25.08.10

Bauwelt
"Klimafragen – Kanzlei und Residenz der Deutschen Botschaft Maskat", Friederike Meyer, 08/10

db deutsche bauzeitung
"Stadt, Haus, Dorf", Carsten Sauerbrei, 08/10

ZDF Exportschlager Architektur
"Deutsche Bauten in Spanien", Claudius Gehr, ZDF Zweites Deutsches Fernsehen, 24.07.10

Leipziger Volkszeitung
"Zwischen Altlast und Denkmal", Andreas Friedrich, 25.06.10

Die Zeit
"Dornröschen und viel Blech", Erich Loest, 02.06.10

welt.de
"Alles nur Fassade", Dankwart Guratzsch, 22.05.10

sz-online.de
"Ende im Streit um Leipziger Blechbüchse in Sicht", 19.05.10

BILD Leipzig
"Die Brühl-Fassade soll hinter Glas", 14.05.10

Der Tagesspiegel
"Ich war eine Büchse", Jürgen Tietz, 02.05.10

faz.net
"Ein zweites Leben für die 'Blechbüchse'", Steffen Uttich, 29.03.10

Berliner Zeitung
"Visionen Raum geben", Jan Ahrenberg, 27.03.10

Frankfurter Allgemeine Zeitung
"Welche Geschichte hätten's denn gern? Leipziger Denkmaldebakel", Arnold Bartetzky, 19.03.10

Oranienburger Generalanzeiger
"Das schönste Haus", 12.03.10

taz. die tageszeitung
"Preis für schmuckes Reihenhäuschen", 12.03.10

Maja (Estonia)
"Berlini ehitusühingud: kogukonnad siselinnas – Berliner Baugruppe: Building Neighbourhoods in the inner-city", Kristien Ring, 03/10

Deutsches Architektenblatt
"Urbane Reihen und dörfliche Höfe", Andreas K. Vetter, 03/10

Handelsblatt
"Innenstadt schlägt grüne Wiese", Handelsblatt Redaktion, 19.02.10

tab.de
"Das 'Brillissimo' in Bremen – Vom 60er-Jahre-Kaufhaus zur begehrten Gewerbeimmobilie", Ralf Dunker, 02/10

HÄUSER
"Adlernest über der City", 02/10

wettbewerbe aktuell
"Ausbildungszentrum der Versuchs- und Lehranstalt für Brauerei, Berlin", 02/10

HÄUSER
"Die besten Häuser von heute", Häuser, 02/10

Architekturführer Berlin-Mitte
"Spandauer Vorstadt", Dorothee Dubrau, 01/10

ELLE Decoration
"Interior Monologue", Cheryl Freedman, 01/10

baunetz.de
"Wohnungsbau am Mauerpark. Architekturpreis Berlin vergeben", 02.11.09

Der Tagesspiegel
"Fassade mit vielen Augen", Falk Jaeger, 01.11.09

wettbewerbe aktuell
"Forschungszentrum für Maschinenbau und Informatik der TU Berlin", 10/09

bmvbs.de
"Lütke Daldrup: 'Neubau der Deutschen Schule Madrid ist wichtiges Projekt für die Präsentation Deutschland im Ausland'", Bundesministerium für Verkehr, Bau und Stadtentwicklung, 15.09.09

baunetz.de
"Organische Figur – Deutsche Schule in Madrid entschieden", 14.09.09

Build-On
"Grüntuch Ernst Architekten – Convertible City", Lukas Feireiss/Robert Klanten (eds.), Die Gestalten Verlag, Berlin 09/09

Deutsches Architektenblatt
"Kann man gute Noten bauen?", Thomas C. Dehmel, 09/09

Bauwelt
"Deutsche Schule Madrid", Friederike Meyer, 09/09

wettbewerbe aktuell
"Deutsche Schule Madrid", 09/09

detail.de
"'Mehr Mitte geht nicht' – Hackesches Quartier in Berlin", Marion Dondelinger, 03.08.09

Deutsches Architektenblatt
"Unreif für die Insel?", Claas Gefroi, 08/09

baunetz.de
"Neues Zentrum am Hackeschen Markt Richtfest in Berlin", 24.07.09

phase eins – Die Architektur von Wettbewerben 2006–2008
"Grüntuch Ernst Architekten Berlin", Benjamin Hossbach/Christian Lehmhaus, 22.06.09

Architektur Berlin 09
"Die Stadt im Dorf lassen – Die neue Gemütlichkeit erobert die Kieze", Uwe Rada, Architektenkammer Berlin (ed.), 06/09

typologie +
"Wohnbebauung Monbijou in Berlin", Peter Ebner/Eva Hermann/Roman Höllbacher/ Markus Kuntscher/Ulrike Wietzorrek, Birkhäuser Verlag, Berlin 05/09

Lübecker Nachrichten
"LN-Kommentar: Mutig, aber gut!", Sebastian Prey, 17.04.09

Lübecker Nachrichten
"Umstritten: Lübecks neuer Blickfang", Sebastian Prey, 17.04.09

baunetz.de
"Vernunft für die Welt – Manifest zur UN-Klima-Konferenz", 23.03.09

Baumeister
"Ein Faible für schwierige Aufgaben", Bernhard Schulz, 03/09

ELLE DECOR Italia
"INTERNI SOFT A LUCE NATURALE", 03/09

maerkischeallgemeine.de
"Am Kreisgymnasium in Dallgow-Döberitz wird im August das zweite Schulhaus eröffnet", Ulrike Klefert, 23.02.09

wettbewerbe aktuell
"Höfe am Brühl", 02/09

europaconcorsi.com
"La 'Deutsche Schule' di Madrid", 15.01.09

Bau und Raum – Jahrbuch 2009/10
"Deutsche Schule Madrid", Bundesamt für Bauwesen und Raumordnung, Junius Verlag, Hamburg 01/09

Baukultur
"Spiegel gesellschaftlichen Wandels", Werner Durth, Paul Siegel, Jovis Verlag, Berlin 01/09

Berliner BDA Architekten Band II
"Berliner BDA Architekten Band 2", Bund Deutscher Architekten Landesverband Berlin (ed.), Jovis Verlag, Berlin 12/08

baunetz.de
"Offene Optionen Wettbewerb in Stuttgart entschieden", 31.10.08

Rakennuslehti (Finland)
"Berliiniin nousee uuden sukupolven kaupunkikiylä", Tarja Nurmi, 16.10.08

Stuttgarter Zeitung
"Hochhaus für ein Hotel oder Wohnungen", Thomas Borgmann, 15.10.08

Die Welt
"Stadthäuser an künstlichem See", Isabell Jürgens, 10.10.08

Der Tagesspiegel
"Wohnen am See auf der Truman Plaza", Cay Dobberke, 08.10.08

AD Architectural Digest
"Die deutsche Schule", Christian Welzbacher, 10/08

AD Architectural Digest
"Radikal Vertikal", Ilka Piepgras, 10/08

Berliner Zeitung
"Schlanke Individualisten", Lea Sophie Lukas, 01.10.08

Berliner Abendblatt
"Grundstein gelegt – Neue Wohnhäuser in Schwedter Straße", bri, 27.09.08

Süddeutsche Zeitung
"Frischzellenkur für Innenstädte", Peter Horn, 26.09.08

Freie Presse Chemnitz
"Architekten kommentieren ihr Werk", Sandra Czabania, 26.09.08

Leipziger Volkszeitung
"Wir haben die Einheit und die Geschichte des Baus betont – Bürgermeister Martin zur Nedden über die alte Brühl-Fassade, LWB und Markthalle", Jens Rometsch, 18.09.08

Berliner Zeitung
"Eine Kultur des Besonderen", Jan Ahrenberg, 06.09.08

Welt am Sonntag
"Berlins Angst vor der Moderne", Isabell Jürgens, 10.08.08

Hannoversche Allgemeine Zeitung
"Klimaschutz beginnt im Boden", 01.10.08

Deutsches Architektenblatt
"Architektur und Kommerz", Ingeborg Wiensowski, 08/08

Berliner Morgenpost
"Die teuersten Adressen in Deutschland", 21.07.08

baunetz.de
"Dallgower Tor und Marie Curie – Grüntuch Ernst bauen im Havelland", 15.07.08

Märkische Allgemeine
"Curie-Architekten bauen den neuen Dallgower Ortseingang", Oliver Fischer, 11.07.08

Welt am Sonntag, Berlin
"Mehr Glanz für die Hauptstadt", Isabell Jürgens, 08.06.08

Der Tagesspiegel
"Luxuswohnen am Mauerpark", Elisabeth Binder, 01.06.08

welt.de
"Berlin bekommt ein Dorf für Reiche in der Stadt", Isabell Jürgens, 24.05.08

baunetz.de
"Hackesches Quartier – Lückenschluss in Berlin-Mitte", 20.05.08

sz-online.de
"Bauausschuss war Bahnhof gucken – In vier Monaten geht der große Umbau los", Anke Schröck, 07.05.08

Betoni (Finland)
"Talo Usealle Sukupolvelle Berliinissä 5", Tarja Nurmi, 03/08

Collection AnArchitecture – Maisons sur l'eau
"Maisons flottantes. Architecture amphibie", Véronique Willemin, Editions alternatives 2008, Paris 02/08

Die Welt
"Letzte große Baulücke in Berlins historischer Mitte wird geschlossen", Isabell Jürgens, 30.01.08

Süddeutsche Zeitung
"Mit Gärten gekrönter Konsumtempel", Hannes Leonard, 18.01.08

Stadt und Haus – Neue Berlinische Architektur im 21. Jahrhundert
"Geschäftshaus in der Leipziger Straße, 2007", Philipp Meuser/Fried Nielsen, DOM publishers, Berlin 01/08

Lufthansa exclusive
"Haus ahoi", Marc Winkelmann, 01/08

Baumeister
"Wettbewerbsentscheidung zur Leipziger Brühlbebauung – Vorhaben bleibt umstritten", nj, 01/08

Architecture of Change, Sustainability and Humanity in the Built Environment
"Marie Curie High School", Kristin Feireiss / Lukas Feireiss (eds.), Die Gestalten Verlag, Berlin 01/08

db deutsche bauzeitung
"Kann eine Shopping-Mall stadtverträglich sein?", Arnold Bartetzky, 01/08

BZ
"Schlaf gut, müder Messe-Gast", Konstantin Marrach, 08.12.07

Der Tagesspiegel
"Spanischer Investor plant Hotelturm am Messegelände", Cay Dobberke, 07.12.07

baunetz.de
"Turm am ICC – Hotelneubau in Berlin geplant", 07.12.07

Bauwelt
"Neubebauung am Leipziger Brühl", Friederike Meyer, 11/07

Süddeutsche Zeitung
"Das tiefe C", Günter Kowa, 21.11.07

Die Welt
"Shopping-Center kehren zurück in die City", rhai, 08.11.07

baunetz.de
"Brühl-Arcaden – Grüntuch Ernst bauen Einkaufszentrum in Leipzig", 07.11.07

Frankfurter Allgemeine Zeitung
"Die Zähmung des Monsters: Leipzig reißt die Brühl-Hochhäuser ab", Arnold Bartetzky, 07.11.07

Space Craft
"Convertible City", Lukas Feireiss/Robert Klanten (eds.), Die Gestalten Verlag, Berlin 09/07

arclife.de
"Sommerwettbewerb Stadt im Wandel", 24.07.07

wirtschaftsblatt.at
"Der Traum vom schwimmenden Haus", Kathrin Gulnerits, 24.07.07

Süddeutsche Zeitung
"Blühende Häuser", Christian Welzbacher, 27.06.07

INSIDE – Interiors of Concrete Stone Wood
"Residential and commercial building, Monbijouplatz, Berlin", Sibylle Kramer/ Iris van Hülst, Verlagshaus Braun, Salenstein, Switzerland 06/07

INSIDE – Interiors of Colour Fabric Glass Light
"Residential and commercial building, Hackescher Markt, Berlin", Sibylle Kramer/ Iris van Hülst, Verlagshaus Braun, Salenstein, Switzerland 06/07

Ausstellungskatalog NEU BAU LAND
"Marie-Curie-Gymnasium, Dallgow-Döberitz", Ernst A. Busche/Oliver G. Hamm/Peter Cachola Schmal/Wolfgang Voigt (eds.), E.A. Seemann Verlag, Leipzig 06/07

Frankfurter Allgemeine Zeitung
"Investoren haben Bremen im Visier", Hans-Jörg Werth, 25.05.07

AREA
"Convertible City. Modalitá di addensamento e dissolvimento dei confini", 04/07

Stern
"Zurück in die Stadt", Sven Rohde, 03/07

Plan
"Die Stadtverbesserer", Britta Nagel, 03/07

Entwurfsatlas Schulen und Kindergärten
"Marie-Curie-Gymnasium", Mark Dudek, Birkhäuser Verlag, Basel 03/07

wettbewerbe aktuell
"Hotelneubau Bredenplatz Bremen", 03/07

H.O.M.E
"Haus-Frauen", Silke Bender, 01/07

FOCUS Schule
"Baustoff Phantasie", Focus Schule, 01/07

Nauja Statyba (Latvia)
"Gimnazijoje visad sauleta", Aida Stelbiene, 12/06

de Architect (The Netherlands)
"Kleuren als potentie/Meerwaarde in de periferie", Claus Käpplinger, 12/06

Detail
"Gymnasium in Dallgow-Döberitz", 12/06

baunetz.de
"Brillissimo. Bremer Stadtdialog mit Grüntuch Ernst", 27.10.06

architektur aktuell
"Grüntuch Ernst Architekten, Polyvalenz in der Peripherie", Claus Käpplinger, 10/06

Frankfurter Allgemeine Zeitung
"Der kalte Herbst der Menschheit", Dieter Bartetzko, 14.09.06

Frankfurter Rundschau
"Das Venedig Protokoll", Reinhart Wustlich, 12.09.06

Berliner Morgenpost
"Unter den Großen ist Berlin klein", Reiner Haubrich, 12.09.06

Welt am Sonntag
"Planen nach Zahlen", Christian Tröster, 10.09.06

Frankfurter Allgemeine Zeitung
"Hauptsache Flachbildschirm", Peter Richter, 10.09.06

Der Tagesspiegel
"Die Stadt ist die Mitte", Bernhard Schulz, 09.09.06

Süddeutsche Zeitung
"Hier wird nichts weniger als die Zukunft der Welt verhandelt", Gerhard Matzig, 09.09.06

Der Tagesspiegel
"Mit dem Badeschiff nach Venedig", Matthias Oloew, 08.09.06

Süddeutsche Zeitung
"Der überfällige Abschied von der grünen Wiese", Frank Thinius, 04.09.06

ARCH+
Catalogue "Convertible City", Armand Grüntuch, Almut Grüntuch-Ernst (guest ed.), 09/06

Deutsches Architektenblatt
"Architekturbiennale Venedig", 01.09.06

build – Das Architekten-Magazin
"Convertible City", Ralf F. Broekman/Olaf Winkler, 08/06

Der Spiegel
"Ich liebe unperfekte Städte", Susanne Beyer, 31.07.06

Westfälische Rundschau
"Die Verwandlung", Michael Braun, 29.07.06

Der Tagesspiegel
"Fliegende Gärten", Jürgen Tietz, 18.07.06

QVEST
"Bauen in Zweisamkeit", 07–08/06

Deutsches Architektenblatt
"Convertible City. Deutscher Pavillon in Venedig", Claudia Schwalfenberg, 01.07.06

Süddeutsche Zeitung
"Im Zeitalter der Städte", Frank Thinius, 09.06.06

baunetz.de
"Convertible City", 02.06.06

baunetz.de
"Neun Freunde", 12.05.06

wettbewerbe aktuell
"Fördehotel Ballastkai 1, Flensburg", 04/06

Süddeutsche Zeitung
"Das Buch zum Bau", Sandra Hofmeister, 15.03.06

aiany.org/eOCULUS
"Dereliction Connects NYC to Berlin", Scott Jardine, 07.03.06

baunetz.de – AppleTalk
"Apple Talk – Grüntuch Ernst Architekten", Benedikt Hotze, 03/06

Baumeister
"Meta City", 02/06

AIT
"Forever young", 02/06

Flensburger Tageblatt
"Bürgerversammlung diskutiert Hotelprojekt am Hafen", 28.01.06

Deutschlandradio
"Neue Kuratoren des Deutschen Pavillons", Carsten Probst, 03.01.06

Pläne Projekte Bauten – Architektur und Städtebau in Hamburg 2005 bis 2015
"Neumühlen 13–15, Bürogebäude am Elbufer", Jörn Walter (ed.), Verlagshaus Braun, Salenstein, Switzerland 01/06

Kunstzeitung
"Grüntuch Ernst Architekten: Venedig ruft", Falk Jaeger, 01/06

baunetz.de
"Stadt als sozialer Raum", 19.12.05

db deutsche bauzeitung
"Biennale Venedig: Deutscher Beitrag zum Thema Stadtentwicklung", 12/05

DBZ Deutsche BauZeitschrift
"Zu zweit in Venedig", 12/05

atd architecture, technology & design
"Designed to 'Cheer up Pupils and Teachers on a Grey-sky Day'", Conray Zhong (ed.), 12/05

AIT
"Architekturbiennale 2006", Ascan Tesdorpf, 12/05

Lebendige Stadt Journal
"Neue Sportstätten: Multifunktional und flexibel", Christiane Harriehausen, 12/05

Kultur Spiegel
"Vitalität in den Zentren", Ingeborg Wiensowski, 12/05

german-architects.com
"Bau der Woche, Konzept Landschaft, Qualität Architektur", Christian Holl, 11/05

Die Welt
"Betreten und Baggern erlaubt", Sabine Gundlach, 15.10.05

Ambientes
"Secundaria Marie Curie – Education creativa", Jeanette Plaut, 10/05

Bauen seit 1980 in Berlin
"Hackescher Markt 2–3, Monbijouplatz 3, Monbijouplatz 5", Rolf Rave, G+H Verlag, Berlin 10/05

CORPORATE ARCHITECTURE
"Corporate Architecture", Jons Messedat, Av Edition, Ludwigsburg 09/05

FOCUS Italia
"Palafitte del 3° millennio", 09/05

Baumeister
"Marie-Curie-Gymnasium in Dallgow-Döberitz – Grüntuch Ernst", Benedikt Hotze, 09/05

A10
"Off the beaten track", Christian Welzbacher, 09/05

Bürobau Atlas
"Bürogebäude am Elbufer, Hamburg", Johann Eisele, Bettina Staniek (eds.), 09/05

vivienda decoración
"La Apuesta Germana", Soledad Salgado S., 09/05

Casa Deco
"Architektur macht Schule", 09/05

wettbewerbe aktuell
"Aufstockung und Umbau der alten Kaufhalle in Bremen", 09/05

BILD
"6 Luftschlösser statt Stadtschlösser", Jan Rentzow, 14.07.05

Berliner Morgenpost
"Palast-Gelände als Minigolfparcours", Sabine Gundlach, 14.07.05

Frankfurter Allgemeine Zeitung
"Auf dem Berg der Republik", Niklas Maak, 10.07.05

Mobil - Das Magazin der Bahn
"Neue Welten auf dem Wasser", Werner W. Klingberg (ed.), 07/05

rbb Dokumentation
"'Da! Architektur'", Grit Lederer, rbb Rundfunk Berlin-Brandenburg, 06/05

Bauwelt
"Umbau der Kaufhalle am Brill", Olaf Bartels, 06/05

architektur aktuell
"Grüntuch Ernst Architekten, Nachrüstung im Speckgürtel", Robert Temel, 06/05

wettbewerbe aktuell
"Marie-Curie-Gymnasium in Dallgow-Döberitz", 06/05

Der Tagesspiegel
"Der Tresor liegt in Trümmern", oew/ling, 30.05.05

baunetz.de
"Grandiose Perspektiven, Wettbewerb für Kaufhalle in Bremen entschieden", 18.05.05

taz Bremen
"Glasfassade am Brill", Peter Kön, 12.05.05

Der Tagesspiegel
"Kunst am Baum", Susanne Kippenberger, 08.05.05

The New Premises of the European Central Bank
"Grüntuch/Ernst Architekten BDA, Berlin Germany", Peter Cachola Schmal/Ingeborg Flagge (eds.), Birkhäuser Verlag, Basel 05/05

Frei Otto – Das Gesamtwerk
"Leicht Bauen. Natürlich Gestalten.", Winfried Nerdinger, Architekturmuseum TU München, Birkhäuser Verlag, Basel 05/05

Water House
"Floating Homes, Berlin", Felix Flesche, Christian Burchard, Prestel Verlag, Munich 05/05

Architektur Berlin 05
"da! Architektur in und aus Berlin 2005", Gerwin Zohlen, Architektenkammer Berlin (ed.), Verlagshaus Braun, Salenstein, Switzerland 04/05

AD Architectural Digest
"Wer baut mit Gefühl?", Alexander Hosch, Wolfgang Stahr, 03/05

Bund Deutscher Architekten Berlin 2005
"Grüntuch Ernst Architekten", BDA (ed.), Jovis Verlag, 03/05

Berliner Morgenpost
"Nach der letzten Party kommt die Abrissbirne", Rainer L. Hein, 26.02.05

build – Das Architekten-Magazin
"Konkrete Sensibilität", Ralf F. Broekman, Olaf Winkler, 02/05

ZDF WISO Magazin
"Wohnen auf dem Wasser – Floating Houses", Bettina Blaß, 11/04

Architektur in Deutschland '03
"Bürohaus in Hamburg-Neumühlen", Werner Durth (ed.), Karl Krämer Verlag, Stuttgart 11/04

Der Tagesspiegel
"Angebote im Schlussverkauf", Ralf Schönball, 11.09.04

Architektur Berlin 04
"Berliner Architekten bauen anderswo: Grüntuch Ernst – Bürohaus in Hamburg", Amber Sayah, Architektenkammer Berlin (ed.), Verlagshaus Braun, Salenstein, Switzerland 09/04

AW Architektur + Wettbewerbe
"Ferienhäuser – Schwimmende Häuser", 09/04

Grüntuch Ernst Architects – Points of Access
"Points of Access", Grüntuch Ernst, Kristin Feireiss (eds.), Prestel Verlag, Munich 09/04

Deutschlandschaften – Epizentren der Peripherie
"Floating Homes", Deutscher Pavillon Biennale Venedig 2004, Hatje Cantz Verlag, Ostfildern 09/04

werk, bauen+wohnen
"Hafenpolis", Klaus-Dieter Weiss, 07/04

wettbewerbe aktuell
"Studentenwohnungen am Stiftsbogen, München", 05/04

Schulen in Deutschland – Neubau und Revitalisierung
"Schule am Mummelsoll", Wüstenrot Stiftung, Karl Krämer Verlag, Stuttgart 05/04

JAM Das Büchermagazin Ausgabe 01/04
"Der offene Blick", Enja Jans, Boris Kagelmann, 04/04

Fassaden – Gebäudehüllen für das 21. Jahrhundert
"Office Building Hamburg, Neumühlen", Dirk U. Hinrichs/Winfried Heusler (eds.), Birkhäuser Verlag, Basel 04/04

GLAS Architektur und Technik
"Bürohaus Oranienburger Straße Berlin", 04/04

db deutsche bauzeitung
"Balthasar-Neumann-Preis 2004, Engere Wahl – Bürohaus Neumühlen", 03/04

Floating Berlin – New Architecture along the Waterfront
"Floating Home", Philipp Meuser/ Shussev Museum for Architecture, Moscow, 03/04

Wallpaper Navigator
"World View – Berlin", Sophie Lovell, 03/04

Süddeutsche Zeitung
"Schwimmende Domizile in der Stadt", 11.02.04

wettbewerbe aktuell
"Schule am Mummelsoll, Berlin", 02/04

DBZ Junge Architekten Januar 2004
"Im Rückblick", Bauverlag, 01/04

Umrisse
"Die Neubauten am Monbijouplatz, die Humbodt-Höfe", 11/03

rbb Sendereihe Stadt, Land, Fluss
"Rund um den Hackeschen Markt", Grit Lederer, rbb Berlin, 21.10.03

Die Welt
"Eine Stadt verändert ihr Gesicht", Gisela Schütte, 15.10.03

A & B Architektura & Biznes (Poland)
"Swiat w szkole", Barbara Nowak-Gildehaus, 10/03

Espacio Experimental de Arquitectura Berlin, La Ciudad Desden 1989
"Berlin – Experimentierfeld der Architektur. Die Stadt nach 1989.", Goethe Institut Madrid, 10/03

Die Welt
"Schwimmende Häuser auf der Spree in futuristischem Design", IM, 07.08.03

Märkische Allgemeine
"Seltenes Ereignis Schulneubau", André Wirsing, 03.08.03

Hamburgs neue Quartiere – 10 × Leben
"Polderbebauung Neumühlen", Freie und Hansestadt Hamburg, Behörde für Bau und Verkehr (ed.), 08/03

Architektur in Hamburg Jahrbuch 2003
"Vier Bürohäuser in Neumühlen", Dirk Meyhöfer, Hamburgische Architektenkammer (ed.), Junius Verlag, Hamburg 07/03

Architektur in Berlin Jahrbuch 2003
"Wohn- und Geschäftshaus Monbijouplatz 3", Ingrid Kultschun, Architektenkammer Berlin (ed.), Junius Verlag, Hamburg 07/03

Architektur in Berlin Jahrbuch 2003
"Warte, bis es dunkel wird...", Frank Peter Jäger, Architektenkammer Berlin (ed.), Junius Verlag, Hamburg 07/03

Die Zeit
"Der dritte Lehrer", Ulla Hanselmann, 18.06.03

ARTE – Metropolis
Beitrag "Floating Homes", Carsten Binsack, Strasbourg, 01.06.03

db deutsche bauzeitung
"Verschiedenes im Gleichen", Gert Kähler, 06/03

architektur aktuell
"Die Schönheit der Konstruktion", Claus Käpplinger, 05/03

Design Berlin – new projects for a changing city
"Grüntuch/Ernst Architekten – Beitrag zum Wettbewerb", Alexander von Vegesack/ Matteo Kries/Britt Angelis, Vitra Design Museum, 05/03

Irish Independent
"Could your future hold a floating home?", Clare Chapman, 04.04.03

Schulen in Deutschland – Neubau und Revitalisierung
"Schule am Mummelsoll", Wüstenrot Stiftung, 04/03

Detail
"Schule für Behinderte in Berlin-Hellersdorf",
03/03

brand eins
"Schmuck oder Zahl", Dirk Meyhöfer, 03/03

HÄUSER
"Freischwimmer", 03/03

db deutsche bauzeitung
"Immaterialität mittels Farbe", Claus Käpplinger,
03/03

The Sunday Times
"Testing the Water", 02.02.03

Bauwelt
"Aufbau", Ulrich Brinkmann, 02/03

BILD
"Jetzt bauen wir schwimmende Häuser",
Jan Meyer, 21.01.03

Süddeutsche Zeitung
"Ein Container für Schneewittchen",
Veronika Schöne, 09.01.03

Brigitte Kultur
"Almut Ernst", Ulla Hanselmann, 01/03

Berlin – A guide to recent architecture
Duane Phillips, Alexandra Geyer, B T Batsford,
London, 01/03

Die erste Skizze
"Grüntuch Ernst Architekten", D. Figa/
G. Nalbach, Förderkreis Dortmunder Modell
Bauwesen, 01/03

DAM Jahrbuch Architektur in Deutschland 2003
"Bürogebäude Neumühlen, Hamburg", Dietmar
Brandenburger, Prestel Verlag, Munich 01/03

Der Tagesspiegel
"Mix aus Ufo und Amphibienfahrzeug", suzi,
01.01.03

Süddeutsche Zeitung
"Die Auserwählten", 01.01.03

Der Tagesspiegel
"Mit Schwung ums Eck", Jürgen Tietz, 28.12.02

Berliner Zeitung
"Auf Wasser gebaut", Marcel Gäding, 20.12.02

Sender Freies Berlin – Sendereihe Stadt,
Land, Fluss
"Schöner lernen – Neue Schulen und Kitas
für Berlin", 12.11.02

MERIAN Hamburg
"Moderne Haus-Arbeit", Niklas Maak, 11/02

2002 Shanghai Biennale – Urban Creation
"Grüntuch & Ernst", Xu Jiang, Shanghai Art
Museum, 11/02

Lofts in Berlin
"Just live in it! Lebhaft!", Tectum Publishers,
Belgium, 10/02

Berliner Zeitung
"The Net has been Mended", Nikolaus Bernau,
22.07.02

faz.net
"Berliner Schlossplatz – Was junge
Architekten denken...", Katja Blombeg, 14.06.02

Indian Architect & Builder, Mumbai
"Grüntuch/Ernst Architects", 06/02

Bauwelt
"Am Mummelsoll", Sebastian Redecke, 05/02

Flash Art
"Plamen Dejanoff", Sonia Campagnola, 04/02

Bauwelt
"Mit leuchtendem Treppenhaus", Kaye Geipel,
01/03

wettbewerbe aktuell
"Gymnasium mit Außenanlagen und Sporthalle
in Dallgow-Döberitz", 02/02

Die Welt
"Wie würde Mies heute bauen?",
Rainer Haubrich, 03.01.02

Die neuen Architekturführer Nr. 37
"Monbijouplatz 5, Monbijouplatz 3, Berlin",
Cornelia Dörris, Stadtwandel Verlag, Berlin 01/02

A&W Architektur & Wohnen
"Hauptstadt-Talente", Dirk Meyhöfer, 01/02

ZOO
"Grüntuch Ernst Projects", Will Compertz, 01/02

Vom Plan zum Bauwerk
"Bauten in der Berliner Innenstadt nach 2000",
Hans Stimmann (ed.), Verlagshaus Braun,
Salenstein, Switzerland 01/02

Das Bauzentrum Baukultur
"Eigensinn. Eigenständigkeit im Kontext", 10/01

Ideales Heim
"Ein Dialog von Alt und Neu", Roland Merz, 10/01

Der Spiegel
"Gefährliche Liebschaft?", 08/01

Frankfurter Allgemeine Zeitung
"Wo, wenn nicht hier?", Oliver Elser, 15.02.01

Berliner Morgenpost
"Big business auf der geilen Meile",
Peter Schubert, 12.02.01

DBZ Deutsche BauZeitschrift
"Wundheilung – Wohn- und Geschäftshaus
in Berlin-Mitte", Anke Wöhler, 11/01

db deutsche bauzeitung
"Neu in ... Berlin", Claus Käpplinger, 01/01

Süddeutsche Zeitung
"Einfach sexy", Peter Richter, 06.12.00

Berlin – Stadt ohne Form
"Triangel am Checkpoint Charlie",
Rudolf Stegers, Prestel Verlag, Munich 12/00

l'ARCA
"Autostadt", Benedetto Camera, 11/00

Der Tagesspiegel
"Gläserner Anschluss", Jürgen Tietz, 16.10.00

Berliner Zeitung
"Schulterschluss zwischen Hausgenerationen",
Michael Mönninger, 11.10.00

architektur aktuell
"Selbstbewusster Dialog", Claus Käpplinger,
10/00

Bauwelt
"Lücke neben den Höfen", Jan Friedrich, 10/00

Süddeutsche Zeitung
"Wilde Zukunft", nma, 12.09.00

Junge deutsche Architekten 2
"Grüntuch/Ernst Berlin", Angelika Schnell,
Birkhäuser Verlag, Basel 06/00

Der Tagesspiegel
"Lernen in Klassen mit Terrassen",
Christian v. Lassen, 13.05.00

Der Tagesspiegel
"Glashaus vom Hackeschen Markt",
Christian v. Lassen, 09.04.00

Die neuen Architekturführer Nr. 26
"Hackescher Markt 2–3 Berlin", Dr. Jürgen Tietz,
Stadtwandel Verlag, Berlin 01/00

World Architecture
"The Glass Canopy to the Consul Hotel",
Ken Yeang, 07/99

Hamburger Morgenpost
"Kossaks Perlenkette: Baubeginn im Mai",
Dirk Rohwedder, 24.04.99

Die Welt
"Der Hafenrand – Die 'Perlenkette' beginnt zu
glänzen", Gisela Schütte, 22.04.99

Der Spiegel
"Die Hauptstadt flackert", Jürgen Hohmeyer,
10/98

wettbewerbe aktuell
"Museum der Bildenden Künste, Leipzig", 01/98

AEDES Katalog
"Architekten Grüntuch/Ernst – Einblicke
Ausblicke", Galerie AEDES: Kristin Freireiss,
Hans-Jürgen Commerell (eds.), 12/97

Berliner Zeitung
"Futuristische Märchenbilder",
Hans Wolfgang Hoffmann, 22.11.97

wettbewerbe aktuell
"Neubau der Landesvertretung Rheinland-Pfalz
in Berlin", 10/97

Schulen für Berlin II – Projekte der 90er Jahre
– Städtebau und Architektur Bericht 30
"Schule für Geistigbehinderte, Eilenburger
Straße, Hellersdorf", Senatsverwaltung für
Bau- und Wohnungswesen Berlin (ed.), 05/97

Neue Architektur – New Architecture Berlin
1990–2000
Martin Kieren, Jovis Verlag, Berlin 01/97

Architectural Design
"Grüntuch/Ernst", Maggie Toy, VCH Publishers,
London 01/96

Architekten Grüntuch/Ernst
"Berliner Projekte 92–95", Philipp Oswalt,
Verlag H. M. Nelte, Wiesbaden 01/96

db deutsche bauzeitung
"Alt und Neu Willkommen, Vordach für das
Hotel Consul", Cornelia Krause, 03/95

Detail
"Wohnhaus in Köln, Treppe", Karl J. Habermann,
05/94

wettbewerbe aktuell
"Schule für Geistigbehinderte, Berlin", 04/94

ARCH+
"Junge Architekten in der Bundesrepublik
– Umbau Reichstag", 09/93

Exhibitions

Chamber of Architects Berlin
"da! Architektur in Berlin 2013"
Berlin, 03/2013

Stiftung Baukultur Rhineland-Palatinate
"Schöner Shoppen? –
Innerstädtische Zentren des Handels"
Mainz, 06-08/2012

Senate Department for Urban
Development
"auf.einander.bauen"
Berlin, 08/2010

BDA Gallery Berlin
"Nach der Mauer. Projekte für eine neue Stadt"
Berlin, 11/2009-01/2010

Chamber of Architects Berlin
"da! Architektur in Berlin 2009"
Berlin, 06-07/2009

C.A.U.E. 5
"Routes of Architecture in Europe"
Strasbourg, 11/2008-01/2009

Chamber of Architects Berlin
"da! Architektur in Berlin 2008"
Berlin, 06-07/2008

DAZ Deutsches Architektur Zentrum
"Berlin – New York Dialogues"
Berlin, 03-05/2008

Center for Architecture
"Berlin – New York Dialogues"
New York, 11/2007-01/2008

German Embassy Minsk
"City & House / New Architecture in Berlin"
Minsk, 11-12/2007

Chamber of Architects Berlin
"da! Architektur in Berlin 2007"
Berlin, 06-07/2007

Senate Department for Urban
Development
"Convertible City"
Berlin, 05-07/2007

BDA Gallery Berlin
"Stadtwohnen – neu"
Berlin, 02-03/2007

KAP Forum Köln
"Convertible City"
Cologne, 01-03/2007

10th International Architecture Exhibition,
Venice Biennale, 2006
Commissioners of the German Contribution
"Convertible City"
Venice, 09-11/2006

Aedes Gallery Berlin
"Grüntuch Ernst Architects: urban upgrade –
Strategien städtischer Verdichtung"
Berlin, 06-07/2006

BDA Gallery Berlin
"Zukunftsfähiges Bauen – Konstruktion"
Berlin, 05-06/2006

EXPO ALEMANIA 2005
"German Architecture: Between Hightech
and Sustainability"
Santiago de Chile, 09/2005

Victoria & Albert Museum
"Deutschlandscape – Epicentres at
the Periphery"
London, 09/2005-01/2006

Chamber of Architects Berlin
"da! Architektur in Berlin 2005"
Berlin, 06-07/2005

stadt.bau.raum Gelsenkirchen
"Deutschlandscape – Epicentres at
the Periphery"
Gelsenkirchen, 03-04/2005

Asian Design Forum 2004
"future urbanism"
Kuala Lumpur, 09/2004

Architecture Biennale 2004 Venice
"Deutschlandscape – Epicentres at
the Periphery"
German Pavilion, Venice, 2004

Shussev Museum for Architecture
"Floating Berlin" Moscow 2004

Goethe Institute Madrid
"Berlin – Experimentierfeld der Architektur.
Die Stadt nach 1989"
Madrid, 10-12/2003

City of Hamburg – Behörde für Bau und Verkehr
"10 × Leben – Hamburgs neue Quartiere"
Hamburg, 09/2003

University of Dortmund and Design
Centre Thuringia
"Die erste Skizze" – "The first sketch"
Weimar, 08-09/2003

Chamber of Architects Berlin
"da! Architektur in Berlin 2003"
Berlin, 06-07/2003

Vitra Design Museum
"Design Berlin! New Projects for a
Changing City"
Touring exhibition: Berlin, Manchester, Madrid,
Berlin, 05/2003

Gallery in the Palais am Festungsgraben
"Floating Homes –
11 Entwürfe für das Wohnen auf dem Wasser"
Berlin, 01-02/2003

Shanghai Biennale 2002
"Urban Creation"
Shanghai Art Museum
Shanghai, 2002

Berlinische Galerie
"Fifty : Fifty"
Berlin, 06-07/2001

Chamber of Architects Berlin
"da! Architektur in Berlin 2001"
Berlin, 06-07/2001

NAi – Netherlands Architecture Institute
"Made in Berlin"
Rotterdam, 05/2001

Aedes Gallery Berlin
"Corporate Architecture Autostadt
Wolfsburg"
Berlin, 07/2000

PS1 - Centre for Contemporary Art (MoMA)
"Children of Berlin"
New York, 1999

Art Forum Berlin, Gallery Volker Diehl
"art peep"
Berlin, 09/1999

berlin biennale
"center peep"
Berlin, 1998

Aedes Gallery Berlin
"Architekten Grüntuch Ernst –
einblicke ausblicke"
Berlin, 12/1997

Museum der Arbeit
"Veränderung am Strom"
Hamburg, Rotterdam, 1997

INTERARCH
"Twenty Young Architects"
Sofia, 1997

Royal Institute of British Architects
"Architecture on the Horizon"
London, 1996

Chamber of Architects Berlin
"Gebaut - Built"
European travelling exhibition 03/1995

Awards

Europahouse Award 2012
Europahouse Foundation
Marthashof, Berlin

Architekturpreis Zukunft Wohnen 2012
Wohnen in der Stadt
Shortlist, Marthashof Berlin

eco-immobilienawardberlin 2011
Distinction for Marthashof, Berlin

BMWi-Award "Architektur mit Energie 2011"
ENOB – Award for energy-optimised building
1rst prize for German School Madrid

Wüstenrot Foundation Award 2010
"Neues Wohnen in der Stadt"
Special commendation for Baugruppenhaus
(co-housing) Auguststr. 51, Berlin

HÄUSER AWARD 2010
"Die Zukunft findet heute statt"
3rd prize for Baugruppenhaus (co-housing)
Auguststr. 51, Berlin

Deutscher Bauherrenpreis 2009/2010
"Hohe Qualität – Tragbare Kosten"
German Association of Cities, Association
of German Architects BDA,
Bundesverband deutscher Wohnungs- und
Immobilienunternehmen
Category: New Building
Baugruppenhaus (co-housing) Auguststr. 51,
Berlin

Europahouse Award 2009
Europahouse Foundation
Baugruppenhaus (co-housing) Auguststr. 51,
Berlin

Architekturpreis Zukunft Wohnen 2009
"Wohnen in der Gemeinschaft"
Shortlist, Baugruppenhaus (co-housing)
Auguststr. 51, Berlin

Berlin Architecture Award 2009
Baugruppenhaus (co-housing) Auguststr. 51,
Berlin

BDA Berlin Award 2009
Special commendation for office building
Leipziger Strasse, Berlin

Best Architects 09
Office building Leipziger Strasse, Berlin

AIT Office Application Award 2008
Category Winner: Best Workplace
Office building Leipziger Strasse, Berlin

Architecture Award
Colour – Texture – Surface 2008
Nomination for office building Leipziger Strasse
and Bruno-H.-Bürgel Primary School, Berlin

Best Architects 08
Police Station Barnim, Bernau

Architecture Award
Colour – Texture – Surface 2006
Recognition for Marie-Curie-Gymnasium,
Dallgow-Döberitz

Deutscher Bauherrenpreis 2006
"High Quality – Reasonable Costs"
German Association of Cities, Association
of German Architects BDA,
Bundesverband deutscher Wohnungs-
und Immobilienunternehmen
Category: New Building
Residential and commercial building at
Monbijouplatz 3, Berlin

Foundation Award 2005
Foundation "Lebendige Stadt"
"Innovative sports venues"
Special Needs School, Berlin-Hellersdorf

Architecture Award Brandenburg 2005
Ministerium für Infrastruktur und Raumordnung
des Landes Brandenburg,
Brandenburgische Architektenkammer
Marie-Curie-Gymnasium, Dallgow-Döberitz

Best German Books 2004
"POINTS OF ACCESS - Grüntuch Ernst
Architects" (Editor Kristin Feireiss),
Prestel, Munich

Balthasar Neumann Award 2004
Bund Deutscher Baumeister, Architekten und
Ingenieure BDB, deutsche bauzeitung db
Shortlist, office building Hamburg-Neumühlen

Architecture Award
Colour – Texture – Surface 2004
Nomination, Special Needs School,
Berlin-Hellersdorf

Light-Architecture Award 2003
Shortlist, office building Hamburg-Neumühlen

German Architecture Award 2003
Federal Chamber of German Architects,
Ruhrgas AG
Recognition for office building
Hamburg-Neumühlen

DuPont Benedictus Award 2003
American Institute of Architects
Category Winner: Education
Special Needs School, Berlin-Hellersdorf

Architekturpreis Zukunft Wohnen 2002
Special commendation for residential and
commercial building Monbijouplatz 3, Berlin

Wüstenrot Foundation Award 2002
Schools in Germany: Recognition for
Special Needs School, Berlin-Hellersdorf

Deubau Junior Award 2002
Building at Hackescher Markt, Berlin

BDA Hamburg Award 2002
3rd prize for office building
Hamburg-Neumühlen

Hans-Schaefers-Award 1996
BDA Berlin Architecture Prize

Conversion of the Reichstag, Berlin, competition 1992

documenta exhibition hall, Kassel
Competition 1989 , with C. Wendt and J. Staudt

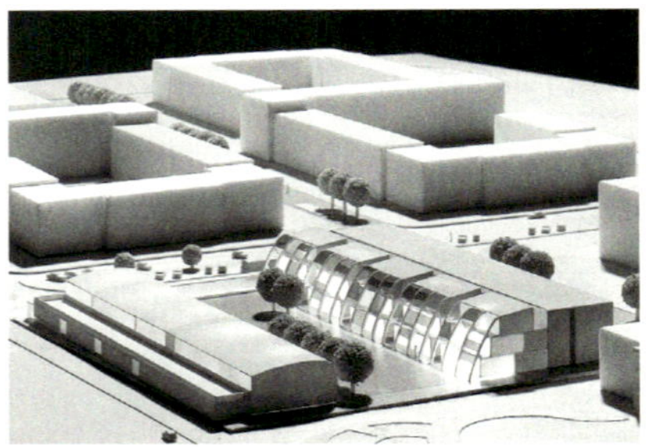

Berlin-Hellersdorf Special Needs School,
1st Prize. Competition 1993, completion 2002

Workshop “Wohltemperierte Architektur” with Cedric Price, Guy Battle, Christopher McCarthy and Jan Kaplický, 1992

Bridge over the Upper Havel, Berlin
Open competition 1993

Office building at Checkpoint Charlie, Berlin, design 1992

Urban development forum, Hamburg, Workshop with Ron Herron and Hadi Teherani, 1993

Office Uhlandstrasse

Architecture and Design School, Wismar, competition 1996

Aedes exhibition "Einblicke Ausblicke"
by Kristin Feireiss, Berlin, 1997

Office building Neumühlen 13–15, Hamburg
1st Prize. Competition 1996, completion 2002

Eternit Headquarters, Berlin, 1st Prize. Competition 1996

Auditorium Lübeck University
Competition 1996

TV tower as an urban barometer, Berlin
Concept 1996

Office Clausewitzstrasse

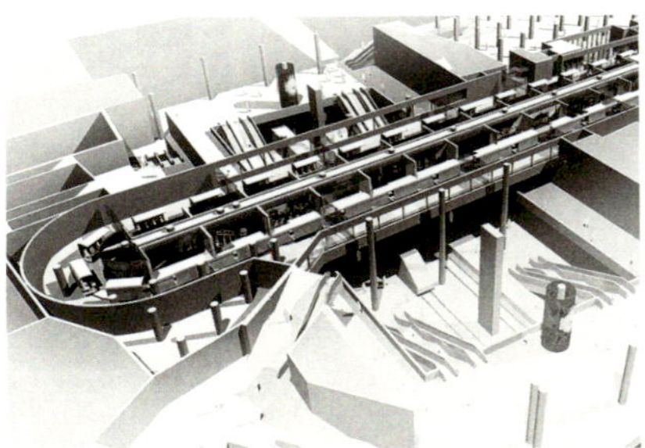
Exhibition "Zeitreise" at the Potsdamer Platz station, 1997

Indian embassy, Berlin
1st Prize. Competition 1997

Museum of Fine Arts, Leipzig
Purchase. Competition 1997

Extension of Stuttgart's main station
Competition 1997

German Pavilion EXPO 2000, Hanover
Competition 1997

Headquarters for the Bayerische Rück, Munich
5th Prize. Competition 1997

Residential and commercial buildings at the Alsterfleet, Hamburg, competition 1997

Federal state building for Rhineland-Palatinate, Berlin
2nd Prize. Competition 1997

Reception building for Brandenburg Psychiatric Hospital, completion 1998

Mobile exhibition Pavilion for Mercedes-Benz, Berlin, competition 1997

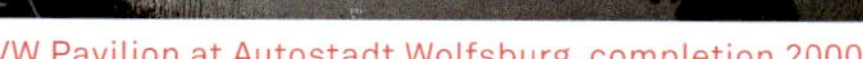

VW Pavilion at Autostadt Wolfsburg, completion 2000

Office excursion EXPO Hannover, 2000

Conversion Kiefholzatelier, Berlin
Completion 2000

Falkenried Hamburg
Competition 1999/2000

Office tower MAX, Frankfurt a. M., competition 1999

Hackescher Markt 2–3, Berlin
Completion 2000

Hotel Checkpoint Charlie, Berlin
Survey 2000

Masterplan District 75, Moscow, International Design Group Workshop, 2000

Marie-Curie-Gymnasium, Dallgow-Döberitz, 1st Prize. Competition 2001, completion 2005

Monbijouplatz 5, Berlin, completion 2001

Müngersdorfer Stadion, Cologne, competition 2001

Leipziger Strasse office building, Berlin
Competitive procurement procedure 2001,
completion 2008

Media Cityport Hamburg, competition 2001

Monbijouplatz 3, Berlin, completion 2001

Office Hackescher Markt

Berlin-Hellersdorf Special Needs School, 1st Prize. Competition 1993, completion 2002

Office building BMW plant Leipzig
4th Prize. Competition 2002

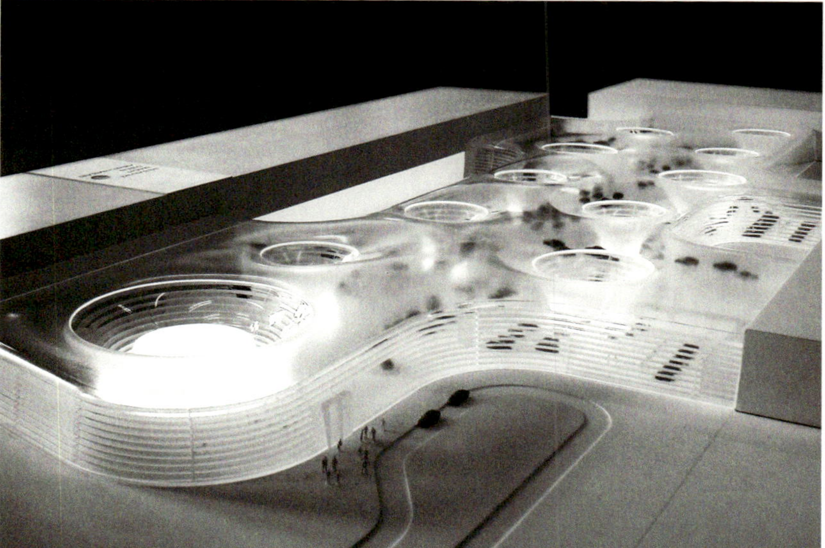

Hotel at the Berlin Fair, Berlin
1st Prize. Competition 2002

European Headquarters Bombardier Transportation, Berlin, 1st Prize. Competition 2001

Conversion “Warenhaus Tietz”,
Klosterstrasse, Berlin
Completion 2002

Humboldt Höfe, Berlin
Completion 2002

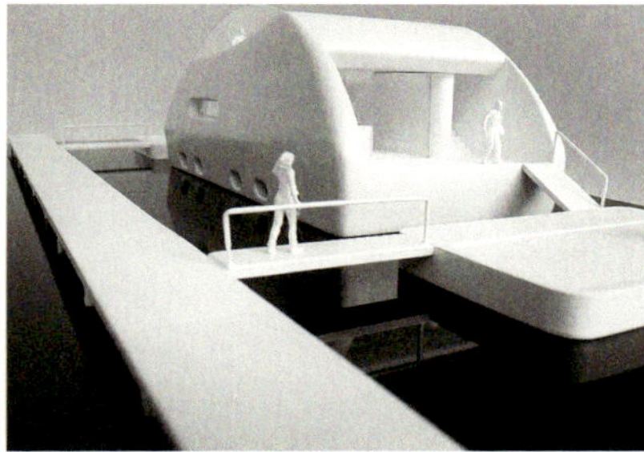

Floating Homes, Berlin
1st Prize. Competition 2002

NAi exhibition opening “MADE IN Berlin”, by Kristin Feireiss, Rotterdam 2002

Office building Neumühlen 13–15, Hamburg
1st Prize. Competition 1996, completion 2002

ABC soccer tournament, 2003

German School in Geneva
Competition 2003

Office building Spreedreieck, Berlin
2nd Prize. Competition 2004

Service building Berlin Fair
1st Prize. Competition 2003, completion 2004

At the 5th Shanghai Biennial
with Yona Friedman, 2004

Temporary entrance of the Kunst-Werke, Berlin
Competition 2004

Conversion Chemnitz train station
1st Prize. Competition 2004, completion 2014

Headquarters of the European Central Bank, Frankfurt a. M., competition 2003 with Frei Otto

Leipzig University Hospital, competition 2003

Office Frei Otto, Warmbronn

Turfclub Masterplan, Penang, Malaysia
2nd Prize. Competition 2005

"Convertible City", German contribution to the 10th Venice Architecture Biennale, 2006

Office building Werftstrasse, Lübeck
1st Prize. Procurement procedure 2007

Townhouse Oberwallstrasse, Berlin
Completion 2008

Conversion Department Store at Brill, Bremen
1st Prize. Competition 2005, completion 2009

Marthashof, Berlin
1st Prize. Competition 2006, completion 2012

Primary School Bruno-H.-Bürgel, Berlin
1st Prize. Procurement procedure 2004, completion 2006

Fördehotel, Flensburg
1st Prize. Competition 2005

Aedes Gallery, "urban upgrade – Strategien städtischer Verdichtung", Berlin, 2006

Police station, Bernau, 1st Prize. Procurement procedure 2003, completion 2006

Residential highrise Stuttgart 21, 1st Prize. Competition 2008

Berlin – New York Dialogues
Exhibition 2007–08

Schlossplatz, Berlin
Concept 2005

Co-housing Auguststrasse 51, Berlin, completion 2008

Höfe am Brühl department store, Leipzig, 1st Prize. Competition 2007, completion 2012

Department store, Lübeck
1st Prize. Competition 2007, completion 2009

BMW Branch Kaiserdamm, Berlin, competition 2007

Hackesches Quartier, Berlin
Competition 2006, completion 2011

Aviary for the Berlin Zoo, competition 2009

German School Madrid
1st Prize. Competition 2009, completion 2015

TU Berlin Research Center, Berlin
Purchase. Competition 2009

Commercial building Alexanderplatz, Berlin
2nd Prize. Competition 2009

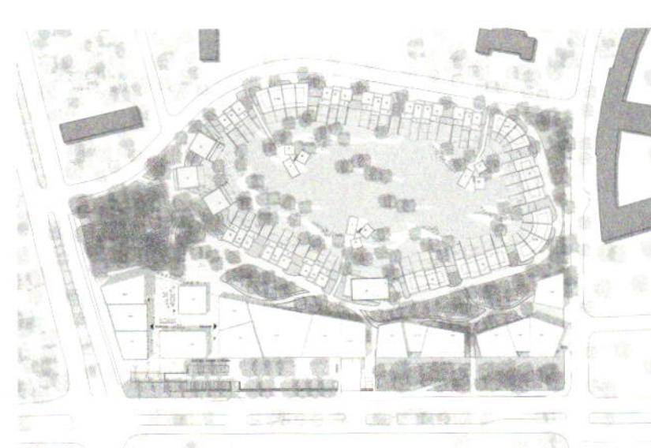

Masterplan (concept) for Truman-Plaza, Berlin, competitive procurement procedure 2009

German embassy Maskat, Oman
2nd Prize. Competition 2010

ABC soccer tournament 2010

Kastanienallee, Berlin
Competitive procurement procedure 2011, completion 2015

Quarter at Mailänder Platz, Stuttgart, 2nd Prize. Competition 2010

Weltkulturen Museum, Frankfurt a. M., competition 2010

"Intelligent Quarters", Hamburg
2nd Prize. Competition 2011

auhaus Museum, Weimar, competition 2011

Former Jewish Girls' School, Berlin
Conversion and reprogramming 2011

Residential development Isoldenstrasse, Munich
1st Prize. Competition 2011

rial Place Ahlem, Hanover
ase. Competition 2011

ThyssenKrupp representative office, Berlin, 2nd Prize. Competition 2011

Sedelhöfe, Ulm, 1st Prize. Competition 2011

Grande Galerie, Erlangen
rize. Competition 2010

Archeological Centre Petriplatz, Berlin, competition 2012

Kirchenweg, Zurich, competition 2011

Höfe am Brühl department store, Leipzig
1st Prize. Competition 2007, completion 2012

Museum for Science and Nature, Jerusalem, Finalist. Competition 2012

Kunstcampus, Berlin
Competition 2012

Conversion Goods Station Wilmersdorf, Berlin
Procurement procedure 2012

Residential building on the Spree riverside, Berlin, competition 2012

Former Women's Prison, Berlin
Conversion and reprogramming 2013

DGUV Headquarters, Berlin
Competitive procurement procedure 2011,
completion 2014

Residential building Pestalozzistrasse, Berlin, survey 2012

Schinkelplatz, Berlin
2nd Prize. Competition 2012

Cultural Forum, Arnsberg
4th Prize. Competition 2012

Schools Binnenfeldredder, Hamburg
2nd Prize. Competition 2012

Approximations
On the Paintings of Asmund Havsteen-Mikkelsen

Jeanette Kunsmann

"Gerhard Richter once said that his paintings were smarter than he is – I often feel the same way." In any case, Asmund Havsteen-Mikkelsen's paintings know more than can be seen at a quick glance. Immediately after the first encounter, his paintings invite the viewer to plunge deeply into his imagery. A dark space reveals itself under bright stairs, a warm yellow disrupts the green façade structure of an office building.

It is certainly something special when a painter portrays the work of an architectural office. On the one hand are the architects, who control their work down to the smallest detail and sometimes alter photographs of their completed projects to remove the wear and tear of everyday life. On the other hand is the painter, who wants to create a work of art with a distinct expression, something beyond a mere copy of reality. But how does such an unusual collaboration even come about? The architects were looking for a special presentation of their buildings – the suggestion to ask a painter to take a different, external look at the work of the architectural office came from the editors. They introduced the architects to the artist Havsteen-Mikkelsen, who in his previous work has often addressed architectural subjects. The cooperation was an experiment: the artist could freely choose his motifs; the architects had a say in the development process. For the artist, that meant reaching compromises in addition to the intensive work of painting, and for the architects it meant learning to let go. Art in architecture, architecture in art: the experiment was an exchange of artistic attitudes, an exciting dialogue.

"There are numerous possibilities for portraying architecture", explains Havsteen-Mikkelsen. "The image has to remain in your head, that's my principle." Stacked in his atelier alongside paint tubes and books are sketches, drawings, and canvases. The artist, who was born in Denmark in 1977, is heir to different disciplines: his architect father, his grandfather, a famous painter – he himself took a roundabout way to painting. He studied literature for seven years before dedicating himself to art studies. "I have the architecture connection from my father, I practically grew up in his office. He wanted me to become an architect, too. My grandfather is a painter. I wanted to be an author. Thus, three movements merge in me." Havsteen-Mikkelsen worked almost exclusively on installations until he came to painting in 2005.

Asmund Havsteen-Mikkelsen is not only interested in a building's message or architecture's effect on everyday life – he goes a step further, or perhaps in the opposite direction: in his work, the artist is searching for what Anthony Vidler called "the architectural uncanny". The uncanny: a feeling that Sigmund Freud examined in an essay from 1919 and that Vidler transferred to architecture. *"Heim, heimilig, heimlich, unheimlich"* ("home, homely, secret, uncanny"): this play on words describes the basis of Havsteen-Mikkelsen's imagery. "A space has a will. There is indeed a connection between architecture and psychology", according to the painter. "Architecture is more than built boundaries: it determines our daily routines, our lives, and our thoughts more than we'd like to believe." Havsteen-Mikkelsen's series "Approximation" can be understood as an approach to this theme; it shows the gap between truth and object. The first picture shows the fiery red stairs that Grüntuch Ernst built for the German Pavilion at the 2006 Biennale in Venice. It is entitled "Coming up for Air", a reference to an essay by George Orwell. The picture forms the point of origin of the entire series; the dominant green tone therein appears in all twelve pictures and becomes the leitmotif.

The result is a sensitive examination of the firm's architecture. The buildings of glass, steel, concrete, and other light materials were a challenge – the painter initially had to find himself in the work of Grüntuch Ernst, a process that took almost half a year. "In the beginning, we had decided on more realistic paintings, in which the buildings were still recognizable in their entirety. You had the feeling with all the sketches: Yes, that's a Grüntuch Ernst building. They were classic photographic positions", remembers Havsteen-Mikkelsen.
"Architectural photography is always beautiful, good lighting, everything is so perfect. A painter, therefore, has to find something different. It took time, but at a certain point the projects were transformed and alienated – the entire painting cycle floats between the whole and the detail". What the paintings still have in common with architectural photographs: "When a picture is empty, it remains open to the viewer", explains the artist. "It's like an invitation – for example, to climb a flight of stairs." Thus, everyone reads a different story into the painting and can develop his or her own view.

For Asmund Havsteen-Mikkelsen, it was his first time painting a large picture cycle of a single architectural studio's work. He looks contentedly through his atelier: "Digital images can be manipulated and copied indefinitely – however, this total reproducibility lacks authenticity, an aura, a value. With painting, it's different: suddenly there are twelve analogue pictures – they have a presence!"

Asmund Havsteen-Mikkelsen
Artist
Born 1977 in Aeroe, Denmark
Lives and works in Berlin

Education

2003–09 MFA, Royal Academy of Fine Arts, Copenhagen
2007–08 Hochschule für bildende Künste, Hamburg
2004–05 CCA Research Program, Kitakyushu, Japan
1996–03 MA in literature and philosophy, University of Copenhagen

Selected Solo Exhibitions

2012 "Blue Devils", Galerie MøllerWitt, Aarhus, Denmark
2011 "The Future Begins at Home", Rønnebæksholm ArtCenter, Denmark
2010 "Meditations on the Uncanny", Helene Nyborg Contemporary, Copenhagen
2008 "Life in the Box", Helene Nyborg Contemporary, Copenhagen

Selected Group Exhibitions

2012 "Needle In A Cloud", Fold Gallery, London
2011 "Enter II", Kunsthallen Brandts, Odense, Denmark
2010 "No Food No Drink No Sticky Lollies", Stadtbad Wedding, Berlin
2009 "Exit", Gl. Strand, Copenhagen
2007 "Autolabor", Brandenburgischer Kunstverein Potsdam e.V., Germany

Pictures as Fragments
Interview with the Photographer Heji Shin

Kristina Herresthal

Heji Shin takes photos in diverse fields of commercial photography and, in addition, shows her work in other contexts, at exhibitions or in books. Last year, for example, she published a modern sex education book, *Make Love,* with Rogner & Bernhard. Her pictures show great affinity for their subjects, creating a feeling of immediacy and intimacy. It seemed natural to ask her to create a photo series that shows how the firm's built projects are inhabited, used, and reshaped.

It is the second picture series in the book that allows an external look at the work of the architectural office. In contrast to Asmund Havsteen-Mikkelsen's paintings, where the projects seem almost otherworldly, Heji Shin's pictures are more atmospheric studies. The viewer has the feeling of being on site, as a quiet observer. She plays with light and reflections; almost like a baroque painting, the motifs are immersed in strong contrasts of light and shadows. Edges dissolve, silhouettes indicate movement and habitation.

Heji Shin has worked in Berlin since 1998. After exhibitions in Berlin and Paris, she recently showed her work in New York. Here, she answers questions about her work and the photo series:

Which subjects generally concern you in your work as a photographer?

I always have my film camera, a Contax T2, and a Polaroid camera with me. I love producing the complete picture at the scene – it never goes to a laboratory or through a computer. A Polaroid photograph is always connected to the place that it shows, like an 18th-century landscape painting, which was also created directly on location. For me, the pictures are fragments. Almost as if you'd taken a stone, a branch, or something else from this place. There are a lot of Polaroids of places that I think no one would believe really exist. But a Polaroid tells the truth, it can't be Photoshopped.

How do you work?

I don't want to stage anything in a studio, because I think that the world is so beautiful and there's so much out there – I'd rather show something that already exists outside. Besides, reality has already surpassed every form of fiction anyway. That's why I don't have a studio. I have something that's more like a developing archive, a collection. None of it was made here, but the things end up with me.

What is your relationship to architecture?

I love being in Manhattan and looking over at New Jersey. All of those high-rises that are built on the shore and how outdated they look. Eerie, a bit threatening. Somehow, you feel the New Yorkers' fear of the America outside of New York. Also, the amazing Tracey Towers in the Bronx, those are two of my favourite buildings by Paul Rudolph. Unfortunately, I think they are supposed to be torn down. The two towers look like a medieval, concrete dungeon. Parts of New York are as bleak as the Middle Ages.

How did you approach the photo series of the Grüntuch Ernst buildings?

It's simple: I got up and ran out and I had a look at them. I think that's the way I approach everything. It's a bit childish, but you don't regret anything either. For me, everything is a part of the same thing, you can't neglect anything.

Has this approach changed in the process?

No, the next day I wanted to do exactly the same. I wanted to ensure that it became a kind of loop that was constantly renewed. I like architecture very much, but after photographing fifteen projects, I thought I had an architectural hangover. Then I looked at everything a bit more slowly and asked more questions.

Is there a project that you especially like?

The Hellersdorf Special Needs School. The project relates to the environment, to the outside world. It integrates itself in its environment, and therefore looks somehow like the landscape itself. At the same time, it seems like a relic – with the prefabricated housing estate and nature as counterparts. A little bit like the work of a land-artist who also doesn't simply put objects in the landscape. It's part of the landscape, yet something else entirely. I really like it.

Heji Shin
Artist, Photographer
Born 1976 in Seoul, South Korea
Lives and works in Berlin

Education

1996–2000 Hochschule für bildende Künste, Hamburg
Department of Design & Photography

Selected Solo Exhibitions

2013 "Camp Habibi", Mathew Gallery, Berlin
2013 "The Great Penetrator", Real Fine Arts, New York
2011 "The Black Object", Anna Catharina Gebbers Bibliothekswohnung, Berlin

Selected Group Exhibitions

2011 "Based in Berlin", Berlin
2003 "White meat & sunlite", Wiensowski und Harbord, Berlin
2002 "Hanayo", Palais de Tokyo, Paris

Published for

032c, The Wire, Die Zeit, brandeins, taz, Die Welt, Spex, Interview Magazine, Another Magazine, Vogue Nippon, Elle Japon, Composite Japan, Ryuku Ishin Japan, Dazed & Confused, The Face etc.

Colophon

Editor
Ilka and Andreas Ruby, textbild, Berlin

Editing
Grüntuch Ernst Architekten, Berlin
Kristina Herresthal

Design
Heimann und Schwantes, Berlin

Interviews
textbild, Berlin

Translations
Alison Kirkland, London (pp. 12–275);
Inez Templeton, Berlin (pp. 1–7, 305, 307)

Copy Editing
Michael Eisenbrey, Berlin; Kirstien Ring, Berlin

Image Editing
Jan Scheffler & Kerstin Wenzel, prints professional, Berlin

Production Management
DISTANZ Verlag, Nicole Rankers

Production
Kösel GmbH & Co. KG, Altusried

The Deutsche Nationalbibliothek holds a record of this publication in the Deutsche Nationalbibliografie; detailed bibliographical data can be found under http://dnb.ddb.de

List of artists
Olafur Eliasson (p. 90),
Paul Hosking (pp. 42, 43),
Sergej Jensen (pp. 81, 89),
Heji Shin (pp. 288–289, 306, XXI–LXVIII),
Marc Sijan (p. 42/statue of policeman)

Frontcover
Asmund Havsteen-Mikkelsen, Berlin
Backcover
Heji Shin, Berlin

Distribution
Gestalten, Berlin
www.gestalten.com
sales@gestalten.com

ISBN 978-3-942405-84-3
Printed in Germany

Published by
DISTANZ Verlag
www.distanz.de

Photo Credits

All unreferenced images (drawings, photographs, renderings) originate from the Grüntuch Ernst archive

Akademie der Künste, Berlin, Hugo-Häring-Archiv, Häring LG 14/5: 128 (t. l.)
Jan Bitter, Berlin: 9–11, 12 (b.), 13–19, 37, 38 (c. and b.), 39 (c.), 40–43, 82–83, 87, 88 (t. r.), 89 (b.), 95, 96, 97, 98 (t. r, b.), 99, 100, 101 (t., c. r.), 102–107, 155 (t.), 156/157, 190, 198 (c.), 251–255, 256 (t.), 257 (t. l., b., b. r.), 259–263, 264/265, 294 (2nd row c., r.), 294 (4th/5th row l.), 297 (t. l.), 297 (3rd row r.), 298 (c.), 301 (2nd row r.), 303 (t. r.)
Bauhaus Archiv, Berlin, Design: Mies van der Rohe, Foto: Markus Hawlik: 128 (t. r.)
Mark Berger, Berlin: 292 (3rd row l.)
Florian Bolk, Berlin: 69, 72 (t.)
Volker Bültmann, Petershagen: 47, 52 (c.), 53 (t. r.)
Celia de Coca, Madrid: 283 (4th row, 2nd from r.)
Constantin Film Verleih GmbH, 2009: filmstill from „The Wave" 181 (b. r.)
Euroluftbild/Grahn: 62 (t. r.)
Walter Fellmann/Lutz-Erich Müller: 198 (t.), from „Der Leipziger Brühl: Geschichte und Geschichten des Rauchwarenhandels"
Flensburger Nachrichten: 140 (t.), 141 (t.)
Christian Gahl, Berlin: 71, 73 (t.), 76–77, 154 (t.), 293 (3rd row r.)
Christoph Gebler, Hamburg: 291 (b. l., b. c.)
Dirk Hasskarl, Berlin: 98 (t. l.)
Achim Hatzius, Berlin: I–XX
Jörg Hempel, Aachen: 75 (b. l.), 172 (r., 2nd from t.), 220 (t. r.), 290 (2nd row r., 3rd row c., r., 4th row r.), 291 (3rd row r., c.)
Oliver Heissner, Hamburg: 216–217, 220 (b.)
Holger Herschel, Berlin: 39 (b., t.)
Frank Hülsbömer, Berlin: 75 (t.)
Werner Huthmacher, Berlin: 134 (c.), 135 (c., b.), 145–148, 151–153, 154 (b.), 155 (c., b.), 156/157, 162–164, 167 (t.), 168–169, 174–175, 176 (b.), 177 (c.,b.), 178, 179, 180 (t., c.), 181 (t., c., b. l.), 182, 183 (t. l., b. r.), 184–185, 215, 218–219, 221, 222 (t., c., b. l.), 223 (c., b.), 224–225, 292 (b. l.), 294 (t. r.), 295 (t. l., b. r.), 295 (3rd row r.), 295 (4th row c.), 297 (3rd row l.), 297 (b. l., c.)
Hans Joosten, Berlin: 73 (b.)
Stefan Korte, Berlin: 39 (c.)
Ulf-Kersten Neelsen, Lübeck: 133
Kiwi Design, Landsberg: 272 (c. r.)
Markus Löffelhardt, Berlin: 65, 298 (c. r.)
Mads Morgensen, Kopenhagen: 70, 73 (c.), 74 (b., t.), 81, 84, 85, 88 (t. l., b.), 89 (t.), 90–91
MFI, Essen: 196 (t.), 298 (4. row l.)
Stefan Müller, Berlin: 64
Müller Reimann Architekten, Berlin: 62 (t. l.)
Patricia Parinejad, Berlin: 38 (c.)
Svea Pietschmann, Berlin: 48–51, 53 (t. li / b. re), 54, 56–57, 294 (3rd row l.)
Thomas Riehle, Bergisch Gladbach: 189, 191–195, 196 (b.), 197 (c., t. r.), 199 (t., c.), 200–203, 300 (b. l.)
Martin Schuppenhauer, Krefeld: 72 (b. r.), 74 (c.), 75 (b. r.)
Schüco International KG: 121 (c.)
Ullrich Schwarz, Berlin: 128 (b. r.)
Senatsverwaltung für Stadtentwicklung und Umwelt, Berlin: 12 (t., aerial)
Stadtgeschichtliches Museum Leipzig: 196 (c. l.)
Elke Stamm, Berlin (for Grüntuch Ernst Architects): 38 (t. l.), 61, 63 (t. r., l.), 100 (b. r.), 101 (c., b.), 103, 156/157 183 (b. l.), 197 (b.), 198 (b. l.), 264/265, 281
Harald Stein, Leipzig: 197 (t. l.)
Torsten Seidel, Berlin: 258
Tafyr S.L., Madrid: 272 (t. r.)
Transsolar, Stuttgart: 275 (diagrams)
Berliner Zeitung, 20.12.02: 112 (t.)
Berliner Zeitung, 08.08.03: 113 (t. r.)
The Sunday Times, 02.02.03: 113 (c.)
GQ Gentlemen's World, 01.11.03: 113 (c. l.)
La Gazzetta del Mezzogiorno, 20.03.05: 113 (b.)
Focus Griechenland Nr. 72, 01.02.06: 113 (t. l.)

Maigrir
Die Montignac Methode

BUGSIER 10

UCS